Seventy Proven Hypnosis Scripts

Robert Hughes, BCH

Seventy Proven Hypnosis Scripts
Copyright © 2015 Robert Hughes, BCH
Cover Art © 2015 Bonnie Masterjohn
All rights reserved.
ISBN: 1514380153
ISBN-13: 978-1514380154
Robert Hughes Publications, Boise ID
hugheshyp@wwdb.org: www.HughesHypnosis.com

This book is dedicated to the hypnotherapy students who over the years virtually demanded that I write down the things they heard me say in session. Without your insistence, and without your willingness to sit still and pretend to let me teach you what you already knew, this book would never have been written.

Robert Hughes.BCH

CONTENTS

INTRODUCTION 1

INDUCTIONS AND DEEPENINGS 5
    Confusion Induction 5
    Two Minute Induction 8
    Dr. John Kresnik's Induction 10
    Dr. Mike Preston's Progressive Relaxation Induction 12
    Dr. Mike Preston's Deepening 14
    Elman Pretend Game Induction and Deepening for Children 16
    Dr. R.D. Longacre's Computer Game Induction for Children 19
    Pocket Watch Induction 22
    Ericksonian Style Induction: Footprints in the Sand 24
    Yellow Flowers Induction 27
    Countdown Deepening 30
    Elevator Deepening 31
    Dr. R.D. Longacre's Yardstick Deepening 33
    Repeat Eye Opening and Closure Deepening 36

SCRIPTS FOR IRRITABLE BOWEL SYNDROME AND ABDOMINAL PAIN 39
    Healing Imagery for Children aged Seven through Eleven 39
    Pain Management for Children Aged Seven though Eleven 43
    Relaxation, for Children, Aged Seven through Eleven 47
    Self-Esteem For Children Aged Seven Through Eleven 50
    Healing Imagery for FAP/IBS: Teens and Adults 54
    Constipation 58

SCRIPTS FOR PAIN 63
Dr. Dan Lester's Endorphin Pump 63
The Pain Shield 67

SCRIPTS FOR STRESS MANAGEMENT 71
The Tropical Lagoon 71
Cleansing the Brain 76
Gaybeth's Coat for Stress 81
The Schoolhouse: Eliminating Negative Feelings and Beliefs 85
The Spider in the Garden 90
Dr. Mike Preston's Library for Depression 94

SCRIPTS FOR FEARS AND APPREHENSIONS 99
Fears, Panic and Anxiety 99
Flying Freely 103
Speaking Freely in Public 108
Overcoming Test Anxiety 113
Freedom from Shyness and Social Apprehension 116

SCRIPTS FOR COMPULSIONS AND ADDICTIONS 121
Smoking Circle of Truth 121
Dr. Mike Preston's Library for Drug and Alcohol Abuse . 127
Nail Biting 132
Freedom from Bulimia 136

SCRIPTS FOR WEIGHT REDUCTION 141
Fool's Appetite, Eating Habits 141
Achieving the Ideal Self 146
Creating the Ideal Self 152
Tom Nicoli's Car 159
The Road of Life for Excess Weight 162
Dr. Roy Hunter's Benefits of Weight Reduction 167
Leptin and Ghrelin 172
Virtual Gastric Bypass 177

SCRIPTS FOR PHYSICAL HEALING..........183
   Immune System Normalization..........183
   Preparing for Surgery..........189
   Radiant Health for Cancer Survivors..........194
   Dr. R. D. Longacre's Childbirth Imagery..........199
   Dave Elman's Childbirth Imagery..........202
   Dental Bruxism..........207
   The Road of Life for Enuresis (Bed Wetting)..........212
   High Blood Pressure..........218
   Insomnia: Sleep Reprogramming..........222
   Insomnia: Sleep Now..........227
   Reverse Diabetes Now 1: Fork in the Road..........231
   Reverse Diabetes Now 2: Circles of Truth..........236
   Reverse Diabetes Now 3: Control Room Metaphor..........241

MISCELLANEOUS SCRIPTS..........247
   Manifesting Abundance..........247
   Self-Esteem for Adults..........252
   Enhancing Spiritual Awareness..........258
   Alleviating Toxic Guilt and Shame..........262
   Grieving..........267
   Healing the Past..........271
   Enhancing Breast Size..........275
   Body Building..........280
   Increasing Concentration and Focus..........284
   Building Powerful Motivation..........288
   Increased Self-confidence..........293

INTRODUCTION

This book is meant as a companion to my book, *Unlocking the Blueprint of the Psyche: Self-Hypnosis for Modern Miracles*. It contains 56 additional therapeutic scripts, and 14 induction or deepening scripts. I have used every one of these scripts, or variations of them, in my hypnotherapy practice over 21 years. Every one of the approaches outlined in these scripts has proven its effectiveness. I do not read scripts to my clients, but the ideas presented in these scripts have become permanent parts of my memory bank. While hypnosis includes many more techniques than the simple direct suggestion of these scripts, direct suggestion is the hypnotist's most basic and most powerful single tool. Every concept and suggestion in these scripts has been tested and proven with my clients, over and over.

These scripts are meant for the individual user to record, or modify and record for purposes of self-hypnosis. The scripts address many common issues that people use hypnosis to address. *Unlocking the Blueprint of the Psyche* teaches you how to write your own recordable self-hypnosis scripts. However, there are occasions when you would like to use effective, professional scripts developed by someone else, if they address your issue. Or you may want to start with a framework of a professional script and modify it to fit you perfectly. This book fills those needs. When you use these scripts for purposes of self-hypnosis, you may record them as-is, and use them without limit for yourself. You may modify them in any way that serves your need. Unless you are a professional hypnotherapist, please do not record these scripts for other people. Let them buy, or borrow, the books and record their own self-hypnosis session.

If you want to use these scripts for purposes of self-hypnosis, I strongly recommend that you purchase my book, *Unlocking the Blue Print of the Psyche: Self-Hypnosis for Modern Miracles*, available online, or from www.blueprintofthepsyche.com. These scripts are most useful in the framework laid out in that book.

I have also written this book for the professional hypnotist. While most of us do not read scripts to our clients, we frequently study scripts developed by other hypnotists in order to generate ideas, and stimulate our own thinking processes. We also keep a library of scripts that can be modified and recorded, so that we can offer our clients supportive, listen-at-home, self-hypnosis recordings. If you are a professional hypnotherapist, you may modify and record these scripts for distribution to your clients. In a spirit of fairness, please give full credit to me, and to anyone I credit, when you record these scripts for others.

A complete self-hypnosis recording is composed of an induction, a deepening if desired, a content or therapeutic script, and an awakening. This book contains 70 inductions, deepenings and therapeutic scripts to complement and expand on the eighteen found in *Unlocking the Blueprint of the Psyche*. This book does not include a script for awakening yourself from a hypnotic state. That is because an awakening is a very simple process. It is enough to say something like the following:

It is time to return to your normal state of consciousness. As I count slowly from one up to five, your inner mind returns you gently to this time and place, bringing all the positive new ideas on the recording out with you.
(Counting Slowly) One... Two... Three... Four... Five...
You find yourself back in this time and place, eyes open and fully alert, bringing all your new truths out with you...
(Repeating the slow count) One... Two... Three... Four... Five...
All the way up and feeling wonderful.

So, counting this short awakening sequence, there are actually 71 recordable scripts in this book. But the awakening script is really too short to count... so the title remains Seventy Proven Hypnosis Scripts.

When you make a self-hypnosis recording for yourself, choose an induction that you like, choose a deepening if you want extra help going deeper, pick a therapeutic script that addresses your issue (or that you can modify to fit your issue exactly), and the above awakening script. Record them in that order. All the scripts are designed to create recordings that are 20-25 minutes in total length. Listen to your recording in a safe, quiet place where you can close your eyes and relax comfortably. Because your eyes are closed when you use these scripts, you never listen to your recording while driving or operating machinery. Expect to relax deeply, and expect miracles to happen. If recording a session for yourself seems daunting, or if you would just prefer to hear the scripts read in my voice, most of them are available for purchase at my website, www.HughesHypnosis.com.

A quick note. Some of these scripts address illnesses and other physical problem. Hypnosis is a complement to regular medical care. **NEVER, EVER**, use these self-hypnosis recordings **in place** of medical care. Use them in addition to professional diagnosis and treatment. Use the Birthing scripts **in addition to** obstetric care, childbirth classes and other pregnancy and birth care. I am not a fan of home births, and would prefer that my scripts are only used in the context of excellent hospital obstetric care. Use the Irritable Bowel protocol scripts **in addition** medical diagnosis. The symptoms of IBS can identical to those of life threatening conditions. Only a doctor can tell you whether you are dealing with a stress-caused functional problem like IBS, or with a physical problem needing immediate medical care. Get the medical care first, and let your doctor be amazed at how much your mind can help. These same ideas hold for all my scripts. They are intended to complement, not replace, care by doctors, chiropractors, psychologists and other health care professional. Never use these scripts in place of regular, professional health care.

Robert Hughes.BCH

INDUCTIONS AND DEEPENINGS

Confusion Induction

A deepening can be added to this induction if desired. It does include an integrated deepening that is usually sufficient. Confusion inductions are very useful for people who have a difficult time entering hypnosis. They are also fun to experience. They work because the conscious mind gets so overwhelmed trying to follow, that it just gives up, and lets you sink into a quiet, subconscious state.

This is a self-relaxation and change recording. Because you may choose to close your eyes and focus inwardly, you only listen to this recording in a place where it is safe to close your eyes,
As we begin, you can help me by not helping me; or not help me by helping me. The choice is yours. And if you choose, you can close your eyes, but only if your eyes want to close and never because you think I want your eyes to close. So don't help me by closing your eyes…. And don't not help me by not closing your eyes. Let your mind drift and don't not close your eyes if they don't want to not open… . And don't not open your eyes if they don't want to not close… just let them do as they want….
And breathe as you want to breathe. Don't not breathe deeply because you think I want you to not breathe in that way or any way and don't not let out a deep gentle exhale unless you truly don't want to not breathe gently and easily… just breathe as you choose, letting each breath not relax you or relax you as you choose.
And your mind can follow my words with exquisite attention or your mind can attend to any exquisite thought it chooses…. or not choose with exquisite balance. And don't not let your mind drift and don't not let your mind focus, but let your mind choose to drift or focus as it chooses. And

no matter what your mind chooses, you are aware of everything and yet you are not aware.

And the more you are aware, the more your inner mind is conscious and your conscious mind is inside. Your subconscious mind is awake and aware and your conscious mind is at peace and choosing to be aware and yet not aware... outside and yet deeply within. Your conscious mind is feeling, hearing and seeing but your subconscious mind is seeing, hearing and feeling <u>everything,</u> and the more you don't not relax, the more your inner mind comes out and your outer mind meets it going in. Your subconscious mind knows and because your subconscious mind knows, your conscious mind can know or not know as you choose. Your outer mind can rest and sleep or it can be present as the inner mind does its magic. The more you don't not rest your outer mind, the more your inner mind doesn't not work its magic. And whatever you choose or don't choose; the magic isn't not working. Your inner mind never doesn't know, and never doesn't work the magic.

Your inner conscious subconscious mind remembers everything so your outer conscious mind can choose what to remember, because your outer conscious mind can't remember everything so it chooses what to not remember but your inner conscious mind is conscious and never doesn't remember. You can remember what you choose to forget or forget what you choose to forget. And in forgetting what you choose, you can choose to remember.... It doesn't matter if your outer mind forgets. It need not remember. Your inner mind remembers what you need to remember and never forgets while your outer mind can choose to not remember, and relax.

Now let your inner mind listen carefully, and your outer mind can listen or not listen as it chooses. And as you continue to listen to my voice, each sound and each breath causes you to relax more deeply and your outer conscious mind focuses on the feelings inside and your inner conscious mind listens and works. Your outer mind drifts in, not caring about the cares of the world, and your outer mind rises out, caring for you as your conscious mind doesn't not sleep and doesn't not rest and recharge itself. And the more you don't not recharge and rest, the more each breath doesn't not carry you into more serene and tranquil inner awareness and control. And the less you try to control the more control you have; and the more you don't not flow with your inner going, the more you don't not find miracles happening in your inner being and outer life. And just letting yourself relax more deeply now, your eyes doing what they naturally want to do; and your breath breathing as it naturally wants to breathe.

As I count in an orderly manner from 10 down to one, your outer mind can try to decipher the order if it chooses, or let the order take care of itself. Every count in _its_ order doesn't not cause your mind to double its relaxation and openness to positive change.

Ten, sleep now or later...
Three, rest deeper now or later...
Eight choosing sleep or rest...
Four, deeper now or later...
Six deeper now or sooner...
Seven, going with the flow, or being the flow...
Two, drifting down or up...
Four. being at peace or peacefully being...
Nine relaxing or resting...
Five so relaxed or so focused ...
One, so calm or so peaceful

Just be where you are now, knowing that every breath you breathe causes your vast inner mind to accept, to embrace and to totally implement every positive and beneficial idea on this recording. Every beat of your heart and every sound in your ears causes you to be more deeply relaxed. Your inner mind thinks at the speed of thought, many thousands of times faster than my outer mind can speak. With every breath you breathe, your inner mind accepts, integrates and implements every good idea on this recording, and makes it true for you. In each and every way, the more you relax your outer mind and heart, the more your powerful inner mind brings about the changes you desire in your outer life.

Two Minute Induction

Once you practice with the longer inductions, and discover how good it feels to be in hypnosis, all you need is a shorter induction. This one has an integrated deepening process, the count down from ten to one. If you want to go deeper, you can add a second ten to one countdown deepening. Or use the feather, or Longacre's yardstick deepening, for a very deep state.

This is a self-hypnosis recording to help you _____. (*Fill in the blank with your specific goal.*). Because you are relaxing deeply, you always use this recording in a safe, quiet place and never while driving a vehicle or operating machinery.

Sit back or lie down in a comfortable place, like an easy chair or your bed. Take a deep breath, and as you let it gently out, let every part of yourself begin to relax. The next 20 minutes is just your time and the cares of the world can simply take care of themselves while you are recharging your mind, heart and body in a deep state of peaceful relaxation. Take in another deep breath and let it out, and you find yourself relaxing even more. It feels so good to just let go and relax. Expect to relax deeply, want to relax deeply, and feel yourself relaxing so deeply.

Focus your attention now on the sound of my voice. For the duration of the recording the sound of my voice and the sound of your thinking are the only important sounds. As you breathe gently, relaxing more with each breath, you let every other sound simply be an invitation to relax more deeply and enjoy the peace that listening to the recording brings you.

Picture or imagine a set of stairs leading down to a beautiful room. That room is a special place, a place of powerful inner peace and learning deep within. In a moment, we are going to walk down those stairs and enter that beautiful room where you can work with your inner mind to attain your deepest desires. As I count from ten down to one, you imagine walking slowly down the stairs and you are amazed to notice that your state of peaceful relaxation doubles with each count. Each number I count is a signal for your mind and body to take another step into relaxation. (Count slowly)

10... every muscle, cell and fiber relaxing
 9... So peaceful, exhaling stress and tension
 8... Serene, calm and tranquil
 7... Letting the cares of the world take care of themselves

6… Your eyes are so relaxed they don't want to open
5… Your body feels tingly and doesn't want to move
4… Breathing in peace and comfort
3… So relaxed now. Doubling mental and physical relaxation with each count
2… The more you relax, the faster things change
1… All the way down now, so peaceful

As you enter that beautiful room at the bottom of the stairs, you notice that it is quiet and softly lit with many glowing candles. Your favorite soft, relaxing music is playing. The room is richly furnished and you know you are always safe to be yourself fully in this deep inner sanctuary. Although the candlelight is soft, you are aware of the rich colors of your room, and notice the comfortable furniture. There is a large, overstuffed chair, your favorite, under a high, arched window. You don't look out yet, but you know somehow that there is an amazing natural wonderland just outside your room.

You feel so safe and serene in your room – so secure and comfortable. The chair is so inviting, as if it would wrap you in a blanket of relaxation and safety. You sit down, and let yourself relax twice as deeply. As you sink down into the wonderful comfort of the chair, sinking into that supporting surface beneath you, your outer mind drifts and floats while your inner mind prepares to do the work. Leaving the past behind, being present in the present. As you float and drift, every beat of your heart and every breath you breathe cause you to relax more comfortably and deeply.

Dr. John Kresnik's Induction

Dr. John Kresnik is a highly skilled and respected hypnotherapist and teacher in Denver, Colorado. This script is my interpretation of his words and style. It also makes a powerful deepening script after another induction. Read this induction slowly, with attention to the rhythm and cadence of your words.

This is a relaxation and stress relief recording to help you _____. (*Fill in the blank* with *your specific goal.*) Never listen to this recording while driving a vehicle or operating machinery.
Please begin by sitting back or lying down in a comfortable place where it is safe to close your eyes. As you settle in to that peaceful place, take in a deep breath and as you let it go, let yourself expect that the next 25 minutes or so is a time of deep rest and recharge for your mind and body as you effortlessly create change in your life.
That's right
Just sit back and allow yourself... to begin to relax.
Feeling yourself... sinking... more deeply in.
To your comfortable resting place...
Letting your mind build a picture for you.
Imagining a beautiful mountain meadow... on a perfect warm spring day.
Hearing the sound of a small stream... seeing the beauty all around.
Aware of the touch of the wind... and the aroma of the trees;
Listening.... to my voice... as you feel yourself...
Drifting and floating.
Floating like a fluffy cloud... drifting across that beautiful mountain sky.
And as you gently drift and float... you feel yourself... swirling and twirling...
Rapidly releasing... floating... enjoying... completely relaxing.
Totally in control... just enjoying the beauty of your mountain meadow.
Totally at peace... just letting the cares of the world take care of themselves.
Listening to my voice...enjoying the beauty of the meadow.
Caring only about the peacefulness... of this moment.
Your body feeling... so light... so relaxed.... Floating and drifting...
With the wind.
Free to be... all you want to be.
Letting go... so completely...

Resting... So tranquil... just sinking into the peace and beauty
Of your private meadow.
Just enjoying who you are.... Where you are
And what you are
That's right.
Yes... allow yourself to relax even more deeply
Imagining your meadow... just being there
Drifting deeper and deeper...
As you imagine yourself in that beautiful meadow
Experiencing the freshness of the meadow
After a soft, gentle spring rain
Feeling the warming sun bursting through the clouds
Warming and caressing your body
The sunlight massaging you... into a deeper relaxation
Looking upward... and relaxing more deeply
Seeing the bright, energizing colors of the rainbow
Across your meadow
The colors brightly and beautifully... showering you
In shades of Red... Orange.... Yellow.... Green... Blue... and Purple
Touching you... Feeling alive and vibrant
Secure... safe and at peace
Grateful for life
Feeling a new sense of meaning... Happiness.... Tranquility.... Joy
Knowing that in this meadow
You are embraced and loved by life
So alert.... So excited.... So peaceful.... So calm and serene
So uplifted.... So tranquil, relaxed and rested
Just enjoying your meadow... totally at peace

And as you gently float in your mountain meadow, every breath you breathe causes your powerful inner mind to be open to, and receptive of, every positive and beneficial suggestion on this recording. And every breath causes you to relax to a deeper state of peaceful awareness, and powerful inner growth and change.

Dr. Mike Preston's Progressive Relaxation Induction

The late Dr. Mike Preston was an amazingly powerful hypnotist and hypnosis teacher who has influenced thousands of hypnotists. This is my rendering of the induction he used for ninety percent of his clients.

This is a self-hypnosis recording to help you _____. (*Fill in the blank* with *your specific goal*.). Never use this recording while driving a vehicle or operating machinery.

To begin, lie down or sit down in a quiet, comfortable place where your head and neck are fully supported. That's right, just lie back, and expect to spend the next 25 minutes on a very pleasant journey of relaxation and comfort. Close your eyes, and let your eyelids gently begin to relax deeply. If you imagine that your eyelids are relaxing so deeply that they don't want to open, you rapidly begin to experience a very pleasant sensation in the muscles of your eyelids, as if they are being stroked softly with a delicate little down feather. And the gentle, massaging sensations cause your eyelid muscles to relax further and further with each breath you breathe. And with each breath you breathe, you are breathing out tension and stress with every exhale, and breathing in comfort and peace with each and every inhale. And with each breath the muscles around your eyelids grow more and more comfortable and relaxed. So comfortable that they just want to stay gently closed as you enjoy this recording. And that peaceful feeling around your eyelids begins to spread with each breath you breathe. You focus on the muscles of your forehead, and as the relaxed, peaceful feelings spread from your eyelids to your forehead, relaxation flows over your forehead like a wonderful coating of a soothing, warming, and penetrating lotion.

You imagine hundreds of tiny fingers gently massaging away every bit of stress, tension, and worry that you have held in your forehead. That wonderful, relaxing, massaging, warming sensation spreads through your jaw... over your scalp and down the muscles of your neck.... As if every part of your head and neck were being gently massaged, rocked and cradled in the kindest, gentlest, and most healing hands. The sensation of a penetrating and soothing massage spreads through your shoulders, and down your arms to your elbow, and with each breath, you feel a wonderful loosening and relaxing of all the muscles of the head, neck, shoulders and upper arms. You continue to allow yourself to imagine a wonderful massaging sensation soothing and relaxing your forearms, and every bit of tension in the arms just bubbles away into the air as your arms relax more deeply with every breath. That pleasant, relaxing sensation spreads into your hands. You may notice them tingling slightly with the sensation of being delicately stroked and massaged. You allow that soothing sensation of comfort and relaxation to fill your hands all the way down to the tips of your fingers, and it feels so good just to let your hands rest, recharge, relax and rejuvenate. And from the top of your head to the tips of your fingers, you allow yourself to simply enjoy this feeling of deep relaxation. And it gets deeper and more pleasant with each and every breath you breathe.

Now send that pleasant relaxing sensation in a wave from your eyelids, through your head and neck, trunk and torso all the way down to the tips of your toes with each pleasant and gentle exhale. Breathing out stress and tension... breathing a deeper wave of relaxation in with each and every gentle, peaceful and relaxing breath...stress and tension out... peace and comfort in... wave after relaxing wave of comfort and peace.... Filling every cell, every fiber and every tissue of your entire being...and that wave of relaxation grows more powerful and more peaceful... with every breath you breathe. You have allowed yourself to relax deeply and peacefully, and every minute you allow yourself to be in this relaxed state is as powerful as 10 minutes of sleep in restoring and recharging your mind, your heart, and your body.

Dr. Mike Preston's Deepening

This deepening is specifically designed to be used with Dr. Preston's induction. It can also be used as a deepening with any of the other inductions. The concepts are his, but the way they are presented is my interpretation of his ideas and style,

It feels so good to just let go and relax. So to deepen this wonderful state of relaxation, imagine a blackboard or whiteboard. In your dominant hand, you are holding a piece of chalk or a marker. And in your other hand, you are holding an eraser. You imagine writing one of the letters of the alphabet on that board, the last letter, the Z. It is made of two straight lines and a diagonal, and as you imagine writing the Z on the board, it causes you to relax a little more. Then you imagine erasing the Z right off the blackboard of your mind, and every time you erase a letter from this blackboard, it causes your powerful mind to double its state of deep and peaceful relaxation... Feel how good it feels to erase and relax

Now write the capital Y on the board in your mind, relaxing a bit more as you do... and with your eraser hand, gently erase the Y from the board and feel yourself relaxing more... doubling your relaxation again. Expect yourself to relax as you erase each letter. Want yourself to relax deeply as you erase each letter. And feel how good it feels to relax into such peaceful comfort.

Now imagine writing the X on your board with your dominant hand, appreciating its shape, and the feel of the crossing lines. And then with your other hand, imagine erasing the X right off the blackboard of your mind, once again doubling your state of calm and pleasant peacefulness... and every letter you erase causes your mind to relax deeply and wonderfully.

Now write all the letters of the alphabet backwards down to P with your writing hand... just imagine putting them up on your board, appreciating all the shapes and realizing how much the letters shape our lives. Relaxing with these familiar symbols of the mind's power to invent... And then, with your eraser hand, in one motion erase all those letters from the mental board... and every letter you erase causes your mind to relax soooo deeply... W...V...U...T...S...R...Q...P – just erasing and dropping now into a deep, focused state of amazing peace and comfort.

Follow with your writing hand putting up the next set of letters in reverse order – from the O down to the H. Such a varied set of straight and curving letters, so elegant and beautiful, so powerful, these letters that let us describe the world in words. And for just this short time, you allow your other hand to temporarily erase these letters from your mind. And as you erase each letter, your state of mental relaxation doubles and doubles and doubles. O...erasing and relaxing...N.... deeper... M...more and more calm... L... K.... J... I.... H... just dropping now into an even deeper, and more focused state of refreshing peace and comfort... Every letter you erase from your imagination causes you to double your state of wonderful relaxation and peace.

And now let your writing hand put up the last seven letters of the alphabet... from G down to A... lots of swirling curves and beautiful that create so much meaning. With your eraser hand, gently erase each letter in turn... slowly, gently erasing, remembering that every letter you erase, causes you to double you wonderful relaxation... G... gently, peacefully letting go... F... fully, totally relaxed... E... erasing and letting all the cares of the world take care of themselves... D... deep, tranquil awareness... C... calm, centered and so serene... B... balanced, relaxed and all is well and... A... absolutely at peace.

Sleep now, deeply at rest, and deeply receptive to new and positive changes. Every breath you breathe causes your mind to be open to, and to implement every positive, beneficial idea on this recording. And every breath you breathe causes you to relax more deeply and be even more receptive to powerful and positive change in your life.

Elman Pretend Game Induction and Deepening for Children

The late Dave Elman, who coined the word "hypnotherapy," used an induction like this one to work with children. It also works very well with adults... particularly those with active and playful imaginations. The concepts are Elman's. This presentation is my interpretation of his concepts. It includes an integrated deepening.

This is a self-hypnosis recording to help you _____. (*Fill the blank with your specific goal.*) Because you close your eyes and relax deeply, you never use this recording while driving or operating machinery.

Now that you are ready to go into deep hypnosis, close your eyes and get relaxed in the chair…. (*Pause 5 seconds*)

Take in a deep breath, and gently let it go… As your breath goes out, you know this is a special time for you, a time to relax and _____ (*achieve your specific goal*)…. That's right; just breathe in and out normally now…

Let's play a pretend game…. I know that you can pretend really well, and we are going to use your powerful ability to dream, pretend and play to help you get so relaxed and feel so good…. and that is *totally awesome*…

I want you to pretend that for the next little while, your eyes are so totally closed that they don't want to open… In fact I want you to pretend that your eyes are so closed that you really can't open them…. And you can show yourself how well you pretend… When you are pretending really hard that your eyes won't open, you can try to open them… and what is really cool, is that when you are pretending you can't open your eyes, they really don't want to open… It's a funny feeling, because you know you can always open your eyes if you want, but the more you pretend they won't open, the heavier they get, and the harder you try to open them the more they stay closed… So, do your very best pretending now, and pretend that your eyes won't open….

That's great, and as soon as you are pretending your very best that your eyes won't open, you can try to open them, and when you are pretending *really hard*, it is *totally cool* because your eyes just won't open and the harder you try, the harder they stay closed… Go ahead and give your eyes a try… (That's right! You are doing great pretending, and the wonderful thing about pretending is the harder you pretend, the more your eyes get totally peaceful and relaxed. (*Pause 2-3 seconds*)

Now let's make your whole body and mind as relaxed as your eyes... Focus on your arms and pretend that your arms are giant pieces of spaghetti... feel your arms and hands get all tingly and heavy... all limp and floppy, just like really well-cooked spaghetti.... Just imagine your arms and hands being loose and limp, and the more you imagine, the heavier and more relaxed your hands become.... You are doing a great job pretending and the more you pretend your arms are like spaghetti, the more relaxed they become.... Great pretending! It feels *totally cool* to have arms like spaghetti... so heavy, and floppy and limp.

Now send that relaxed feeling from your arms into your legs and body... that's right, just pretend that your whole body is getting as relaxed as your eyes and arms.... Pretend that your whole body is as heavy and floppy as a bowlful of spaghetti... and the more you pretend, the heavier and looser and more relaxed your whole body begins to feel. You are doing a great job pretending and the harder you pretend the deeper you relax. (*Pause for 2-3 seconds*)

You are really good at this! And the great thing about pretending is that the more you pretend that your body is loose and floppy, the more you begin to sink into the chair and the more *totally awesome* you feel because you are doing such a great job of relaxing... and the more you pretend, the more relaxed you really get. Notice how slow and peaceful and rhythmic your breathing has become because you are doing such a great job pretending to be like a heavy, floppy, relaxed plate of spaghetti! Notice how light and nice your mind feels as your body get all relaxed and floppy!

Now let's do the coolest pretending of all... for the rest of our session, I want you to pretend you can't remember your ABCs... Now I know that you are really smart and could never really forget your ABCs, but let's just pretend that all the letters of the alphabet are getting ready to march right out of your mind, just like a parade... Imagine all the letters of the alphabet lining up and getting ready to march out of your mind for a little while... Now pretend they are going away, just disappearing.... There goes the Z now. Pretend the Z just marched right out of your mind.... It will come back as soon as your stop pretending to forget it... but every time you pretend a letter is marching away, your whole mind and body get more and more relaxed, and the harder you pretend, the more relaxed you get. And you are doing a great job of pretending. Feel how good it feels to pretend the Z is fading right out of your mind.... And as it fades away, you relax even deeper.

And now, pretend that the Y is following the Z right our of your mind.... And every letter you pretend to forget causes your mind to get more and more peaceful.... Now pretend that the X fades away too, and feel how good it feels to relax more and more as more letters fade away.... (*Pause 2-3 seconds*)

Now lets do some really good pretending and imagine a whole bunch of letters leaving at once.... W... V.... U... T... S... R.... Q.... P.... Pretend those letters are going, going, gone... and the harder you pretend the more the letters really march right out of your mind for a little while....

And the harder you pretend you are sending the letters away, the harder it is to remember the next letter to send and the better you feel... And the O fades away all by itself, and the N, the M, the L... and it feels so good to just relax totally and let all the letters fade away all at once and you pretend that you can't even remember what letter comes next and all the letters all the way down to the A just fade right out of your mind. Just pretend the letters are all gone now. And the coolest thing is that the harder you pretend, the more the ABCs really fade away. And your mind relaxes deeper and deeper as each letter fades temporarily out of your mind. (*Pause 2-3 seconds*)

You are doing great! You are <u>so good</u> at pretending that you are really in totally great hypnosis. And every breath you breathe makes you more relaxed. And every breath you breathe makes your mind open up and accept all the good ideas you hear about all the positive changes you want in your life. And the more you relax the more those wonderful changes happen effortlessly and automatically.

Dr. R.D. Longacre's Computer Game Induction for Children

The late R.D. (Sean) Longacre developed this induction for children, but adult who play computer games may find that it works well for them too. It doesn't require a deepening, but a countdown deepening goes well with it. The concept is Sean's. The execution is my style.

This is a relaxation recording to help you _____. (*Fill in the blank with your specific goal.*) Never use this recording while driving or operating machinery.

Begin by taking a deep breath in and letting it out – like this (*inhale and exhale audibly.*) And as you let out your breath, close your eyes and let's play the pretend game together. All you have to do is to pretend that your eyes are so closed that they just don't want to open. That's right, pretend that your eyes just don't want to open, and pretend that the harder you pretend your eyes don't want to open, the more closed they get. And as long as you keep pretending your eyes don't want to open, everything on this recording sinks into your mind, and you feel great. So pretend that your eyes just want to stay closed until the session is over. And let all the good ideas on the recording sink into your mind.

Pretending your eyes don't want to open gives you a nice kind of funny feeling. Because when you are pretending really hard, if you try to open your eyes, the more you try to open them, the more they stay closed. And because you are really good at pretending, they don't want to open. And since you want the help this recording gives you, it is so easy to pretend your eyes want to stay totally closed. (*Pause 2-3 seconds*)

Now that your eyes are so relaxed that they don't want to open, let's pretend that you are a computer. Your head is the top of the computer, and your fingers are the mouse and keyboard that give your computer instructions. So just pretend that your computer is warming up and getting ready to help you relax even more. (*Pause 2-3 seconds*)

Take another deep breath and feel yourself beginning to relax as you play the computer game called "turning off the switches." This is a very simple game and you play it by moving the pointer finger on one of your hands. Every time you move the pointer finger, you are turning off the switches that control your muscles and you are relaxing and feeling really good.

Each time you move your finger, it turns off a switch that controls a different part of your body. It's really cool because you feel more relaxed and calmer every time a muscle relaxes. And you can turn off switches and relax different parts of your body. As each part of your body relaxes, your pointer finger gets more relaxed too and it barely moves as you turn off switch after switch. Every time you lift your finger, a different part of your body relaxes and your finger gets more relaxed too. And when a part of your body relaxes, it feels really good, like it is sleepy. And that part of your body may stretch and yawn or just feel different; like pretending to be tired or heavy and that's OK because you are in control of the computer, and you can turn the switches on or off whenever you want.

So moving the pointer finger and turning off the switch to your head makes your whole head and neck feel loose and heavy and tired and so relaxed and feeling so good *(Pause)*. Go ahead and lift the pointer finger NOW to turn off the muscles in your head and neck and your whole head and neck relax and go very peaceful NOW and your pointer finger relaxes right along with your head and neck. (*Pause five seconds*)

When you turn off the switch to your chest and back, it makes the whole middle of your body feel so good and so peaceful. So lift your pointer finger again NOW and relax your whole chest and back. And your finger is getting so much heavier that it can just barely move, but even thinking about moving it causes you to relax the next part of your body. And your whole chest and back just relax and sink deeper into the chair. Sleep now. Like your body is sleepy but your mind is alert and awake. (*Pause five seconds*)

Think about lifting your pointer finger again NOW, and just thinking about lifting it turns off the muscles of your arms and legs NOW and your whole body feels so good and your arms and legs get so relaxed and peaceful and heavy and your whole body feels good, just the way you want it to feel. And you are so relaxed, and as your body gets so relaxed, even the insides of your body relax and begin to feel good.

And when your whole body is relaxing and starting to feel sooo good, you turn on the switch to the main computer so you can program your mind and body computer just the way you want it to run. And you are programming your mind with all it needs to help you feel healthy and strong and good, and you know how to turn on the main control for achieving your goals and feeling great. You turn on the main control for feeling great by moving the pointer finger again, and even if your pointer finger feels like it is too relaxed to move, just thinking about moving your pointer finger NOW turns on the main control for learning to achieve all your goals. You may not even feel your finger move, but just thinking about moving your pointer finger turns on the learning center now and you are ready to program your inner computer so it works for you.

Pocket Watch Induction

This induction uses your imagination to lead yourself into hypnosis using the image we have all seen of a hypnotist waving a watch on a chain. Since an imaginary watch is just as real to your subconscious as an actual watch, this induction works like a charm. You can add a deepening if desired. A countdown deepening or Dr. Longacre's yardstick work well. Read this one slowly... with lots of Pauses... so that your imagination can keep up with your words.

This is a self-hypnosis recording. Because your eyes are closed and you are deeply relaxed, you never listen to this recording while driving or operating machinery.

Close and eyes.... Take a deep breath, and slowly let it out as you begin to relax... you are relaxing deeply today by using your amazing and powerful imagination.

Begin by imagining that you are holding and swinging a shiny gold pocket watch slowly on a chain right in front of your eyes... you know, just like the movies and cartoons where someone gets hypnotized when the hypnotist says "watch the watch..." Only today, the watch is imaginary, and you are the hypnotist, swinging your imaginary watch gently in front of your own eyes.

Picture and imagine that beautiful watch swinging gently and easily on its golden chain... Let it swing gently in your imagination and just watch it swing.... Take another deep breath, and when you are ready to go into hypnosis, just let your breath out gently and let your eyes relax so deeply that they don't want to open... watch the watch in your mind and let your eyes lock down...

That's good... now imagine the weight of the watch and how it pulls down on your hand as you swing it gently in front of your eyes...
Let your breathing go gently but deeply into your tummy, and feel how good it feels to breathe in and out...
And imagine that the watch is getting heavier and heavier with every swing, pulling your imaginary arm down toward your lap...
And with every gentle swing, imagine the watch getting heavier and heavier...

And with every exhale, the watch is getting heavier and heavier
And pretty soon, it starts to pull your hand gently down toward your lap
Heavier and heavier with every swing…. And you picture your imaginary hand and arm beginning to slowly, slowly move down toward your lap… See it in your mind's eye… imagine it… and feel your whole body and mind getting more and more relaxed as you imagine the watch pulling your arm down to your body….

That's great… and as you imagine your hand moving slowly down, you relax more and more… and every swing of your imaginary watch causes you to feel calm and peaceful…. And even more peaceful and calm with every breath you breathe…
Want it to happen… Expect yourself to relax more and more with every imaginary swing of your watch…
That's right; just let yourself relax more and more…
The watch is almost down to your lap now, and the instant the watch touches you… imagine your entire body being as relaxed and floppy as a bowl of noodles…
The instant you imagine the watch touching you, your imaginary arm collapses and you feel a whole wave of relaxation flow through your entire body relaxing you ten times deeper…

Sleep now, deeply asleep, and every breath causes you to relax even deeper… Not asleep like at night… just a gentle sleep of the nervous system… deeper and deeper with every gentle exhale…

You are in deep hypnosis and every breath causes your mind to be open to great new ideas that make Your life better… Every breath causes you to go deeper and more relaxed…

Ericksonian Style Induction: Footprints in the Sand

This induction is particularly good for clients with strong Christian beliefs. They will recognize the story, and find it a very comforting way to focus the mind and relax. It is a very good induction to use when low self-esteem is part of the underlying problem, because of its message of being cherished by God is a powerful anodyne for self-hatred. I use it both as an induction and as a healing metaphor. The story can be adapted for almost any religion. Instead of telling a story about Jesus walking with a person on a beach, it can be modified to be about the Buddha helping one cross the mountains, or about Mohammed accompanying one on a pilgrimage across the desert. For a recording, modify it to fit your spiritual and religious beliefs. My guess is that other hypnotists have used this induction, but I developed it independently from the anonymous story, Footprints in the Sand. It is written here as if the client were a young girl. Change the words to fit if you are older or male.

Begin by closing your eyes and listen to this wonderful story which is so close to your heart. Because you are relaxing so deeply, you never listen to this story while driving or operating machinery.

That's good...now just settle back in the chair and get really comfortable... Settle in and sink into the chair. You have heard this story before, and as you begin to recognize it, the sound of my voice telling the story causes you to relax deeply and quickly. And even if this is the first time you have heard the story, just following along with my voice is so comforting and so relaxing...

The story is about a girl (*or boy, or man or woman, depending on you*) who lived on a beach, and spent her (*his*) whole, long, healthy life walking down that beach, leaving footprints in the sand behind her (*him*). And as you hear the words "footprints in the sand" you recognize the story and feel yourself relaxing so fast because it is such a beautiful story.

The girl walked down that beach on sunny days and cloudy days, through storms and perfect weather, through the fog and through the moonlight, always leaving footprints in the soft beach sand as she walked. Sometimes the breakers purred and sometimes they roared and thundered, but she kept walking down the beach leaving footprints to mark her journey.

One day, after a long hard walk, she noticed that the beach ahead of her was clear and empty... there were no footprints in front of her... But when she looked back, she saw to her incredible surprise that there were two sets of footprints stretching behind her down the beach... just imagine what it is like to look behind you and see two sets of footprints where you expected only one, and let yourself relax even more... (*Pause*)

So, looking into that place she had never really looked before, she saw that right along side her, matching her step for step, all the long way down the beach, was Jesus, the master, walking with her stride for stride...

And she felt a deep wave of comfort and peace come over her because she realized that when the Lord said: "I am with you always," he really meant it. And looking deeply into the Lord's eyes, she felt a love that she had never felt before... and she knew she could trust Him to help her with anything... And you are relaxing now so deeply and sinking into infinite love...

And looking back over her journey, she noticed that there were places on the beach where there were only one set of footprints... All those times she had felt hopeless, powerless, sick, enraged, afraid, overwhelmed or lost... in all those times, there was only one set of footprints in the sand.

Turning to Jesus, she asked: "Lord why, in all those times when I was afraid, enraged, lost, or hopeless, in all those times when I was sick and felt powerless, why did you leave me alone in those times?"

And Jesus, holding her hand gently, replied: "beloved daughter, beloved friend, in those times when you were most hopeless, afraid, lost or enraged, in those times when you were most sick or powerless, in those times, I did not leave you... **In those times I carried you**..."

And as the words "**I carried you**" echo through your heart and mind, you feel so peaceful and calm and every breath relaxes you more... just rest on that wonderful beach in your mind and let a healing peace fill you.

And there is a secret about this story you didn't know... even though you have heard the story before, and the secret is that the story is about you... YOU are the girl on that beach, walking always and forever side by side with the Lord, and He is always there for you when you relax and visit this beautiful beach within... relaxing so deeply now, into the peace beyond understanding...

Now just rest deeply and know that God's plan for you calls for perfect health, (*or your specific goal*) and that as we work, the Lord is always there, to carry you whenever you need help. Know deeply that your heart, mind and soul are open to receive the grace of inner healing (*or powerful change*). And the more your mind visits your beautiful beach, the more quickly and deeply you return to full and radiant health (*or your specific goals*). Just sleep now in the peace of the Lord...

Every breath you breathe causes all the good ideas for healing and change to take root and grow in your mind, as beautiful as the lilies of the field. And every breath you breathe causes you to relax more deeply and feel the divine love that is always with you.

Sleep now, in the arms of the Lord... At peace and at rest... Changing and healing.... So calm, so relaxed and so refreshed.

Yellow Flowers Induction

This is a variation of the Beach Induction presented in Unlocking the Blueprint of the Psyche. *It was inspired by the Chilean Poet, Pablo Neruda, and by Dr. Ernest Holmes. It is a particularly good induction for people with a strong spiritual awareness. It is meant to be read slowly, like a poem, allowing the mind to form the pictures of the beach and flowers.*

Sit back, or lie back and allow yourself to begin a journey of deep relaxation and powerful inner healing and change. Take in a deep breath, and as you let it out, sink into your comfortable surface, letting your eyes close down, and letting every muscle in your body start to relax.

Now imagine that you are on a beautiful, sandy ocean beach...
Imagine yourself walking along the sand...
Feeling the softness of the sand between your toes
And the cool caress of the waves as they gently wash your feet and ankles
And every breath you breathe, and every sight, sound and sensation on your beach cause you to relax deeply and swiftly... mind, body and spirit

There are seabirds overhead
Soaring in harmony with the waves
You breathe deeply filling your lungs with the aromas along the shore
You can taste the salt in the air
And relax ten times more deeply

Looking over the vastness of the ocean, you marvel at the magnitude
Of the sea,
And of the entire world and the universe, of which
You are an indispensable part.
As you continue to walk along the strand, you are aware of,
And awed by, the immense rolling sea
Developing her myth, her mission
Her vast ferment of life, her vast participation
In the divine miracle of creation
And the rhythm of the breaking waves causes you to relax more deeply yet.

You turn from the ocean and walk a path up an emerald green hill

Robert Hughes.BCH

You reach the top and are joyously amazed
By a vast panorama of sand, water, sun and sky
The blues reflecting and shifting against one another
The gold of the sand and the white of clouds fill your eyes
And you relax even more deeply

Far out in the ocean, you see dolphins and tuna dancing
You see giant whales swimming by
And you marvel at the beauty and complexity of God
Revealing in all creation
And then it dawns on you
That you are also one of those marvels
And a unique part of that creation
And you relax even more deeply into the welcoming arms of a loving Universe

As you begin to walk back down the path
Your eyes are rooted to the beauty
Of three small yellow flowers
And they are so compelling that your eyes desert
The sea and her majesty, the sky and his vastness
And you see in the small, brilliant flowers an even deeper affirmation
Of the spirit in all things
Your eyes flee the power of the sea and the endlessness of the sky
Your heart leaps in joy at the flowers springing in bloom
Against all the vastness around
You feel the presence of God in this smallest
Most routine of miracles
The flowers of spring blooming impossibly yellow and brilliant
Into the fleeting joy of being
Knowing that though they are here but briefly
They return again, and again and again
And in their own way they are as eternal as the sea and sky
And they are divine love on a human scale
Perhaps we cannot encompass the entire sea
But our eyes can feast and our hearts can dance
To the song of daffodils dancing in the wind

You dance the eternal dance of life
Feeling God within and in everything

Feeling a renewed love, a regenerated strength and purpose
A vast awareness of God in the oceanic whole
And a vaster awareness of God in every tiny flowering detail
And in yourself
Dancing between the ocean and the flowers.
Just floating and drifting now, in the miracle of being you
A flower of pure being,
Dancing in the heart of God
And as you float in your awareness of your connection to all creation,
Your mind is open to, and accepting of every positive and beneficial suggestion on this recording.
Every breath you breathe causes you to relax more deeply
And every breath you breathe causes your inner mind to do whatever healthy thing it takes so that you _____ (*achieve your specific goal.*)

Countdown Deepening

This is the shortest and simplest deepening technique I know, but it is very effective. Read it slowly with short Pauses between steps.

And as I count from 10 down to one, every number I count causes you to relax twice as deeply into the deepest relaxation you can imagine and ten times deeper than that.
Ten: Calm, relaxed and totally at peace, doubling your relaxation
Nine: Deep, serene, comfortable, twice as relaxed again
Eight: So inwardly alert, but so calm
Seven: Sinking into the chair or bed, doubling the relaxation
Six: Doubling the depth again, every gentle exhale takes you deeper
Five: Halfway down, so deep calm and peaceful
Four: Doubling that relaxation with every count, so rested, so uplifted, so peaceful
Three: Serene, tranquil, so peaceful, as deep as you can imagine relaxing
Two: Relaxing even deeper, so totally peaceful
One: Ten times deeper than you ever believed you could relax, but so inwardly alert and so ready for change

Every breath you breathe causes your inner mind to be open to, and to be accepting of every positive and beneficial idea on this recording. And every breath you breathe, and every beat of your heart, cause you to relax more deeply and to accept and implement all the beneficial ideas on the recording.

Elevator Deepening

Now that you are good and relaxed, let's go really deep. Imagine an elevator that goes a long way down into the basement of relaxation... in fact imagine that there are three levels of basement... The A level of relaxation basement is 10 times more relaxed than you are right now... the B level of the basement of relaxation is ten times deeper than that, and the C level of relaxation is the deepest level of relaxation and it is even 10 times deeper than the B level.

We are going to take that elevator all the way down to the C level, the incredibly deep level of relaxation where healing (*or change*) is so easy...

As you look at the elevator, you realize it is under your control... you decide how deep you go and how fast you get there...

So when you are ready to get totally relaxed, you can push the down button on the outside of the elevator. You wait for the door to open, relaxing more deeply with every breath you breathe. (*Pause to give yourself time to follow the instruction*)

The elevator door opens and you see that there are numbered buttons for all the floors going up, and buttons with letters for the deep basements of relaxation marked A, B, and C. When you are ready, push the button for the C basement, the deepest basement of relaxation. Push the C button now. (*Pause 2-3 seconds*)

That's good... The door closes, and your elevator starts to move slowly down... You can feel the slight lightness you feel on an elevator going down. And you sense your elevator very gently rocking and vibrating as it descends so deeply at just the perfect speed for you. And you feel yourself relaxing deeper and deeper the more the elevator gently and slowly carries you down. The elevator won't stop at the A basement of relaxation, but as it goes by the A will light up.... The A basement of relaxation is ten times deeper than when you got on. Just feel yourself gently relaxing as the elevator slides gently down. And as you relax, notice when the light for A goes on, letting you know that you are passing the A level of relaxation... (*Pause 5-10 seconds to let yourself go by A*)

Wonderful! You are letting your elevator carry you deeper at the perfect pace for you... just feel the elevator carrying you down, rocking gently as it descends to B, and you are relaxing so deeply so quickly... B is ten times deeper than A, and the light comes on as you go past the B basement of relaxation... just relaxing even more deeply at the perfect pace for you, and watching as the light goes on for the B level of relaxation. (*Pause 10 seconds to let yourself go by B.*)

(*Reading slowly*) Gently rocking, you relax more deeply with every gentle exhale... totally in control of your relaxation, just like your inner mind is totally in control of helping you heal (*or change or achieve your specific goal*) at the perfect pace for you.... Just riding past the B level of relaxation and going all the way down to the C level of relaxation at your own perfect pace... hearing, sensing, feeling and imagining your elevator moving down, and every movement causes your body and mind to relax deeper and deeper... the deeper you go, the more effortlessly you _____ (*ill in the blank with your specific goal*)

(*Reading slowly*) And when your elevator reaches the C level, and takes you all the way to the deep basement of relaxation, the C light comes on and you feel your elevator gently come to a stop... As the door opens on the deepest relaxation you have ever felt or imagined, step off your elevator into the depths of your incredible inner mind, knowing that the deeper you relax, the more powerfully you _____. (*Fill in the blank with your specific goal*) Every breath you breathe for the rest of the recording causes your mind to follow the elevator deeper.

Dr. R.D. Longacre's Yardstick Deepening

Sean Longacre called this technique "the hypnodepthmeter." But since it uses an imaginary yardstick, I just refer to it as Longacre's yardstick. The beauty of this deepening is that it allows you to control precisely how deeply you relax and how quickly you get there. It works well with any of the inductions. I use it most with the shorter inductions. Like all deepenings it can also be used as a stand-alone induction, just by changing the first sentence to: "begin by closing your eyes and taking a deep breath and going into deep hypnosis so your inner mind can help you…." Read this more slowly, with short Pauses if you want more time to go deep. Read it more steadily if you don't need as much time to relax deeply.

You have done a great job going into hypnosis… now let's go deeper so your inner mind can really help you _____. (*Fill in the blank with your specific goal*) To help you relax super deeply, I want you to imagine a yardstick… just picture or imagine it in your mind.

Your yardstick is three feet long, and has markings from 0 to 36. Your yardstick can be any color you want, as long as you can see or imagine the numbers. Now imagine there is an indicator that slides along your yardstick. 36 on your yardstick represents your normal, outer state of mind, and 0 on your yardstick represents the <u>deepest you can even imagine</u> relaxing. Your indicator is pointing to a number that tells you where you are right now between 36 and 0. When you can see or sense where the indicator is right now, notice that you are already relaxing. Whatever number you see is perfect… the more you use this recording the faster you relax deeply…

This beautiful yardstick is a magical yardstick…. It doesn't just show you how relaxed you are; it lets you control your level of relaxation. Every time you move the indicator down or up, your level of relaxation follows the indicator. Try it now… When you are ready to relax more deeply, you can imagine sliding your indicator from wherever it is down to 14. And you feel yourself moving deeper at you own pace. So when you are ready, move the indicator to 14, and watch and feel as your mind follows the indicator… Want yourself to relax to level 14, expect to relax to level 14 and feel yourself relaxing deeper at the perfect pace for you… Your body heavy and peaceful, your mind so totally calm and yet so inwardly alert…

(Pause to allow yourself to reach 14)

Great work! Your yardstick is magic because it lets you relax just as fast and just as deeply as you want to go. And the deeper you go, the better the hypnosis works. *(Pause briefly)*

Now move the indicator from 14 down to 10. And your mind responds to the indicator by relaxing you even more, at just the right pace for you, feel yourself sinking deeper into the chair, feeling so pleasant, calm and serene... as you float down at your perfect pace, expecting to relax to 10, wanting it, and feeling yourself relax so effortlessly...*(Pause to give yourself a moment to reach 10)*

You are so peaceful, and it feels so wonderful to know that you are in total control of how deeply you relax and how fast you get there. Let's go deeper yet by moving the indicator down to 5. As you do, feel yourself automatically relaxing more and more, just deeply relaxing.... It feels so good... your eyes don't want to open, your body doesn't want to move... Sleep now. A gentle, alert sleep of the nervous system... The more you relax, the more worries, stress and discomforts just fade away.... Let yourself continue relaxing at your own perfect pace... deeply asleep now... *(Pause to let yourself get to 5)*

Perfect. It is so wonderful that you can relax yourself and take total control of how deep you go and how fast you get there! Remember that zero on your yardstick is the deepest you could even imagine relaxing when we started, but now that you are at 5, down near the bottom; you can see that there is plenty of room to relax below zero. In fact there is a whole second yardstick. 36 on the old yardstick connects to zero on the first one. And zero on the new yardstick is many, many times deeper than you ever dreamed you could relax and still be alert and aware.

So if you like, you can just pull the indicator down to zero on the first yardstick because that is plenty deep enough for good hypnosis. But if you would like to experiment with going even deeper than you ever dreamed possible, you can slide the indicator right off the first yardstick, onto the second one, and keep right on relaxing even deeper than you dreamed you could go. So go ahead and slide the indicator down to the level you want. And let your mind automatically take you to those wonderful deep levels of relaxation where all stress, pain and discomfort automatically fade away and you feel totally great. Just let yourself relax deeper and deeper down, as deeply as you want to go, and Sleep now. (*Pause before continuing with the rest of the recording to let yourself achieve your desired depth.*)

Every breath you breathe, for the rest of this recording, causes you to relax more deeply. And every breath you breathe causes your amazing subconscious mind to accept, and integrate every positive suggestion on this recording into you inner mind so that you effortlessly _____. (*Fill in the blank with your specific goal*)

Repeat Eye Opening and Closure Deepening

You have done such a great job relaxing that you are already in hypnosis... focused and awake, in control of your own mind and really feeling comfortable... Just to prove things are different inside, in a moment, I am going to ask you to stay really relaxed and peaceful in your whole mind and body, but let your eyes open just a little so you can see what the world looks like when you are in hypnosis. (*Pause 2-3 seconds*)

So when you are ready, let you eyes open just a little bit... notice how heavy your eyes are.... They really would rather stay closed, but just let them open up a crack... and notice that when you are in hypnosis, everything looks the same, but different at the same time... like more vibrant, or like everything is filled with energy... In fact, beautiful and awesome. But I know your eyes really want to close, so when I count from 3 down to 1, let your eyes close down, and as your eyes close again, your entire body relaxes 10 times deeper. Three... Two... One... SLEEP NOW! Not asleep like at night, just a deep restful hypnotic sleep. (*Pause about 5 seconds*)

Great work, now let's relax even deeper. Let your eyes open again, even though it is getting really hard to open them, just open them a crack (*Pause 2-3 seconds to let the eyes open*) good work... and as I count again, your eyes close down and you relax 20 times deeper.... Three... Two... One... SLEEP NOW! Close your eyes and feel yourself relaxing as deeply as you can imagine. (*Pause about 5 seconds*)

Wonderful job! You are so awesome at going into hypnosis! Your eyes really want to stay closed, but one more time, give your eyes a little try, noticing that they may not even really open.... They may be too relaxed to really open... Just pretend they are opening. And the next time your eyes close, you go 100 times deeper relaxed... (*Pause*)... Three... Two... One... eyes closed...
SLEEP NOW! 100 times deeper!

And your eyes are so relaxed they just don't want to open no matter how hard you try, but give them a little try anyway *(Pause one second)* SLEEP NOW! Eyes totally closed! Deeper than you ever imagined you could relax!

For the rest of this recording every breath carries you deeper, and causes you to relax more deeply and to integrate every beneficial idea on this recording so that you automatically _____." (*Fill in the blank with your goal*)

SCRIPTS FOR IRRITABLE BOWEL SYNDROME AND ABDOMINAL PAIN

*The six scripts in this session were designed for children and adults with stress caused tummy and intestinal pain and problems. I developed these scripts under the direction of pediatric gastroenterologists to use with their young patients. These scripts are meant to supplement medical care. They are **never** a replacement for appropriate professional diagnosis and treatment. Never use these recordings for relief of tummy pain until your doctor rules out serious physical problems that need medical intervention. Recurrent tummy pain, constipation, diarrhea, nausea and vomiting may be irritable bowel syndrome, which responds well to hypnosis. But the same symptoms could also indicate a tumor, an inflamed appendix or a number of other problems that need immediate attention from a doctor. If I were experiencing the symptoms of IBS or stress-caused tummy pain, I would not listen to my own recording until AFTER my doctor ruled out the life-threatening conditions. Please use the same caution I would use myself. Only use these and other physical healing scripts IN ADDITION TO PROFESSIONAL HEALTH CARE. If your doctor prescribes medications and dietary changes, take your medicine and make the changes. Let the scripts add to and augment your healing. But please, never replace health care with these scripts.*

Healing Imagery for Children aged Seven through Eleven

Although this script is originally designed for children, it works effectively for adults. Of course you can modify it to reflect your preferred words and concepts.

Your body is a truly wonderful thing... it knows how to be relaxed and totally healthy. Your body knows how to make your stomach and intestines and all your internal organs work perfectly, free of pain and doing what your body is designed to do just as naturally as breathing. You don't have to tell your body how to breathe or how to make your heart beat. It just knows. So you don't have to tell your body in detail how to make your stomach and intestines work perfectly. Your body already knows. And the more you relax and make your mind calm, the more automatically your body can start operating just the way it was always meant to. Every breath you breathe causes you to relax more deeply and every breath you breathe causes your mind to be open to every positive and beneficial idea on this recording.

And while your body relaxes totally, your mind goes to the control room in your brain. The control room is a place filled with levers and buttons and computers and all kinds of controls. It looks like the controls for a jet plane, only bigger and more complicated. And as you look at the controls for your body, you realize that someone has turned on the autopilot. And that means there are some things going on in your body that aren't quite right. And you know that you have to take control and set things back to normal. So you turn off the autopilot while you fix things. Imagine the autopilot switch, and imagine turning it to OFF, <u>Now</u>, so that you can set things right.

The first thing that you notice is that there is a red warning light flashing over a control lever for your adrenal glands. The adrenal glands make something called adrenaline. And your adrenal gland lever is set to high. Whenever we make too much adrenaline, it causes our tummies to slow down and it keeps us from digesting our food. So you pull that adrenaline lever down with your mind until the red warning light goes off and the green normal operation light goes on. And that means that you just don't worry about things as much as you used to. Most things have a way of taking care of themselves if we just wait long enough. And so you just tell your body to relax and let things take care of themselves.

Next you look at your stomach controls. There is another red flashing warning light. When your stomach is operating normally, it gets food from your mouth, mixes it up with digesting chemicals, and sends that food into your intestines. The warning light means that your stomach is acting too slowly, or mixing in the wrong chemicals. You find the stomach lever, and set it into the normal position. You don't have to tell the stomach exactly what to do... all you have to do is tell it to go back to normal. Your stomach knows how to do that perfectly. So you adjust the control lever until the flashing red light goes off, and the green normal operation light comes on. And as you adjust the lever, your stomach begins operating normally, just the way nature intended it to... mixing your food and moving it into your intestines to be absorbed in the perfect amount of time... and mixing your food with exactly the right chemicals for perfect digestion.

There is another warning light over your intestines. Your intestines have two jobs. First, they absorb the things in your food that your body needs. And second, they move all the waste that your body doesn't need out of your body as poop. The warning light might mean your intestines are working too slowly, or working too fast, or that they aren't letting you poop normally. You don't have to know exactly what the warning light means, and you don't have to tell your intestines how to work right. They already know how to work. All you have to do is set the control lever back to normal. So you adjust the control lever until the flashing red light goes off, and the green normal operation light comes on. And as the green light goes on, your intestines go back to perfect normal operation. Your intestines absorb all the things from your food that make your body strong and healthy. And they turn everything that your body doesn't need in to regular, normal poop. And they do every bit of their work in the normal time... easily and free of pain. And it feels so good to you to feel your intestines settle down and get back to work just the way they were always meant to.

Now look around your control room. Anywhere you might see a red flashing warning light, you find the lever, and adjust it until the red light quits flashing and the green normal operation light comes on. You don't even have to know what each light means or what each lever controls. When you set the control levers to normal, and the green lights come on, your inner mind automatically causes everything in your body to return to normal, healthy operation. All pain and discomfort fades away. And every part of your body starts working at its very normal best.

Now that you have corrected all the warning lights, you can turn your body's autopilot back on. And your body just works by itself it in the normal, healthy way it was always meant to work. Your tummy feels great most of the time. Your poop is normal and easy. All the pain just fades away. And your body is getting all the healthy nutrients it needs from your food, and you feel great almost all the time. And any time you listen to this recording, your powerful inner mind checks the control room and makes sure that all your body's controls are set to normal. Every time you hear my voice on this recording, it causes your powerful subconscious mind to magnify every good thing on the recording a thousand times. Every day you feel better and healthier. Every day you worry less and less. And every day, in every way, your life gets better and better.

Pain Management for Children Aged Seven though Eleven

Although developed as a part of my pediatric functional abdominal pain protocol, this script may be used (with slight modification) for any pain problem in children and adults, not just for IBS and functional abdominal pain. As written here, it uses Dr. Longacre's computer game induction.

One of the things that is really cool about the computer game we are playing is that there are switches that control every part of your mind. There are switches that help you control pain, and switches that help your stomach work better. And coolest of all, every time you play the "I'm a computer game", and relax by turning off the muscle switches, your mind automatically turns on the switches for a normal tummy and turns off the switches for pain. Your pointer finger controls the relaxing switches and your thumb controls the pain switches. Every time you think about moving your pointer finger it causes your muscles to relax and it causes your mind to get really calm. And every time you think about moving your thumb, it causes your mind to forget about pain, and it causes your body to work normally. And when you think about moving your thumb, it causes you to be mentally at peace, and feeling great.

Try it now. First, think about moving your pointer finger <u>now</u>, and even if you can't feel it move, just thinking about moving your pointer finger makes your whole body and all its muscles feel more relaxed, more heavy, more like sleepy and peaceful. It feels so good to just relax and every time you think about moving your pointer finger you feel more calm and peaceful.

And now that you are very relaxed and peaceful, think about moving your thumb. Moving your thumb turns off the pain feelings in your tummy, and even thinking about moving your thumb causes your whole body to relax and start working normally. When you move your thumb or imagine moving your thumb, your **stomach begins to relax and digest your food the way nature intends it to**. When you think about moving your thumb, **your intestines relax and begin working normally**. Whenever you imagine moving your thumb, it is a signal for your mind to relax and tell your entire body that it is safe and OK to operate normally. And when your body is operating normally, all the pain just fades away, and you start feeling great. The pain goes away and you start feeling great all the time. When you listen to my voice, the pain automatically starts fading away and the more you relax the more the pain stays away and the more normally your whole body is working. And when your body is working normally and you are free of pain, it feels so good to do all the things you enjoy the most. And the more you practice moving the pointer finger to relax, with this recording, or on your own, the less and less pain you have. And the better your body works, the better and better you feel every single day. You **eat better, you digest better and you poop better** every single day. And you feel better and better every single day. (*For other types of pain, remove the references to stomach and intestines* **in bold**, *and replace them with your specific type of pain*)

And the more your practice moving your thumb, the more you are sending your mind a signal to turn off the pain inside, and let everything return to normal and healthy operation. Practice now – just think about lifting your thumb NOW, and a wave of good feeling fills your **tummy**, everything starts working just the way nature intended, and you feel so good.
(*Pause... for other types of pain, remove the references to tummy,* **in bold**, *and replace it with your painful area*)

You don't have to be listening to this recording for your thumb to work. From now on, every time you lift your thumb, no matter where you are, lifting your thumb causes a wave of wonderful relaxation and peace to fill your **tummy**, everything starts working normally, and any pain just fades away and you feel great. Try it again... lift your thumb NOW and another wave of good feeling flows all through your **tummy** and you feel great. (*For other types of pain, remove the references to tummy,* **in bold**, *and replace them with your painful area*)

Sometimes in the past, you have had really bad pain in your **tummy**. If that ever happens again, you can use your switches and your powerful mind to turn the bad pain off. Whenever you have really bad pain, the first thing you do is find a quiet place to sit down or lie down so that you can relax yourself using your pointer finger. You just pretend your eyes don't want to open, and begin moving your pointer finger, and your body automatically starts feeling relaxed, calm and heavy. You don't have to be listening to this recording. Anytime you close your eyes and play the pretend game with the pointer finger, you automatically begin relaxing. And as you start relaxing, the pain starts fading away. The pain fades away the more you relax. Then you think about moving your thumb and just thinking about moving your thumb turns off all the pain switches and turns on all the normal operation switches in your body. And within a couple of minutes the pain is fading away and you are feeling great. Even thinking about moving your thumb tells all your body's inner organs to begin working normally and to turn off pain. It is so good to know that you are in charge of how your body feels, and your magical and powerful inner computer is working all the time to keep you feeling great. (*For other types of pain, remove the references to tummy,* **in bold***, and replace them with your painful area*)

Moving your thumb is one switch that turns off pain, but your mind has an even more powerful way of turning off pain and turning on good feelings.
If you imagine your pain is like a big hot, red ball of fire **in your tummy**, you can use your mind to make the pain go away by imagining doing things that put out the fire. (*For other types of pain, remove the references to tummy,* **in bold***, and replace it with your painful area*)

Practice with me now. Remember how it felt the last time you had a really bad pain **in your tummy**. Now, imagine that you can see the pain, and it looks like a big, hot red ball of fire. Now imagine a wonderful water hose spraying a cooling spray of water on that fire. Imagine your mind being like a firefighter, putting out the fire. And notice that as you put out the fire, the pain and discomfort start fading away. Anytime **your tummy hurts**, you can make it feel better with your mind. All you have to do is take a deep breath, close your eyes, and imagine that the pain is a big ball of fire **in your tummy**, and then you imagine putting the fire out with a wonderful water hose, and as soon as your mind imagines spraying water on the fire, the pain and discomfort begin to fade away. And you feel peaceful, calm, relaxed and in control. (*For other types of pain, remove the references to tummy,* **in bold***, and them with your painful area*)

Let's practice again: Remember another time you really had a lot of discomfort **in your tummy**. Take another deep breath and let it out, and pretend you can actually see the pain, and it looks like a big, hot red ball of fire **in your tummy**. Now imagine that your mind is like a firefighter spraying that ball of fire with a really big fire hose, and putting the fire all the way out. As the fire goes out, the pain starts fading rapidly away. And your body starts working perfectly and smoothly, And **you poop easily and naturally.** As the pain fades away, your whole body returns to normal. (*For other types of pain, remove the references to tummy and poop,* **in bold**, *and them with your painful area and functions*)

You can use your powerful fire hose technique any time you want. You don't have to be in hypnosis, or even be very relaxed. All you have to do is close you eyes and imagine that the pain is a big ball of fire inside. Then imagine putting the fire out with a very powerful fire hose. And as soon as you imagine the fire going out, your mind totally removes the pain, and leaves you feeling totally great.

You can use your finger switches to relax and your thumb switch to turn off pain whenever you like. And every time you listen to this recording, your switches get more and more powerful. And your fire hose gets stronger every time you use it to put out the big ball of flame **in your tummy**. And every time you listen to any of my recordingss, all these good ideas work better and better. (*For other types of pain, remove the references to tummy,* **in bold**, *and it with your painful area*)

Relaxation, for Children, Aged Seven through Eleven

Although developed specifically as part of my protocol for pediatric functional abdominal pain, this script can be used for adults as well. As presented here, it uses Dr. Longacre's computer game induction.

You have such a powerful and great imagination that can really help yourself to feel good. So let's begin by imagining a very beautiful and peaceful place where you can always go to feel good. This is a secret place that you imagine, and no one else has to know about it. Maybe your secret, special place is a wonderful beach, or a special garden. It can be a mountain meadow or even a special room in a building. But wherever it is, it is just your place.

Let your mind show you your special place. Imagine everything you see there. Listen to all the sounds of your special place. Feel everything you can touch.... Even smell all the aromas of your special place. This place is yours, and yours alone. Nobody else knows about it, and you can always come to this place when you want to feel comfortable and peaceful. You are always comfortable and peaceful when you think about this special place. Whenever you want to feel comfortable and happy, you can close your eyes and think about this special place. And you feel really good. You don't have to be listening to this recording to visit your special place. All you have to do is close your eyes and think about it and your mind takes you to this relaxing and wonderful place. And every time you think about your private, beautiful place, you feel calm and warm and peaceful.

And whether it is inside a building or out in nature, your special place has a big television in it. It's a beautiful wide screen, giant television the size of a movie screen. There is always something interesting playing on this television... some program that makes your mind feel good, and helps your body to relax. Whenever you think about this special place, your television is always playing a program that helps you with whatever is going on in your outer life.

Today, your television is playing a program that shows you how to be relaxed and calm almost all the time, no matter what is happening in your life. Today, your television is playing a program that is teaching you how to be peaceful and calm no matter what happens in your life. As you watch the TV in your special place, your mind is getting all sorts of good ideas about how to be more happy and peaceful all the time. The program on the TV reminds you that you can handle everything life brings you because you are getting stronger and healthier every day of your life.

And the program teaches you how to stay relaxed about almost everything. There is a wise old grandfather or grandmother on the program who is reminding you that when you relax, nothing bothers you. And they are reminding you that you are much stronger and better than you think; and that you are safe and calm. Every time you listen to this recording, that wise and kind old man or woman has a special message just for you.

Sometimes the wise, kind. old person tells you secrets about how to stay relaxed about life, no matter what is going on. Sometimes they tell you secrets about how to love yourself and take care of yourself more. Sometimes they remind you what a special person you are. Sometimes they remind you of all the ways you can take care of your heart and your body. Some times they tell you more and more about how to relax and just let yourself be comfortable all the time.

Let's watch and listen to your special program now. The wise old person on the screen has something very special to tell you today; something that makes your life easier and more peaceful. So I am going be quiet for a whole minute, and as soon as I am quiet, your special wise person inside begins to tell you what you most need to hear today so that your life gets better and better. The minute of silence for you to watch and listen to that special program begins <u>now</u>.

(Pause one full minute)

Come back to my voice now, and your powerful inner mind locks every good thing your wise mind told you. And here is a secret: That wise, kindly old man or woman is really a part of you! Deep inside your mind there is a wise, grandparent part of your mind, and it is always there to help you with whatever is going on in life. And when you listen to this recording, you are talking to the wise woman or wise man inside you. And they are always there for you.

Now let's relax even more. Take a deep breath and let it out gently... and relax your heart and mind just as deeply as your body. Just thinking about relaxing more deeply causes your whole body to relax more and more. Take another deep breath and think about relaxing even deeper. Just thinking about moving your finger causes your powerful mental computer to make your body even more relaxed, and to make your mind even more peaceful.

And it feels so good to just let go and relax. You don't have to do anything or think about anything. Just being relaxed like this causes your body to begin healing, and just relaxing causes your mind to be totally at peace, and even after you finish the recording and come up to the surface, you are so calm that nothing bothers you. You go through every day being relaxed and calm. Most of the things we worry about never happen anyway, so nothing bothers you any more. You take care of the things that are in your power to do something about, and you let everything else take care of itself. And best of all, the more you listen to your recordings, the better you feel. You listen to one recording at least once a day, and every time you listen to the recordings you feel stronger, healthier, and much more relaxed about everything in your life.

Self-Esteem For Children Aged Seven Through Eleven

This script was also developed as part of my functional abdominal pain protocol for children, but it can be used as a stand-alone script whenever self-esteem is an issue, in either children or adults. This script is directly adapted from one by Dr. John Kresnik, and influenced by Dr. Mike Preston. I like to use Dave Elman's pretend game induction.

You are a wonderful, creative and powerful dreamer and imaginer, and the more you use that great imagination, the better you feel about your life and the better your body feels. So let's use that powerful and amazing imagination of yours, and the more you imagine the things I am describing, the more all the awesome ideas on this recording sink into your mind and become true for you.

Now imagine a big video store – a special video store – that is filled with rows and rows of shelves. And every shelf is filled top to bottom with videos. Just imagine that video store as if you were standing in the doorway looking at all those amazing shelves just filled with videos. And there are all sorts of aisles of shelves of videos. One of them has adventure movies. Another aisle has cartoons. Another aisle is filled with comedies. But the most important aisle is filled with all the videos of your life. One side of the aisle, the shelves on the right, has videos of all the good things that have ever happened to you. It has all the great experiences, and everything that you have learned, and all the memories that are important to you. Every video on the right side of the aisle shows you as the smart, pleasant, talented, bright, friendly and amazing person you are.

On the other side of the aisle, the not-so-nice side of the aisle, there are a bunch of negative videos. These videos contain all the problems in your life. They show you all the stresses and worries of your life. They are videos of all the negative things you have ever thought about yourself, and videos of all the negative things that other people have ever said about you. There are videos of all the negative thoughts, feelings and behaviors you have ever had, and videos of all the things you think you can't have or be or do on the not-so-nice side of the aisle.

And as you look at all the videos about your life, you realize that your inner mind has been spending too much time watching the videos on the negative side. Enough is enough! Your mind is spending too much time with worries and fears. Your mind is playing too many negative inner videos! It is time to get rid of all these negative videos in your mind, so that your mind can remember what an incredible and wonderful person you are.

At the end of the aisle, there is a big trashcan. Next to the trash container there is a shredding machine. It is a place where you can throw away negative videos, and shred them up, so that your mind never has to watch them again. You begin with the videos of all the things you worry about, and all the things you stress out about. You take the worry videos off the shelf, you hold your worries in your hands, and you carry all your worries to the shredder. You put your worry videos in the shredding machine and let the machine cut all your worries into little tiny pieces. Then you take all the shredded worries and throw them into the trash container. And as you throw your worries away, you remember one of life's biggest secrets. The secret is that most of the things people worry about never happen. So worry never helps anything. It feels so good to just shred those worries up and throw them away. Your mind now lets the cares of the world take care of themselves, and all your worries fade away.

Feeling great, you go back to the negative side of the video aisle, and pick up a whole bunch of videos that contain all the negative thoughts you have ever had about yourself, and all the negative things other people have said about you, and you take all your negative thoughts back shredding machine. You toss all those negative thoughts into the shredder and let it rip your negative thoughts to pieces, and you toss the pieces into the trash. And then you go and get all the videos of negative feeling that you have ever had, and you take your negative feelings to shredder and shred them too, And you throw all the negative feelings into the trash bin. And it feels so good to just empty your mind of all the negative thoughts and feeling, and to just throw away all the negative things anyone else has ever said,

Next, you find the videos of all the negative actions you have ever connected with yourself. And you take those negative behaviors back to the shredder and tear them to pieces. Then you throw all the negative behaviors into the trash along with all the other negative junk, and you feel just great.

Finally, feeling really good, you go and get your video of "I can'ts." This is the video of all the things you have ever believed you can't do. You get your video of sadness... the video of all the things that have ever made you sad. And you take all your sadness, and all your "I can'ts" and you take them back to the shredder and tear them to pieces. And all the things that have ever made you sad just fade away as you throw them in the trash. And all your beliefs about what you can't do or be just fade away as you throw the shredded "I can'ts" into the trash. And you know that you can have or be or do whatever you can dream of, if you put your mind to it. It feels so good to empty all the sadness and "I can'ts" out of your mind and out of your life.

And now that you have thrown away all your negative videos, your mind never has to watch them again. And you never have to accept negative thoughts and words about you, no matter who says them. All that is left are the videos on the good side of the aisle.

You go and look at those videos on the good side of the aisle, and they have titles and labels that reflect the real you. These title and labels talk about all the wonderful, good, talented, special and great things that make you the awesome person you are. You read these titles and they say things like confident, skilled, talented, cool, special, precious, worthwhile, remarkable, important, great, fun, intelligent, and happy. You stand there feeling a warm wave of good feelings because you know those videos show you the way you really are. You realize that the ways you think, the ways you feel and the ways you act are wonderfully good and that you are a wonderful person who is making your own dreams come true. Your deep, wonderful, thoughts and feelings and actions are the real you, and they make you feel great.

You begin to remember who you really are, and you think of yourself as a great kid who is growing up to be a wonderful adult. (*Modify the last sentence for adults.*) You believe in yourself. You feel smart, talented, valuable and worthwhile in every way. As you let your new good feelings fill your heart and become true for you, and as you know that you love yourself and appreciate yourself more than ever before, you notice that there are some special videos on the nice side of the aisle that your inner mind really wants to watch. One is your video of your deepest dreams. It contains all the deepest dreams of your heart and soul. Another is your video of "Who I Really Am" and it is all about the special gifts you have to share with the world. And the third special video seems kind of funny. It is a surfing video; all about the special things we can learn from surfing. And even if you have never been to the ocean, you decide that you want to watch it. So you take your three special videos, your video of deepest dreams, your video of your special gifts, and your surfing video to the back of the room, where there is a great chair and a huge wide screen TV. And you just sit back and relax while your inner mind puts the videos on and begins to watch. And even after this recording is over, your inner mind keeps watching those videos of dreams and gifts. And your inner mind is working full time now to bring your dreams into your conscious mind, and your inner mind is doing whatever it takes to help you unfold your gifts and share them with the world. Each person has their own private dreams and gifts. Nobody knows what your special dreams and gifts are but you. And your inner mind is doing whatever it takes to unfold your dreams and gifts and to make them real.

The surfing video is one we can all watch. You are amazed to watch men and women, and boys and girls, surfing on huge waves in the ocean. And you realize that there is a lesson for your mind. You notice that the best surfers don't try to control the ocean. Nobody can do that. They just work to control their balance on the board, no matter what the ocean sends. And as you watch them, sometimes they have great rides and sometimes they wipe out. But it doesn't matter. Even when they fall off, they just get back on the board and try again. It's no big deal to fall off. Falling off just teaches you how to balance better the next time. And you realize nobody can control the waves that life sends us. All we can do is keep our balance whatever comes. And even if we mess up or even totally wipeout, we know we can get back on the board and do better next time. And you feel so much calmer about everything in life, and you feel so good to know your inner mind is studying your deepest gifts and deepest dreams, and helping them come true. And you go through life like a surfer now, going with whatever wave life brings you and keeping your balance through everything. You know, more and more with every day, what a relaxed and wonderful person you are. And you know that life is getting better every day.

Healing Imagery for FAP/IBS: Teens and Adults

This script is very similar to the one I developed for children, but the language is directed to more mature people. It can be modified for any physical condition that has a stress component by replacing the words and phrases related to the digestive system with words and phrases that reflect your body. Any induction or deepening will work, but as written here, it uses the feather induction or deepening.

And while your body relaxes totally, and your mind just floats like a feather, the more you relax and focus your inner mind on the healing images and words on this recording, the more you are feeling healthier, stronger and in control of your body and your life. Your powerful subconscious mind has the ability to return you to vibrant good health and to living the way you want to live, and the more you listen to these self-hypnosis recordings, the better you feel, and in each and every day, in every way you are becoming healthier and stronger.

Your powerful imagination, the part of your mind that makes pictures and images, is the key to helping you heal and improve... Imagine the control room in your brain. The control room is a place filled with levers and buttons and computers and all kinds of controls. It looks like the controls for a jet plane, only much bigger and much more complicated. Your control room has all the controls for everything your body does. Each control has red and green indicator lights showing whether things are operating normally or not. And as you look at the controls for your body, you realize that the autopilot is on, and everything in your body is happening automatically, but some things that are going on in your body aren't quite right. And you know that you have to take control and set things back to normal. So you turn off the autopilot while you fix things. Imagine the autopilot switch, it is right in front of you, and imagine turning it to OFF, NOW, so that you can set things right.

The first thing that you notice is that there is a red warning light flashing over the control lever for your adrenal glands. The adrenal glands make adrenaline. And your adrenal gland lever is set to high. Whenever we make too much adrenaline, it causes our digestion to slow down and it keeps us from digesting our food. So you pull that adrenaline lever down with your mind until the warning light goes off and the green normal operation light goes on. And that means that you just don't worry about things as much as you used to. Most things have a way of taking care of themselves if we just wait long enough, and so you tell your body and your mind to just relax and let things take care of themselves. As you set the adrenaline lever to normal, and as the green light replaces the flashing red warning light, you may feel a wave of even deeper relaxation flow through you. You think about this adrenaline control lever, even when you aren't in hypnosis, and anytime you even imagine pulling the adrenaline lever down to normal, a wave of peacefulness fills you and you can concentrate on all the important things in life.

Next you look at your controls for your stomach. There may be one or more red flashing warning light. When your stomach is operating normally, it gets food from your mouth, mashes the food, mixes it up with digesting chemicals, and sends that food into your intestines. Red warning lights means that your stomach is acting too slowly, or mixing in the wrong chemicals. You don't have to consciously know what is going wrong. Your stomach knows what normal, perfect function is. You find the stomach controls, and set each one into the normal position. And the stomach lights return to normal healthy green. You don't have to tell the stomach exactly what to do... all you have to do is tell it to go back to normal. Your stomach knows how to do that perfectly. So you adjust the control levers until the flashing red lights go off, and the green normal operation lights comes on. And as you adjust the levers, your stomach begins operating normally, just the way nature intended it to; mixing your food at the perfect speed and pressure; and moving it into your intestines to be absorbed in the perfect amount of time, and mixing your food with exactly the right chemicals. As your stomach operates normally, you feel a wave of good feelings fill your body and mind. And you can imagine this control room even when you are not in hypnosis. Any time you imagine setting the stomach control levers to normal, your powerful inner mind reestablishes normal operation in your stomach, and a wave of physical good feeling fills you. And your mind feels SO GOOD.

There are more flashing red warning lights over the control levers for your intestines. Your intestines have two jobs. First, they absorb the things in your food that your body needs. And second, they move all the waste that your body doesn't need out of your body as poop. The warning lights might mean your intestines are working too slowly, or absorbing food inadequately, or working too fast, or that they aren't letting you poop normally. You don't have to consciously know exactly what the warning lights mean. Your subconscious knows exactly what they mean. And you don't have to consciously tell your intestines exactly how to work right. They already know how to work. All you have to do is set the control levers back to normal. So you adjust each of your control levers until the flashing red lights go off, and the green normal operation lights comes on. And as the green light goes on, your intestines go back to perfect normal operation. Your intestines absorb all the things from your food that make your body strong and healthy. And they turn everything that your body doesn't need into regular, normal poop. And they work at just the speed nature intended. They do every bit of their work easily and free of pain. And it feels so good to you to feel your intestines settle down and get back to work just the way they were always meant to. And anytime you imagine setting your intestine controls back to normal, whether you are listening to this recording or not, your powerful inner mind responds instantly by making your intestines work just the way nature intended, in a perfect rhythm, and you feel a wave of relief and good feelings.

Now look all around your control room for any other red warning lights. And anywhere else you see a red flashing warning light, you find the lever, and adjust the lever until the red light quits flashing and the green normal operation light comes on. You don't even have to know what each light means or what each lever controls. Your inner mind always knows. When you set the control levers to normal, and the green lights come on, your inner mind automatically causes everything in your body to return to normal, healthy operation. All pain and discomfort fades away and every part of your body starts working at its very normal best.

Now that you have corrected all the warning lights, you can turn your body's autopilot back on. When you turn your autopilot on, your body just works by itself it in the normal, healthy way it was always meant to work. Your autopilot switch integrates all the healing changes you have made into your deepest mind. And your body simply feels great. Your stomach and intestines feels great almost all of the time. Your poop is normal and easy. All the pain just fades away. And your body is getting all the healthy nutrients it needs from your food. You feel great almost all the time. And any time you listen to this recording, your powerful inner mind checks the control room and makes sure that all your body's controls are set to normal. Every day you feel better and healthier. Every day you worry less and less. And every day, in every way, your life gets better and better.

You can also return to this control room any time you want just by thinking about it. You don't even have to be in hypnosis. And any time you visit the control room in your mind, and set the control levers back to normal, your mind and body instantly respond by making every part of your body work normally and harmoniously. The more you imagine setting the control levers to normal, the better you feel.

And now it is time to return to the surface of the mind, but you bring back with you, all the powerful and wonderful healing ideas from this recording, and you rise to the surface knowing that your powerful inner mind is back on automatic pilot, automatically helping every part of your body work at its very best.

Constipation

As presented here, this script uses a Kresnick style induction and a feather deepening.

Your beautiful natural haven is a perfect place to learn about natural processes... and digestion and elimination are natural processes. As you rest and drift peacefully in this perfect inner sanctuary, enjoying nature at its best, your powerful inner mind accepts the positive ideas on this recording about digestion and elimination, and your vast inner mind does whatever healthy thing is necessary to implement those positive ideas and make them the truth for you. Every breath you breathe causes your inner mind to accept, implement and totally reinforce every positive and beneficial idea on this recording.

Letting your conscious mind simply rest in the beauty of nature, your inner mind now focuses on the entire cycle of eating, digesting and eliminating. This cycle is the basic natural building block of life. Your body's natural programming is for the entire process to be smooth and easy. Your digestive system is like a natural factory. Your mouth is the receiving dock where raw materials flow in and are unpacked. Your throat and esophagus are the conveyor system that carries the raw materials onward. Your stomach is where the processing begins. Your small intestine is where the useful products, like fuel and building blocks for your body, are absorbed and distributed to your body's cells. And your large intestine is where waste products are collected for elimination from the system.

This natural factory is designed to work perfectly and automatically. It is based on a natural conveyor system. Your entire digestive system is essentially a long tube of muscles that rhythmically relax and contract, to move the raw materials through the system. Chewing and swallowing are the first rhythmic contractions of muscles that start the system working. Chewing and swallowing stimulate the rhythmic contraction of the stomach, which breaks down and mixes the food. The stomach contractions stimulate the small intestine to begin its rhythmic squeezing and relaxing which cause the food to move along, as the useful parts are absorbed and carried to the body. In turn the small intestine's contractions move the waste product into the large intestine and stimulate the large intestine to contract and relax, pushing waste products all the way to the end where it collects in the rectum. When the rectum is full, the contractions of the large intestine stimulate the rectum muscles to contract and relax, and we have the feeling of needing to eliminate. We then find a toilet, and voluntarily relax the last ring of muscles, and eliminate the waste products from our system. This process of contracting and relaxing muscles is called peristalsis. Peristalsis is the basis for natural digestion and elimination.

Your inner mind is now remembering what it had temporarily forgotten. The entire process of peristalsis – eating, digesting and eliminating – is designed to be a single integrated, connected process.

Chewing stimulates the esophagus to swallow. Swallowing stimulates the stomach to contract and relax in rhythm. The stomach's contractions cause the small intestine to begin peristalsis. The small intestine's waves of peristalsis cause the large intestine to begin squeezing the waste along as it leaves the small intestine. And finally, the large intestine's peristaltic waves of contraction and relaxation cause the waste to fill the rectum, and stimulate the rectum to easily discharge its waste in a timely manner.

From this moment onward, your inner mind resets your digestive system so that it acts in harmony, as an interconnected, single process. The act of chewing and swallowing food is now a signal to your body to maintain normal peristaltic muscle rhythms throughout the your system. The more thoroughly you chew your food, the more effectively chewing stimulates the rest of the system. So you now chew every bite of food thoroughly and completely before swallowing. Swallowing causes your stomach to mix, mash, and breakdown your food at the perfect speed for the perfect amount of time with the perfect balance of digestive chemicals. Your stomach's contractions now perfectly stimulate your small intestine to absorb food and pass waste onward in perfect harmony with the rest of the system. Your large intestine takes the peristaltic signals from the small intestine and passes the waste onward in a timely manner, absorbing only the perfect amount of fluid so that the waste arrives in your rectum soft, and compact, ready for easy elimination. As your rectum fills, the peristalsis from the large intestine stimulates the feeling of having to eliminate. You always pay attention when your body feels like eliminating. **You never** ignore the feeling of needing to go. You always use the toilet when your body says it is time to go. And you are always aware of your rectum being full and ready to go, because the large intestine's peristaltic waves stimulate the rectum to contract and push.

When you sit on the toilet, you easily relax your outer ring of muscles. The contractions of your rectum naturally and easily push the waste outward. There is absolutely no need to strain. Your rectum now naturally and easily pushes the waste outward.

You have learned that putting your feet up on a small stool when you sit on the toilet puts your body in a more natural position for elimination, and makes the rectum's job of pushing out the waste much easier. You have also learned that incorporating fiber in your diet and drinking plenty of fluids makes your internal factory work more smoothly. Fiber and fluids in your body are like lubricants on an assembly line. They make the whole process move more smoothly. Your inner mind now remembers that the entire system is connected, as a single large conveyor. And every step along the way, the rhythmic contractions of one part of the system stimulates the next part to do it own rhythmic, peristaltic contraction and relaxation, sending the food and waste effortlessly and easily onward. Every time you eat, it is a signal for the rest of the system to move in harmony. Every rhythmic chewing motion stimulates peristalsis throughout the entire system. You chew you food longer and more thoroughly. And the long, thorough, chewing stimulates every part of your digestion and elimination system to work in perfect harmony.

When you eat, the rhythmic contraction and relaxation begins... in your mouth as you chew... in your esophagus as you swallow... in your stomach as you mix and process... in your small intestine as you sort and adsorb... in your large intestine as you compact and shape... and in your rectum as you smoothly and easily eliminate. The whole process is automatic and working in perfect rhythm and harmony. You only have to think about one thing. As your rectum begins its peristaltic contracting and relaxing, your conscious mind notices the feeling of having to eliminate, and you **immediately** respond by finding a toilet and relaxing the final voluntary muscles, so that the rectum can effortlessly push out the waste. When you sit on the toilet, it is an automatic signal for the last voluntary muscles, the sphincter muscles, to relax and pulsate. And as the sphincter relaxes, the normal peristalsis of the rectum gently and easily propels the waste out of your body.

Your inner mind is reconnecting all the pieces of the digestive and elimination system **now**, so that they work in perfect harmony. Shortly after listening to this recording, you feel the feeling of having to eliminate. You always respond to that signal immediately. You sit on the toilet and allow your sphincter to relax so that your rectum can propel the waste out naturally and effortlessly. You are eliminating more often and more easily than you ever dreamed possible. And you are feeling healthier and better with every passing day.

If all these positive and beneficial ideas for effortless and natural, smooth and easy elimination are acceptable to you, you simply continue breathing… just as you are. And your vast and powerful inner mind multiplies and magnifies these powerful ideas and makes them absolutely true for you. Every time you listen to this recording, these ideas become more and more powerful and true for you, magnifying themselves over and over and billions of times over.

Now just float in your beautiful, natural haven for a few moments of silent rest. As you float and drift, your inner mind studies all the harmonious, interacting processes of nature, and continues doing every healthy thing it needs to do inside to restore healthy, smooth, easy, natural elimination to your life.

Pause 30 seconds

Returning to my voice, knowing that you can effortlessly return to your inner sanctuary just by closing your eyes and thinking about it. And every time you hear the word "feather" or think about your special place, your inner mind strengthens every positive and beneficial idea on this recording billions of times over. And now it is time to return to the outer world, totally relaxed and ready for smooth and natural elimination.

SCRIPTS FOR PAIN

Dr. Dan Lester's Endorphin Pump

This script is my attempt to replicate a demonstration by Dr. Dan Lester, a master hypnotist now living near Richmond, VA. Any of the induction and deepening scripts will work well.

As you rest, peacefully and comfortably in this tranquil state of relaxation, your inner mind focuses on the task of reducing and managing discomfort while your outer mind floats comfortably. Simply being in a pleasant hypnotic state is automatically anesthetic, and the more you relax with every breath, the more comfortable you become in every way. And every breath causes you to relax more deeply... breathing out stress and tension with each exhale... breathing in deeper comfort and peace with each inhale. There is nothing your outer mind has to do... just be. Breathing, and relaxing more deeply with every rhythmic breath. Each gentle breath causes you to feel more and more peaceful and comfortable.

You have a magic phrase that helps you relax instantly and deeply to this peaceful state of mind. Your magical phrase is "calm and relaxed." Any time you want to relax yourself quickly and deeply, all you have to do is sit down in a safe place, close your eyes and whisper your magic phrase "calm and relaxed," silently in your own mind. Every time you whisper your magic phrase silently to yourself, you feel a wave of peaceful relaxation fill you and you feel all the comfortable good feelings you are feeling right now. Practice with me now. Take a gentle breath in, and as you let it go, repeat your magic phrase to yourself: "Calm and relaxed". And feel the good feelings magnify as an even deeper wave of relaxation flows through you, bringing you an even more pleasant sense of peace and comfort. "Calm and relaxed."

You don't have to be using this recording or even be in hypnosis to use your magic phrase, "calm and relaxed." All you have to do is sit in a safe place, close your eyes and repeat the words, "calm and relaxed" silently inside your own mind. And the instant you repeat your magic phrase, "calm and relaxed," you feel a wave of relaxation, comfort and peace. And any discomfort you feel diminishes and fades away. Every time you hear or repeat your magic phrase, "calm and relaxed", it gets ten times more powerful for you. Every time you hear or repeat your magic phrase, "calm and relaxed", you relax twice as deeply, twice as quickly and your magic phrase becomes ten times more powerful for you.

You have been experiencing pain or discomfort in your body that is limiting your actions and choices. Pain is meant to be a warning that something is wrong or that you have been injured. Most pain is totally useless because we are already aware of a problem. Our bodies are designed to use pain as a signal and then let it fade away. We have an almost magical set of internal chemicals that are designed to reduce pain to nothing once it has served its purpose. The problem is that fear and worry interfere with our bodies' built- in pain relief system.

There is a chemical called noradrenalin produced by our adrenal glands. The purpose of noradrenalin is to calm our bodies and establish normal operating processes. Noradrenalin does the opposite of adrenalin, which winds us up and prepares our bodies for fighting or running away when we are threatened. One of the most important jobs noradrenalin does is stimulate our bodies to release endorphins to control pain. Endorphins are internal chemicals made by our bodies for pain control. Endorphins are 100 times more powerful than morphine. And since they are our bodies' own natural chemicals, they have no negative side effects. The problem for most of us is that endorphins can only be released when noradrenalin is flowing from our adrenal glands. Fear, anxiety, worry and stress cause the adrenal glands to quit producing noradrenalin and begin producing adrenalin. When we are getting adrenalin in our systems, the endorphins are trapped and can't do their magic pain relief work. Fear and worry make pain worse. Calm relaxation allows our bodies to work their endorphin magic and eliminate pain.

Self-hypnosis is automatically anesthetic because when we relax, we produce less adrenalin and more noradrenalin. And that means our brains can release our natural pain relieving endorphins into the blood stream to diminish or eliminate the uncomfortable feelings. Your magic phrase, "calm and relaxed," causes you to relax in mind and body. That causes your adrenal glands to produce noradrenalin. And that leads to release of the incredibly powerful pain reducing endorphins. So the more you are calm and relaxed, the more the discomfort and pain fades away.

You can use the power of your vast subconscious mind to increase the flow of endorphins to any part of your body that hurts. Focus your mind now, on the place where you have been feeling the most discomfort. Imagine a long, flexible, pipeline running from the painful area up into the center of your brain. This is your endorphin pipeline. Your brain sends endorphins through this pipeline to reduce pain and stimulate healing in the affected area. Imagine a small gate at the top of your pipeline, deep in your brain. Your inner mind opens and closes this gate in order to send the magical endorphins down the pipeline to the area that hurts.

Now repeat your magic phrase, "calm and relaxed" silently inside. "Calm and Relaxed..." As another deeper wave of relaxation flows through your body and mind, the gate opens and a beautiful golden fluid begins dripping down the pipeline directly to the place where it hurts. As you imagine this awesome golden fluid arriving where you hurt, you begin to feel an amazing sense of comfort and peace...the golden drops of endorphins coat and flow all through the places that hurt; and all the discomfort begins fading away. Your magic phrase, "calm and relaxed," is your mind's signal to release endorphins down the pipeline. It doesn't take much. Endorphins are 100 times more powerful than opium or morphine, and they quickly diminish and eliminate pain. And because your endorphins are your body's natural chemicals, the discomfort fades away, and you are totally alert and aware.

Practice with me again... Focus on the place where you are most uncomfortable, and imagine the endorphin pipeline running from your brain to the place that hurts. As you repeat your magic phrase, "calm and relaxed," along with me now... "Calm and relaxed..." the beautiful golden, soothing, easing and healing endorphins flow down the pipeline and the discomfort fades away. The more you use your magic phrase, the more comfortable you feel.

There is an endorphin pipeline from the pain control areas of your brain to every place in your body that hurts. Just imagine that intricate and beautiful web of endorphin tubes connecting your brain to every place in your body that hurts. Every time you use your magic phrase, "calm and relaxed" it causes your mind and brain to flood the painful areas with endorphins. You do not have to be using this recording for it to work. You do not have to be in hypnosis or any special state for it to work. All you have to do is sit down in a safe place, close your eyes and repeat your magic phrase, "calm and relaxed." And every time you use your magic phrase, "calm and relaxed," you feel a wonderful wave of peaceful relaxation, and an amazing flow of comfort as your brain releases a soothing flow of endorphins to each and every area of discomfort in your body. The more you practice using your magic phrase, "calm and relaxed," the more powerful and effective it becomes. And you are a person in balance with your body's natural healing and you are free of pain. The discomfort fades away and healing commences. And in each and every way, you are more calm and relaxed, more free of discomfort, stronger, and healthier with each and every day.

If all the positive and beneficial ideas on this recording are acceptable to you, you simply continue breathing... just as you are. And every breath you breathe causes your powerful inner mind to magnify and reinforce the ideas on the recording thousands of times over, locking them into the most powerful parts of your brain and mind where they simply become the truth for you.

The Pain Shield

As you continue relaxing more deeply with every breath, you remember and experience the natural anesthesia that comes with being in a deeply relaxed and peaceful state. When your muscles are relaxed, and your heart and mind are at peace, your adrenal glands are producing noradrenalin, and that stimulates your body to produce endorphins, your body's own natural internal pain relieving hormones. Endorphins are 100 times more powerful pain relievers than morphine, and have none of the unwanted side effects. In fact, they speed healing of any part of your body that is injured. The deeper you relax, the more your brain releases endorphins, and the better you feel. The more your body produces endorphins, the more the pain fades away to nothing. So you relax more deeply with each exhale, knowing that your body is producing endorphins that stimulate long-term pain relief and healing.

One way that you can keep your mind relaxed, and return to a calm and relaxed state instantly, is to have a special place in your mind that you can visit any time you wish to relax and be at peace. Imagine some beautiful, relaxing place… a tropical beach, a mountain meadow, a special garden, or even a rich, relaxing private room… (*Pause 5 seconds*)… This is your special place, and whenever you close your eyes and imagine this special place, a wave of relaxation fills you… Simply picturing or imagining your special place causes your inner mind to fill you with a wave of peace, comfort and serenity. And as that wave of serenity fills you; your adrenal glands relax and produce noradrenalin. In response to the noradrenaline, your body releases endorphins. And the endorphins immediately set to work diminishing and eliminating any discomfort in your body. You can think about your special place anywhere, anytime, as long as it is safe to close your eyes for a few moments. And every time you visit the special place in your mind, a wave of tranquil serenity fills you. Your muscles relax. And your mind and heart return to their natural state of peaceful calm. You carry on with your daily activities, calm, relaxed and filled with hours of endorphin comfort.

You visit your special place often, and every time you imagine it, the wave of calm and serenity is greater and greater, and the discomfort fades away like fog evaporating in the sunshine.

You have also learned to picture the pain you have been feeling as if it were an object of some kind, and you have learned that when you imagine changes in the symbolic object, your subconscious mind makes the same changes in the pain or discomfort itself. So take a moment now to imagine your discomfort....

What kind of object is it today? It may be same as always, or it may be changing... Just notice what kind of object your pain would be today... (*Pause 5 seconds*)... Notice how big it is today... the bigger it is, the more intense the discomfort you are feeling... (*Pause one breath*)... Notice its shape... is it all points and sharp edges, or is it becoming softer... (*Pause one breath*)... Notice its color... is it black or fiery red, or is it getting to be a more soothing color... (*Pause one breath*)... How heavy is it? (*Pause one breath*)... How much of your visual field does it fill? How close is that object? Notice everything about that object of pain

And as you notice everything about that pain object, you remember that if you use your imagination to change the object, you are giving your brain direct instructions to make the same changes in the way it experiences the sensations it thinks of as painful. When you shrink your object and make it smaller, your brain reduces the sensations of discomfort.... (*Pause one breath*)... When you push the object further from you, the pain fades into the distance... (*Pause one breath*)... When you change its color from dark or fiery, to soft and soothing, the pain itself fades and your feel a wave of soothing comfort... (*Pause one breath*)... Every positive change you imagine in the object causes a similar change in the pain itself.

Now, as my voice takes a short break, you take a minute to make the changes you would like to make in the object. And as you make those changes, the pain fades to nothing.

(Pause 30 seconds)

Return to my voice **feeling great**, knowing that you have the power to modify and reduce pain to nothing any time you wish. Whenever you are in a place where it is safe to close your eyes, you can use this technique. All you have to do is sit or rest comfortably, close your eyes and imagine your pain object. Notice how it appears, and then make the changes in the object that you want in the discomfort itself. And within a very few seconds, your inner mind responds by reducing and relieving the discomfort. When you open your eyes after a minute, your new state of peace and comfort goes with you for hours, and you can repeat this technique, and even combine it with your special place as often as you like to remain calm and at peace. You don't have to be listening to this recording or even in a state of hypnosis. Any time you close your eyes and make changes in the object of pain, the actual discomfort fades away almost instantly.

Now notice how good you are feeling after using your powerful mind to take control of the discomfort. It is amazing to realize the power of your own mind to help you live comfortably and at peace. Now let's use that same powerful imagination and mind to picture or imagine a wave of energy, like a healing white and golden light. And your wave of light and energy is flowing from your brain, down your spine, and through your nerves to the places in your body that have been sore or tender. And that wave of energy forms a shield of light over the formerly tender spots. That shield stays in place, the light fills the problem area, and your entire brain and body focus their attention on healing any underlying problems at the spots where the pain was. The light forms a shield that keeps away all sensations of pain or discomfort for hours. And all sensations of discomfort simply bounce off your shield of light, and your body feels calm, serene and comfortable. Every time you picture or imagine this shield of light around the areas that have felt tender, your body produces more healing endorphins, you relax more deeply, the pain fades away and your healing increases. You don't have to be in hypnosis to use your shield of healing light and energy. All you have to do is be in a place where you can safely close your eyes. And, as soon as you close your eyes and picture or imagine your shield of light, another wave of comfort and peace fill you, wherever you are. The more you picture and imagine your shield of light, the stronger it becomes, and its effects last for hours. The more you practice the stronger your shield becomes.

Practice now... Take in a deep, calm breath, and as you exhale, imagine and picture your shield of protective energy flowing from your brain to form a shield over any areas in your body that have been sensitive or uncomfortable. Feel a wave of deeper peace and comfort fill you... Just relax into that wave as the golden energy forms a shield of peace and healing that totally protects any tender spots... Expect the discomfort to fade away. Expect the waves of peace and comfort to grow with every breath you breathe... The more you picture and imagine it, the stronger your protective, healing shield becomes... And it feels so good to just relax and feel the comfort... calm and relaxed now

Every time you imagine your shield of golden light, your shield grows stronger and more healing. Every time you imagine your golden healing energy shield, your body heals and the discomfort fades further from your life. You don't have to be listening to this recording, or even be in hypnosis to imagine your shield. All you have to do is be in a place where it is safe to close your eyes. Any time you feel discomfort or pain, you can sit down in a safe place, close your eyes for a moment, and picture or imagine your shield of beautiful protective, healing light. And immediately, pain relieving and healing endorphins fill the tender areas... The discomfort fades away so fast it is amazing. And a wave of comfort and peace fills you totally... The more you imagine your golden healing energy shield, the stronger it becomes.

Every time you listen to this recording, your mind gets more and more powerful and you take more and more control. You are relaxed, serene and tranquil, and your peacefulness astounds your doctors and amazes everyone who knows you. You are totally awesome and getting stronger and more amazing every time you practice your techniques.

And now, it is time to return with me gently to the surface, bringing out with you a comfort and anesthesia that last for hours. You can listen to this recording as often as you like, and use the techniques whenever you want. And every time you do, your inner mind magnifies and reinforces all your powerful techniques and seals them in place in the most powerful parts of your mind. And you are more calm, more relaxed and more comfortable and healing each and every day.

SCRIPTS FOR STRESS MANAGEMENT

The Tropical Lagoon

Picture and imagine that you are sitting on a beautiful tropical beach on a perfect day. And as you picture that beautiful beach, touch the thumb and forefinger together on one hand and then release them. That is the signal for your mind to take you to this wonderful and relaxed place every time you do it. Any time you close your eyes and bring your thumb and forefinger together, it is a signal for your mind to bring you to this wonderful state of relaxation, and onto this perfect beach you have created as a private mental get-away....

Deeply asleep now, not asleep like at night, but just a gentle sleep of the nervous system...fully alert and aware, but very relaxed and very peaceful. Deeply asleep.... just imaging and enjoying your wonderful, tropical beach.

Sometimes our poor overworked outer minds don't know how to rest because they don't have enough practice taking a vacation, and so they keep sending thought after interfering thought to disturb our rest because that is all they know how to do. But remember this... every thought has to have an energy source. Every thought needs energy to become and stay conscious. So when an interfering thought comes through your busy outer mind, you can help your mind take a much-needed rest by simply unplugging the thought. It is as if every thought has an electric cord that plugs into your mind. You can help your mind take a rest by imagining that you are unplugging your thoughts every time one comes up to disturb your relaxation. Just reach up and pull that thought's electric power cord right out of the wall. Picture and imagine yourself unplugging the thought every time a negative or interfering thought comes up. As you pull the plug, the thought simply shrivels up and drifts away, knowing that it can come back later if it is really important.

Bring your thumb and forefinger together again and release. That is also the signal for your mind to pull the power cord on any interfering thought from your busy outer mind... Squeezing your thumb and forefinger is your signal for your outer mind go back and get the rest it deserves so much. When you touch your thumb and forefinger together, it is a signal to your mind to pull the power cord on interfering thoughts, and to let you drift in this peaceful, tranquil feeling of serenity and relaxation. And the interfering thoughts just shrivel up and drift away.

Now picture or imagine your beautiful tropical beach... the most calm and beautiful beach in the world. There is a warm sun shining on the beach, and as you notice the sunshine, a special ray of the sun comes and shines especially for you... The sunlight pours over your body just like wonderful healing golden oil, or like warm honey... It is so beautiful here. You can hear the wind in the palm trees and the sounds of the gentle ocean breakers rolling up the beach. The sand is so warm that you can imagine how it would feel if your legs were buried in the sand... so warm and inviting. The sun overhead is a brilliant golden ball in a perfectly blue and cloudless sky shining down on the radiant blue green of the tropical sea and pure white sand in your little lagoon. Birds fly overhead and fish are jumping. You look and listen, and there is no one else on this beach. It is all yours.

You find yourself floating on the peaceful water of the lagoon in a lovely yellow boat. You can feel the gentle waves of the lagoon rocking your boat just like it was a cradle. Outside the lagoon, a coral reef protects you from the power of the mighty ocean and you can hear the ocean breaking loudly on the reef. A pelican flies over and you watch as it comes in to land and float a few feet away from your boat. Everything is so peaceful. It is a tropical paradise.

You notice that in the bottom of your boat there are a number of old leaves. You realize that each leaf is a symbol for some obstacle to you learning to relax and heal. Some of the leaves are big and some are small, but each one is some obstacle in your mind to relaxing and healing.

You pick up the largest leaf and hold it in front of you. It is the largest obstacle to you learning to relax and heal. As you do, you may become aware of its name and what it symbolizes. It is OK if you don't consciously understand what the leaf symbolizes for you, because your powerful inner mind, your subconscious mind, knows exactly what it means. As you look at the leaf, you realize that it has actually been there helping you, and even though it is an obstacle now, at one time it was a friend protecting you from something or helping you with some problem in your life. And as you look at the leaf and let your powerful inner mind come to understand it, you realize that you no longer need it. So you thank the leaf for all its past service to you, with true gratitude in your heart, because the obstacle has been a servant in the past. But then you tell the leaf, "I don't need you any longer...I am learning better ways to deal with that problem you came to help me with, and I no longer need you to get in the way of my relaxation and healing." Then you gently release the leaf into the water and watch it float off toward the reef where the pounding surf, brilliant sunlight and pure water work to recycle the leaf and release its energy back into your system to help you heal.

Then you pick up the next largest leaf and hold it in front of you. It is the next largest obstacle to you learning to relax and heal. Your inner mind, and perhaps your conscious mind recognize this leaf and know its name. It is another obstacle to healing that began in some way to help you with some problem in the mind, or to protect you from something that was too big for your mind to handle at the time. And as you look at the leaf and let your powerful inner mind come to understand it, you realize that you no longer need it. So you thank the leaf for all its past service to you, with true gratitude in your heart because the obstacle has been a servant in the past. Then you tell the second leaf, "Thank you for your past service, but I don't need you any longer... I am learning better ways to deal with that problem you came to help me with, and I no longer need you to get in the way of my relaxation and healing." Then you gently release the leaf into the water and watch it float off toward the reef where the pounding surf, brilliant sunlight and pure water work to recycle the leaf and release its energy back into your system to help you heal.

Then you pick up the third largest leaf and hold it in front of you. It is the next largest obstacle to you learning to relax and heal. Your inner mind, and perhaps your conscious mind, recognizes this leaf and knows its name. Your inner mind always knows. This third leaf symbolizes another obstacle to relaxing or healing that began in order to help you with some problem in the mind, or to protect you from something that was too big for your mind to handle at the time. And as you look at the leaf and let your powerful inner mind come to understand it, you realize that you no longer need it. So you thank the leaf for all its past service to you, with true gratitude in your heart, because the obstacle has been a servant in the past. You tell the third leaf, "Thank you for your past service, but I don't need you any longer... I am learning better ways to deal with that problem you came to help me with, and I no longer need you to get in the way of my relaxation and healing." Then you gently release the leaf into the water and watch it float off toward the reef where the pounding surf, brilliant sunlight and pure water work to recycle the leaf and release its energy back into your system to help you relax, grow, heal and change.

And somehow, something almost magic begins to happen in your mind. You realize that the next time you listen to this recording, you are able to relax much more deeply... and in that relaxation, your inner mind is exploring ways to help you heal or change in whatever ways you wish to change or grow. You understand with pride and satisfaction, that you are learning to relax and be yourself. You are learning to find your own special path to personal change and healing, and to taking control in your own life. You realize that you do have the ability to relax, and even more important, the ability to heal, and to begin making positive and beneficial changes in your life.

Touch your thumb and forefinger lightly together again and then release them. As you release, it is your mind's signal to return you to your beautiful beach. Any time you touch and release the thumb and forefinger together, it will immediately take you to this wonderful place of powerful inner knowledge and change. Of course you will only do so when it is safe and convenient to close your eyes and relax for a moment.

Now take a full two minutes to just float in this wonderful and peaceful state, enjoying your beach, letting your mind simply float in this wonderful state of peaceful relaxation, knowing that this state of mind is the place from which all change and healing begins...

Pause two minutes then segue into the awakening sequence.

And now it is time to return to my voice, and to your normal state of awareness, bringing all you new inner calm and relaxation out with you. Every time you listen to this recording, and every time you squeeze your thumb and forefinger together in a safe place, you relax more deeply, you unplug interfering thoughts, and you drift and float in your tropical lagoon, totally at peace... relaxing, changing, healing and growing... and so it is.

Cleansing the Brain

My deep thanks go to Jerry Kein for teaching this process. Don't record this one if you have strong negative reactions to visualizing the inside of your body! Use Dr. Kresnick's induction.

And as you let yourself relax in your meadow, you notice that the stream that runs through it is very slightly steaming... it is a warm stream, and you realize there must be a mountain hot spring nearby, You walk upstream, following the creek to its source. And as you walk through the meadow, the steaming creek branches off the main stream, and you know you have found the outlet for the hot spring. Turning and following the warm spring water to its source, you come to the tree line at the edge of the meadow. And in the trees at the edge of your private and beautiful meadow, there is a beautiful mountain chalet built over the hot spring. You recognize this chalet as an age-old place of healing and renewal that has always been there for you. There is a sign that invites you to enter and leave the cares of the world behind... to enter and find peace.

As you enter the building, there is a pleasant outer room, and an inner room that sits directly over the spring. You move through the outer room and enter the spring room. And in the room that is built directly over that warm, natural healing spring of water, there are two beautiful basins filled with warm, natural healing spring water. And there is a beautiful mirror between the two basins.

The basins are carved from blocks of the silver and white granite of the mountains, and they are polished so highly they seem to glow. The water within the basins reflects the beauty of the granite and looks so inviting. One of the basins is filled with healing spring water and soap bubbles... It is a cleansing basin. The other is a rinse basin, filled only with the pure, healing, natural, warm, mineral spring water itself. The mirror is framed in beautiful polished wood and gold. The entire room is so comfortable and so rich that you know you have always been welcome here.

And as you approach the basins and the mirror, you do something that seems a little silly. But in this gorgeous healing resort it seems as natural as breathing. Standing in front of the mirror, you reach up to your head and gently find and begin to unzip the zipper that holds the top of your head on... And as you unzip the zipper and pull the top of your head back, you can see your marvelous and amazing brain.

And you have a bit of a shock, because as you look at your brain's reflection in the mirror, it is grey and dull looking. You know that we refer to brains as "grey matter", but you also know that living brains are not supposed to be grey. Brain cells are only grey when they are pickled in formaldehyde in a lab. Living brains are filled with flowing blood and vast electrical activity. Living brains are a rich, rosy, glowing electrical red in color. So it shocks you a bit to see your brain all grey in the mirror.

Looking closely, you realize that your beautiful and marvelous brain is not really grey; it has simply been slimed over with a sticky, tarry, nasty layer of grey stress, worry and tension. Every worry or stress that you have been carrying around, has slimed your brain over with this sticky, ugly gray tar. Your incredible brain was never designed to be tarred over with stress. It was meant to process stressful situation and let them go. Your brain was never meant to store and warehouse stress. It was never meant to become all coated over with tension.

So, deciding that your brain has been slimed over with stress and tension for far too long, you gently and lovingly lift your brain out of your head, and carefully set it into the soapy washbasin... And you let that wonderful warm soapy wash water begin to soak away and dissolve away the stress, tension, and worries that have polluted your amazing and beautiful brain... Soaking away all the miserable slimy, tension, worry, stress and fear. All the worries that have been weighing you down, all the problems that have been tightening you up... Just letting them all begin to soak away in that lovely warm mineral healing water.

You reach into the water, and scrape off all the heavy, outer layers of grey, nasty, tarry stress and tension. Gently wash that beautiful brain of yours. And the water in the basin turns dirty and black as that powerful healing spring water begins to wash away all the outer layers of stress and tension... Washing away all your worries, problems and concerns. And as they wash away, you are beginning to see the rosy electric rich color of your amazing living brain showing through the grime, worry, and stress.

You pull the drain plug in the washbasin, and allow the water to drain out, carrying all the heavy, outer layers of stress and tension down the drain and out of your life forever. And it feels so good knowing that your brain is beginning to operate the way it was meant to, processing stressful situations, and then letting the stress drain away.

You fill the basin with more of that natural, healing mineral warm spring water. And you squeeze in more of the cleansing soap. Then you set to work scrubbing all the deep stress and tension out of every corner of your incredible and magnificent brain. You soak away and scrub away every worry, every fear, and every stress, from every fold and sulcus of that richly glowing and abundant brain. You see the rosy rich glow of color and feel the bright awareness of your brain operating at its very natural best, as all the stored up stress, tension and fear washes away in that healing warm spring water. You gently clean out every fold and every crevice of your brain, removing every last bit of that nasty tarry mess of tension and stress, worry and fear. Your brain positively shines and glows its natural rich electric rosy red... It radiates vitality and health. And all the nasty stress and tension simply dissolves away. You pull the drain plug again, and let the dirty water down the drain... And as it drains away, it carries all of the accumulated stress and tension right out of your life forever. It carries away all the worries, concerns and fears as the worthless nothing that they are.

You gently lift your brain from the washbasin, and place it in the rinse basin, where the pure natural spring water washes away all the soap and any last traces of stress. The minerals in the water soak inside and provide your brain the perfect balance of nutrients to let it repair any damage the stress has done, so that it can work at its very most efficient for your best and highest good. The rinse water penetrates inside, bringing its soothing warmth and natural nutrient balance to every single cell, fiber, and tissue of your brain and nervous system. You simply allow your brain to soak up and enjoy all the soothing comfort of your natural spring water.

You notice that there are some essential, aromatic oils on a small shelf above the rinse basin... oils like frankincense for ancient wisdom, myrrh for protection and healing, peppermint for vitality, and rose for glowing health. And many others, including all your favorite healing and protecting aromas... And you take your very favorite energizing, healing and protecting oils and shake a few drops of each into the rinse water. And those energizing and healing oils spread to form a protective coating over your brain... almost like a Teflon or wax coating over your powerful and astounding brain. So that from this moment onward, stress, tension, fears and anxieties never stick to your brain again. They simply slide off as your brain processes stressful or fearful situations, and then lets them go.

There is one special vial of protective oil on the shelf marked "Serenity Blend" that you intuitively know will polish your brain to its brightest, glowing rosy state of perfect operation. You take the serenity blend off the shelf and drop a few drops of the oil into the rinse water where it spreads out to penetrate every last corner of your brain with a new set of operating principles that help maintain your brain's natural rosy electric power at its very highest best.

And the new operating instructions that your brain now adopts follow the principles of the Serenity Affirmation: "I live each moment in the serenity of simply accepting, without worry, the things I cannot change in this moment... I choose to act with the courage and strength necessary to change what I can in this moment... and I affirm that I have the internal guidance and wisdom to know the difference in each and every moment of my full and abundant life."

Listening to the Serenity affirmation once again, your brain accepts this affirmation as a part of its operating system, and locks the Serenity affirmation into place. Your brain never warehouses stress again. From now on, your brain processes every stressful situation in life and lets it go. And the serenity affirmation becomes 10,000 times stronger every time you hear it again:

'I live each moment in the serenity of simply accepting, without worry, the things I cannot change in this moment... I choose to act with the courage and strength necessary to change what I can in this moment... and I accept that I have the internal guidance and wisdom to know the difference in each and every moment of my full and abundant life."

'I live each moment in the serenity of simply accepting, without worry, the things I cannot change in this moment... I choose to act with the courage and strength necessary to change what I can in this moment... and I accept that I have the internal guidance and wisdom to know the difference in each and every moment of my full and abundant life."

The serenity affirmation oils polish your brain to a wonderful glowing, rosy electric red that shines and shines. You gently and lovingly place your renewed and rejuvenated brain back into your head. You zip up the zipper that holds the top of your head on, and step out of your hot springs temple feeling incredibly refreshed and energized. You return to your meadow, knowing that you can return to this wonderful, healing warm spring any time you like... by listening to this recording again, or simply by thinking about it in a relaxed and peaceful place. And knowing that you can return to this healing spring any time you like, it is easy now to return to the outer world bringing all your new found peace and serenity back with you into your outer life.

Gaybeth's Coat for Stress

Gaybeth Brown is a remarkable woman who delivered her first child using hypnosis. For her second child, no hypnotist was available to help her, so she learned hypnosis herself for the birth. She spent 20 years after that doing professional hypnotherapy. She generously shared the idea for this script with me. I use a beach induction.

As you rest, you see something odd on your beach. Just a little way down, there is a full size mirror in a golden frame standing at the high surf line. The highest waves come nearly up to it, but it is just above them. The sun glints off the frame, and it looks to you like solid gold. The mirror itself is reflecting the sky and sea with a deep beauty. You feel a deep inner desire to look into this mirror and see your reflection.

You stand and begin to walk toward the mirror and as you do, every step causes you to feel more at peace and more curious. As you approach the mirror, you can see a sign on it that reads "Mirror of Truth, Reflecting Inner Peace". And you realize that the mirror doesn't reflect your clothing or body, it reflects the inner truth of your being.

And as you begin to see yourself in that mirror, you are amazed, perhaps a bit shocked, to see that you are wearing a very heavy, sodden, uncomfortable coat. And as you stare at the coat in the mirror, you realize that the coat represents all the stresses, strains and concerns that have been weighing you down and making your life heavy and constrained.

As you look more closely at that coat, you recognize the things that have been weighing you down: the worries and fears that make everything in life so much heavier... the stresses and tensions that add to life's burdens... the anxieties, uncertainties and overwork that press in on you.

Take a moment, and just let yourself study and understand, for you, all the specific worries, fears, difficulties and stresses that have been weighing you down and making life heavy... (*Pause 10 seconds*)

And as you recognize that coating of fears, anxieties and worries that you are carrying, a thought comes to you that it is pointless to carry all those worries around. You realize, guided by what you see in the mirror, that stress, anxiety, tension, and worry never help anything... they just make life worse. Your mirror reminds you that 80% of the things people worry about don't happen... Another 10% of our worries are about trivial stuff we can handle effortlessly... And the other 10% are situations that are totally out of our control. The mirror reminds you that it is pointless to spend even a moment fretting about things. It is useless to worry about things that never happen. It is pointless to worry about things we can handle. And it is totally worthless to worry for even an instant about things that are outside our control.

You realize that enough is enough, and that you have been weighed down by that worthless, constricting coat of stress and worries for far to long, So you walk down to the breakers and take off that worthless coat of fears, stress and tension. You hold all your worry, stress, tension, anxiety, and fear at arms length, and refuse to ever let them coat you and weigh you down again.

You drop that miserable heavy coat of fear and stress into the sea and let the beautiful, majestic and eternal sea begin to break apart, dissolve and recycle that coat thoroughly and effortlessly... leaving you free of fear, free of stress, free of tension, free of worry.
Free to enjoy life in each moment
Free to discover the gift in each experience
Free to live with energy, enthusiasm, and joy
Free to be

You return to the mirror, and watch and listen, as it tells you what you most need to hear about peacefulness and calm... Your mirror tells you or shows you ways to bring a deeper personal peace into your life. And as your mind studies and integrates what you see in your mirror, you feel yourself accepting that there is a deep peace at the center of your being... a deep knowledge that life never brings you anything that you can't handle... It never has and never will... You will not only survive every challenge life brings you... you will thrive!

And your mirror reminds you of the ancient wisdom that anything that doesn't kill us makes us stronger, and you realize what a truly strong and resilient human being you are.

Wave after wave of peacefulness fills you. Wave after wave of water flows up onto the sand of your beach. And your inner peacefulness grows with each wave. You now relax into the rhythmic peaceful waves and let them fill you with calm and relaxed awareness of your ability to handle everything that life brings your way.

The flowing waves repeat, over and over again, a simple refrain. The waves come in sets of two, one a large wave, the next one smaller, and each set of waves sing a new truth into your life. The first wave tells you "don't sweat the small stuff" and the second wave reminds you that it is all small stuff. And you realize that 90% of everything is small stuff and the other 10% is out of our direct control anyway, so you refuse to sweat the small stuff in any part of your life. Wave after wave the message locks into your mind – Don't sweat the small stuff (*Pause one breath*)... It's all small stuff ... (*Pause one breath*)... don't sweat the small stuff (*Pause one breath*)... it's all small stuff (*Pause one breath*)... Don't sweat the small stuff (*Pause one breath*)... It's all small stuff (*Pause one breath*)... Wave after wave, your mind adopts and integrates this powerful new awareness... And locks the message into your mind

You return your attention to your mirror and again, it has a personal, timely message for you. The mirror tells you or shows you specific and personal ways in which you can increase the contentment and peace in your life, and ways that you can creatively and continuously drop stress permanently off your shoulders. Your inner mind now realizes that stress, tension, worry, anxiety and fear never help anything, and that your natural way of being is as peaceful as the ocean on a perfect day. (*Pause 15 seconds*)

Your mind gathers all the peace on this beach, and everything that you have learned here. And your mind leaves all the stresses in your life behind for the sea to recycle. Your mind integrates the positive and beneficial new information that you have gathered here. And your inner mind locks every new and useful thought and feeling deep into the most powerful part of your mind and makes it true for you. These new thoughts and behaviors are simply the way you are now: calm, peaceful, and knowing that you can effortlessly handle anything that life brings you.

Return to my voice now, knowing it is time to return to the surface of the mind. As you rise up, you are bringing all your powerful new thoughts and feelings out with you.

The Schoolhouse: Eliminating Negative Feelings and Beliefs

Use one of the inductions, like the Beach Induction from Unlocking the Blueprint of the Psyche, *or Dr. Kresnick's Induction, that take you to a special place. The contents of this script can be easily modified to help you erase any specific limiting beliefs or to ingrain any new positive truths you want.*

Gently squeeze the thumb and forefinger together on one hand and then release them. That is the signal for your mind to take you to this wonderful and relaxed place every time you do it. Any time you close your eyes and bring your thumb and forefinger together, it is a signal for your mind to bring you to this wonderful state of relaxation, and into this perfect place you have chosen. Whenever you squeeze and release a thumb and finger, it sends a wave of peaceful relaxation through you. Try it now, gently squeeze and release your thumb and forefinger and just enjoy that pleasant wave of relaxation taking you deeper. (*Pause to follow directions*)

As you look around your special place, you notice a one-room schoolhouse, painted red, with a silver bell above the door. Even if you do not actually "see" this schoolhouse or hear its beautiful bell, if you can imagine them they are there for you. This schoolhouse is the place all your lessons from childhood are stored. But it is much more than that. It is a place of powerful inner learning where old negative lessons and patterns can be unlearned and new ones learned at any time in your life.

The magical silver bell rings and you walk up the steps into the school. Inside it is much vaster than outside. The sound of the bell is so peaceful, melodious and welcoming, that you realize joyously that this time the lessons will be different. You peer in the door and are most amazed to see a very kind, wonderfully beautiful woman within. She positively glows with energy and with kindness. You know instantly that she teaches only with love... never with fear or punishment. She is your own Inner Wisdom, come to this schoolhouse to help you free yourself of the old lessons of the past and to teach new lessons of abundance, love, strength and serenity.

Your Inner Wisdom shows you the blackboards and they are covered with the old, limiting, punitive and self-destructive lessons of your past. These are the lessons you have learned in your past from shame, abandonment, hurt, punishment, trauma, loss, fear and anger. They are the limiting, old, obsolete, mistaken lessons that are poisoning your life. Inner Wisdom is here to help you erase them and replace them with new lessons of love, patience and peace. The words on the board are all the old, false lessons; that you are somehow not enough, or that there is not enough love or abundance for you. These worthless old lessons include every limiting, critical or demeaning thing you have ever believed about yourself, or that anyone has ever said about you.

Inner Wisdom gives you a magic eraser and tells you to erase all the old, worn out lessons of fear, pain, loneliness, anger, and shame from the blackboards of your mind. Your magic eraser glows with power and hums with excitement to replace the old toxic lessons of the past with the life-affirming lessons of your new present.

You begin with the simplest, least toxic of the old lessons. As you erase them, your confidence builds that you can erase all your old toxic beliefs and replace them with new lessons of wisdom, joy, triumph, and tranquility. For example, perhaps you learned from punishment or abandonment that "there is never enough money, food, love or comfort for me". You erase that toxic old, life- destroying message and write in the new lesson. "The Universe and my own soul support me with everything I need. There is plenty of love for me and a wealth of resources that arrive just as I need them."

Or perhaps you learned through shaming that "I am not enough, not smart enough, not attractive enough, not cool enough, or not good enough." You erase those ridiculous old beliefs with your magic eraser and write in a new lesson "I am all I need to be, and I have the resources and talent to meet any life challenge and thrive."

Or perhaps pain taught you that you are separate and unimportant. You erase that absurdity and replace it with the truth that "I am a child of my own soul and divine love and I reflect them in all I am and all I do"

Your inner mind didn't know it has permission to erase and change toxic lessons, but your inner mind knows it now! Guided by Inner Wisdom, your inner mind is erasing the toxic lessons that have diminished your life. Give your powerful inner mind your full permission to erase the old, negative lessons of the past and replace them with lessons that fully affirm your life.

Perhaps you learned a series of subtle wrong lessons that have set up harmful patterns in your life. Examples of such toxic lessons might be:
Relationships lead to fear and pain
Fat equals protection
Closeness causes danger
Touch is always power abuse and hurt
Being alive means being alone and lost
Anger and rage keep me alive
Food or alcohol takes away pain
Smoking or drugs replace love
Other people are threatening
I am bad
(*Add or modify this list to reflect your specific toxic or limiting beliefs.*)

You may have internalized many other similar toxic lessons that are limiting your ability to live a full and abundant life. Just notice other toxic lessons that have filled your mind. They are written on the board. (*Pause 10 seconds*)

Your magic eraser works overtime to erase all of these obsolete, worthless, life-destroying lessons that keep you from reaching your fullest potentials of joy, success, health, abundance, love, and harmony as the wonderful, unique and miraculous human being that you are. Every time your magic eraser erases an old toxic lesson, your Inner Wisdom replaces it with new truths that reflect your true inner strength and wisdom.

Your have erased many of the relatively minor toxic lessons of the past, and replaced them with life affirming new truths. Now it is time to get rid of the major toxic inner beliefs and lessons. Squeeze and release your thumb and forefinger, your signal to relax ten times deeper.

Now Inner Wisdom, your marvelous teacher, shows you the place on the board where your MOST terrible lesson is written. This is the belief that has most injured you or distorted your life with painful recurrent negative patterns. You may recognize this lesson consciously or perhaps your inner mind chooses not to make it conscious at this time. But that painful, central toxic lesson lives in the subconscious and injures your life. And your powerful subconscious mind is perfectly capable of erasing that lesson so that it never harms you again. And your magic eraser goes after that most major toxic lesson with a fury, erasing it, and every trace of it, from your life. And then your Inner Wisdom writes in a new, life-affirming lesson to completely and totally change the effects of that previous belief. The new lesson frees your subconscious mind to recreate your life and your choices in patterns of freedom, health, abundance and love. She writes: "I am a beloved child of divine energy and my own soul, and my life is a miraculous adventure." And she adds anything else that totally reverses the old negative belief. (*Pause 10 seconds*)

As Inner Wisdom writes the new, life affirming truths, you feel a deep desire to return to this recording often, and to rewrite your new lessons over and over until every last vestige of the old destructive pattern is replaced by a new, flowing, peaceful and creative life. You absorb the new lessons of love, abundance and radiant wellbeing. And they simply become true for you. Your entire life changes to reflect your beautiful new inner truth. Squeeze and release your thumb and forefinger, relaxing 10 times more deeply, and as you do, your new truth locks into place and gets 1,000 times stronger.

You return to this recording often. And every time you do, your Inner Wisdom guides you in erasing and replacing all the old poisons of the past with new and peaceful truths from your present. You realize that the ancient truth; "whatever doesn't kill us makes us stronger," is totally true for you, and you realize that you are a totally strong, resilient and incredible human being who is all you need to be to meet any challenge in life and thrive through it. You are a powerful being, and you can accomplish whatever you can dream or imagine.

The more often you listen to this recording the more conscious you become of the new lessons. And the more the old destructive or painful patterns leave your life... replaced forever by new patterns of love, prosperity, harmony, serenity abundance, accomplishment and power. Every time you listen to this recording, the new life-affirming truths get stronger and stronger.

You are now free to create the life your were intended to have. And in that freedom, you find a miraculous set of changes that move your life to its highest potentials. Your deepest new truth is that you are totally free to have, do, or be whatever you can imagine or dream. And you are a powerful dreamer. Stand in that power and look out on a changed world.

You thank Inner Wisdom for her work, and promise to return often to this schoolroom to undo the old lessons of the past and replace them forever with life giving truths of abundance, peace, harmony, freedom and love.

The Spider in the Garden

I like to do this with a two-minute induction, and a Feather deepening, or even just a Feather induction.

Gently squeeze the thumb and forefinger together on one hand and then release them. That is the signal for your mind to take you to this wonderful and relaxed place every time you do it. Any time you close your eyes and bring your thumb and forefinger together, it is a signal for your mind to bring you to this wonderful state of relaxation, and into this perfect place you have chosen. Whenever you squeeze and release a thumb and finger, it sends a wave of peaceful relaxation through you. Try it now, squeeze and release your thumb and forefinger and just enjoy that pleasant wave of relaxation taking you deeper... Now just rest and imagine yourself to be just like a little child as I tell you a story. Every breath you breathe causes your mind to be open to, and to apply the lessons of this story.

Once upon a time, or even right now, right here where you are sitting, in a part of your special place, there is a beautiful garden... a wonderful place filled with flowers, and vegetables and healing herbs of all kinds. And tending your garden is a most marvelous person. The gardener is a wise old man or wise old woman... but you know the gardener is special because the gardener glows with a wonderful energy. And birds land close by and sing sweet songs. You listen to this story pretending to have all the wonder of a child. This wise old being is your own Inner Healer, a very wise inner aspect of your wholeness. Inner Healer is always willing to share vast wisdom with you about whatever needs healing in your life when you become quiet and visit the garden. But Inner Healer never interferes with your outer life unless you ask for help because of a profound respect for your free will. Inner Healer is here today because you have become quiet and gone to the garden.

Inner Healer takes you to one side of the garden and points out something very sad. In the garden, there is a little spider whose original job was to keep the garden free of flies and mosquitoes. But this little spider got big ideas and spun her web bigger and bigger. It is much too big a web for such a little spider. It covers a third of the garden, and she keeps on spinning it. She is like an addict and doesn't know how to stop spinning her web. She doesn't know how to set reasonable limits on the size of the web. The spider is totally out of control. The web has grown to gigantic proportions and is choking off the richest part of the garden.

A beautiful songbird, a lark or a nightingale, flew into the web by accident and got caught. As you sense or imagine the web, you realize that the songbird is completely enmeshed in the web... completely caught. The more the bird struggles to get free, the more it gets tangled in the sticky strands of the web. The songbird has struggled to get free for so long that she is now almost totally wrapped in webbing and she is almost totally exhausted from the struggle to get free.

Your beautiful bird is much, much bigger than the tiny garden spider, and the spider wants nothing to do with such a huge captive. The spider only eats flies and mosquitoes. The web just grew all out of control and captured the songbird as if by accident. The spider is ignoring the bird and spinning a bigger and bigger web. And the bird is exhausting itself almost to the point of death.

You can help. Inner Healer has scissors, tweezers and swabs for you. Very carefully, you begin to cut the strands that hold the bird in the web. Strand by strand, all around the bird. Strand by patient strand. Just float peacefully and let your inner mind cut the strands away. Your inner mind thinks in symbols and feelings more than in words. As you cut each strand, your powerful inner mind knows exactly what the bird means for you, what the spider represents, and what the web symbolizes. And even if your conscious mind doesn't remember what these things symbolize, your inner mind is healing powerfully, setting your mind free of the webs that have trapped it. And you can feel the energy move as you cut away the strands.

You patiently trim the web away until the bird is out of the web and in your hand. And then, with tweezers and swabs, you painstaking remove the sticky strands from the bird's feathers and wings. Watch and imagine her reaction as you clean every last bit of webbing away. The bird trusts you utterly and just sits in your hand as you clean, removing every last sticky trace of webbing. Float peacefully as you imagine cleaning your beautiful bird from beak to tail feathers.

When the bird is clean and free of web material, bring her water and food in an eyedropper and watch her gratefully take them in. She quickly regains the strength to fly. She is taking the courage and strength from your heart and kindness.

When the bird is ready, set it free. She may land in a tree and stay in the garden. Or she may fly gloriously out into the world outside, singing a song of joy and thanks. But wherever she flies, she fills your heart with her gladness and freedom.

As you watch the bird fly, as you hear her song and feel her joy, Inner Healer guides you back to the spider web. You take whatever tools you need to cut away the huge, overgrown web. You trim and cut the web in every direction, until just a little bit is left, just big enough for a tiny spider to catch the flies and mosquitoes that visit the garden.

Your inner mind thinks in pictures and symbols, and has been learning a profound lesson about the possibility of freedom and about the steps to attain it. Perhaps the spider represents your ego, or perhaps it represents defense mechanisms that have gotten completely out of control. Perhaps the bird represents your true self or your hidden talents or strengths. Or perhaps they mean other things for you all together. It is not important for you to consciously understand what the symbols mean. Your powerful inner mind is totally aware and has learned that it is possible to live free of the insidious trap. It is possible to be free, possible to live your deepest truth, possible to get free of whatever webs your mind has been trapped in. And at a deep inner level, your inner mind has learned and adopted the steps you must take to get free. Trust your inner mind. It is subtle, yet powerful beyond imagining. Change is happening right now, and moving toward your outer reality at the speed of thought. The more you listen to this recording the faster the changes happen, and the faster you achieve freedom.

Know that inside, you are learning. And the new, web-free reality is emerging into your outer reality as fast as you are ready for it. Expect your freedom. It is happening now, moving from the inside of your mind to your outer life. Your subconscious mind knows what freedom means now and is changing your outer reality to reflect your inner freedom even as we speak. Expect miraculous freeing transformation. **It is yours!** And as you listen to this story with all the wide-eyed wonder of a child, you pretend that every word on this recording has been meaningful to your inner mind. And the harder you pretend, the more real it becomes.

Inner Healer brings you to your special and peaceful place. And you remember pretending that once upon a time there was a bird caught in an overgrown spider web in the middle of the most beautiful garden. And you remember helping set that bird free. And you feel a deep satisfaction and peace that your inner mind now knows how to keep the garden in perfect harmony and balance. And Once Upon a Time is now, and now is forever, as your subconscious mind remembers the story and applies everything it has learned about setting you well and truly free of anything that traps the beautiful bird of your being.

Now take a full minute to just float in this wonderful and peaceful state, letting your mind simply enjoy this wonderful state of peaceful relaxation, knowing that this state of mind is the place from which all change and healing begins. Squeeze and release your thumb and forefinger, and feel yourself relax 10 times more deeply as your inner mind takes the next minute to magnify everything your mind is learning about freedom one thousand times. Your minute of silence begins NOW. (*Pause for one full minute*)

Returning to my voice, you find yourself floating gently into awareness of your special place. You thank your Inner Healer for helping you set the birds of your spirit free. You know that you can return to this garden any time you wish simply by listening to this recording or by squeezing and releasing your thumb and forefinger. **You are free to have, to do or to be whatever you can imagine or dream, and you are a powerful dreamer.** Once again, gently squeeze and release your thumb and forefinger. Any time you squeeze and release, it is signal for your mind to send you a wave of comfort and peace, and to magnify everything you have learned about freedom 10,000 times.

(*Use the affirmation,* "**You are free to have, to do or to be whatever you can imagine or dream, and you are a powerful dreamer**" *three times in the awakening sequence.*)

Dr. Mike Preston's Library for Depression

The format for this script was developed by Dr. Mike Preston. The specific language is mine. Use his induction and deepening. This script can be adapted for any problem simply by replacing the book of depression with a book for your specific problem.

As you drift in this deep, peaceful state, I would like you to imagine a library. A library is a big building with aisles and aisles of books on shelves, and as you picture and imagine your library, you realize the most important aisle there contains all the books of your life. Just picture and imagine your library, the one that contains all the books of your life. And imagine that one special aisle that contains the books that record every instant of your life.

The aisle of the books of your life has books on the right side, and books on the other side. The right side of the aisle is filled with all the positive books that record your dreams, goals, positive memories, and every positive learning experience of your life. The good side of the aisle records every positive thing you have learned from every situation in your life, even the difficult ones. On the right side of the aisle there is a book for every one of your skills and talents, even the ones you have yet to discover. You realize that the books on the right side of the aisle describe you as you truly are, at your very natural best. As you study the positive side of the aisle, you feel a bit surprised and saddened that your subconscious mind hasn't spent much time with the books on the positive side of the aisle because all the covers are new and unworn.

The other side of the aisle, the not-so-nice side of the aisle, is filled with books that record all the negative thoughts and feelings you have ever had about yourself. It has books for every problem in your life, physical, emotional, mental, social, or financial. It has books that contain all the stress and tension in your life. It has books that contain all the obstacles to you living a peaceful life of rich experience. And it has books about all your fears and self-imposed limitations. All the books on the negative side of your aisle are from the past and are still affecting you today. It is with a shock that you realize your subconscious mind has been spending far too much time reading these negative books… All the spines are broken and bent, the pages are dog-eared and the covers are ragged. And deciding that enough is enough, you decide you have carried these negative books around too long, and wasted too much time with them.

So beginning with the books that contain all the negative thoughts, feelings, or behaviors that you have ever associated with yourself, you take your negative self thoughts and negative self feelings and negative behaviors off the shelf, and load them onto a library cart. You push your negative thoughts, feelings, and behaviors to the back of the aisle where there is a very large recycling bin. Without even bothering to read them, you hold your past negative self-definitions in your hands and tear them to shreds until only the cover is left. Then, realizing that even the covers of books that define you negatively are no longer worthy of you, you rip the covers of those negative feelings, thoughts and behaviors to shreds and recycle them too.

Next, returning to the not-so-nice side of the aisle, you load the books that contain all your stresses and tensions, worries and concerns on to the cart, and push them back to the back of the aisle. You realize that 90% of what we worry about or stress over never happens or can be handled easily. And the other 10% is out of our control. So worry and stress are totally worthless emotions. You hold your stress, tension, worries and concerns in your hands, remember that they are useless to you. And one by one, you tear up every stress, every tension, every worry and every last concern in your life and recycle them, tossing away every useless worry and stress in your life... and they are _all_ useless.

Feeling lighter and more courageous now, you return to the negative side of the aisle and to the book that contains your major obstacle to living fully. It is the biggest, blackest and heaviest book on the shelf, and it is titled: "My Book of Depression." The depression book contains all the roots and causes of depression in your life. It contains all the sad feelings and low energy. It contains the pain and lack of interest and everything else that goes with depression. And you realize that enough is enough! You choose that today really is the beginning of a new life. You choose that everything changes for the better NOW. With all your courage and skill, you reach up and take that heavy, heavy book of depression off the shelf. Holding the depression in your hands, you take it back to the recycle bin and you rip your depression to shreds and throw it away with all the other worthless trash. It feels so good to throw that problem out of your life forever.

And finally, feeling great, you return to the aisle, and find your books of limitations and fears... your books of "I Can't and "Excuses". These books contain all the limitations you have ever accepted as true about you. They contain all the fears and anxieties that have kept you from experiencing life as richly and fully as you were born to. All of these fears and limitations are from the past, and even though you have accepted them, they were given to you by other people. Other people's negative limitations on you are no longer part of your life. Remembering that you are an incredible being of vast and unlimited potential, you take your fears and limitations, your I can'ts and your excuses, into your hands. You carry them to the recycle bin. Then you rip every one of those fears and limitations to shreds and throw them out of your mind forever, even ripping up the covers so that your mind never collects other people's fears and limitations again. All your I cant's and excuses are ripped to shreds along with the covers. And you are free to have, do or be whatever you can dream or imagine. And you are a powerful dreamer.

Now, moving back to the nice right side of the aisle, you pick up some books that you want your subconscious mind to absorb and act upon. First, there is a book, which is even a book in the outer world... the title is "Don't Sweat the Small Stuff – And It's All Small Stuff". You direct your subconscious mind to read this inner book thoroughly, and to integrate its instruction not to sweat the small stuff 100% into your outer life.

Next there is your "Book of Undiscovered Talents, Interests and Joys" You pick it up knowing that you have vast internal resources and interests that you have yet to uncover, and that the things in this book can open your life to unexpected joy.

There is your book of "Deepest Dreams, Goals and Desires" that record the soul-deep dreams of your spirit: your reasons for being alive, and all the things you want to accomplish in your time here. You pick it up, knowing that your subconscious mind has the power to read these deepest dreams, goal and desires, and to make them conscious and guide you in making them manifest and real in your life.

Finally, there is your book, "How to Enjoy Every Moment of Your Life as You Find It". Knowing that this book is filled with personal information about how your can enjoy every instant of your life as it occurs, even the difficult moments, you take this book with you.

Out in the front of the aisle, there is a reading area with a perfect, large, overstuffed reading chair. You sit down in an open and relaxed state, settling into your chair, knowing that your subconscious mind is now focusing on these great new books to read. As you rest in the chair, simply letting your outer conscious mind float and drift, your powerful inner mind begins reading your new books... "Don't Sweat the Small Stuff"... "Undiscovered Talents"... "Deepest Dreams... and "How to Enjoy Life".

Your subconscious mind reads these books here in the chair. It reads these powerful new books when you are sleeping and dreaming. It reads these books in every relaxed and quiet moment. And your subconscious mind begins making the information in these books conscious. It begins integrating all the deep wisdom in these inner books into your outer conscious life just as rapidly as you can assimilate the information and the new ways of thinking, feeling and acting. You find yourself living life like a surfer on the Ocean, always going with the flow but directing your ride across life's waves in the way that brings you the best ride. You find worries and fears being replaced by calm acceptance. You have a wonderful new sense that no matter what life brings, you will not only survive, you will thrive. In each and every day, in each and every way your life is becoming more abundant, healthier, more relaxed, and more filled with the simple joy of being. You feel positive, optimistic, and whole. You know that you have within you, all you need to accomplish all your many wonderful goals. Your dreams are rich and fulfilling. You look forward to the adventure and gift in each new day and in every moment. Life is magic and you are both the magician and the living result of the magic. In each and every day you are experiencing richer and richer choices in life and each day brings you joy. And if all these positive and beneficial ideas are acceptable to your inner mind, you simply continue breathing... just as you are.

Every time you listen to this recording or relax in any way, your subconscious mind continues reading the books on the nice side of the aisle, filling your mind with wonderful and joyous new, and relaxed ways of living fully. Every breath you breathe causes your inner mind to create joy and abundant choices in your life. Take a moment of silence now, and allow your inner mind to fill itself with the deep inner wisdom that has always been in your inner library and when that minute of silence ends, it will be time to return to the surface, feeling absolutely wonderful and filled with exciting new ways to live life free of stress. (*Pause 60 seconds*)

Return to my voice… it is almost time to return to the outer world, knowing that you are internally and automatically learning powerful new ways to let go of depression and live abundantly. And your inner mind is doing every healthy thing necessary to alleviate depression and open your life to peace and joy. Every breath you breathe strengthens, magnifies and reinforces all the positive and beneficial changes happening within. And you are amazed at how rapidly your life gets better and better… every day in every way.

SCRIPTS FOR FEARS AND APPREHENSIONS

Fears, Panic and Anxiety

Try this with a short induction and a Feather deepening, or use Dr. Preston's induction or deepening. You can also try the Pretend Game induction or the Confusion induction if you are adventurous.

Imagine now, a peaceful place of total safety... perhaps a mountain meadow, a special beach or a beautiful garden. The place you imagine is a safe place, a place where you are always calm and at peace. Just let that special and beautiful place fill your mind. Your safe place is a place of learning, where your powerful inner mind can rapidly unlearn the mistakes of the past and learn healthy, new and exciting ways of living in the present. Whenever you visit this special place in your mind, a wave of comfort fills you. Your inner mind now associates all the peaceful feelings that you are feeling right now with your special inner sanctuary. And whenever you think about this beautiful place, you feel a calming wave of all the serene and peaceful feelings you are feeling right now. You don't have to be in hypnosis to feel these wonderful feelings. All you have to do is close your eyes and picture or imagine your beautiful place, and a wave of pleasant calm and relaxation fills you. No matter what you are doing, or what is going on in your life, every time you even think about your special place, a sense of safety, tranquility and peace fill you. Your nervous system can only feel one emotion at a time. And calm, peacefulness always drives out fear.

As your outer mind continues simply to rest in the peace of your special place, your inner mind is receptive to the ideas on this recording. Your inner mind accepts every positive and beneficial idea on this recording and makes them true for you. Your entire life changes in the most exciting and positive ways as your inner mind rapidly integrates the ideas on this recording into your outer life. The more you listen to this recording and the more you visit the special place in your mind, the faster the positive and exciting changes occur.

The first thing for your subconscious mind to know is that fear is a mistake of the mind. Whenever fear… by any name, panic, anxiety, worry… whenever fear paralyzes you, limits your choices or stops you from achieving your goals, that fear is based on a mental mistake. Fear is always a mental mistake. Intense fear never helps anything, it only make life worse. Your subconscious mind learned fear, and whatever you mind learned can be unlearned.

Sometime, a long time ago, you faced some difficult situation or challenge, and you also just happened to be feeling a little fear. You survived the situation or challenge, because you were prepared, because you had what you needed, because you had help, or even perhaps because you were lucky. But your inner mind saw the fear and made the mistake of thinking the fear caused you to be OK. And that is the basic mistake the mind made. Then your inner mind compounded the mistake by deciding that if a little fear helped in that situation, then sending you lots of fear would help you even more. And bit-by-bit, your inner mind increased the amount of fear so that it has become totally paralyzing and distracting, actually causing you far more damage than any situation you face ever could. Fear by any name: worry, anxiety, concern, phobia, terror… Fear is always a mistake of the mind.

As you listen to this tape in the safety of your special place several times, you may actually consciously remember the specific event where your inner mind made the mistake of thinking fear keeps you safe. But it isn't necessary for you to remember that first event consciously. Because your inner mind knows exactly what it is. Your inner mind always knows. And as your outer conscious mind rests in the special place, just relaxing in the safety, your powerful and dynamic inner mind reviews all the times you have felt the fear, all the way back to the very first time. And your subconscious mind, guided by your highest wisdom, reviews that very first experience of the fear. And your inner mind realizes that the reasons you survived or succeeded had nothing to do with fear. The fear just happened to be there, but had nothing to do with your survival or success. Your inner mind recognizes the mistake it made, and now realizes a new truth. That new truth is that fear never helps anything. No matter what name we use for it, anxiety, panic, or worry; fear never helps anything. At best fear is a distraction, and at worst it totally poisons our lives. Your inner mind, at lightning speed, reviews every time you felt those fears and realizes that each and every time, sending you the fear was a mistake that actually made everything worse. Fear never helps anything; it only makes things worse.

And your inner mind is discovering the power of calm peacefulness. When you are calm and peaceful, your thinking is clear, and you can access all of your deepest resources not only to survive, but to thrive through every challenge in your life. Whenever you feel the least trace of anxiety, panic or fear building, even subconsciously, your inner mind instantly brings an image of your special place into your mind. And you immediately feel a wave of calm and peaceful focus fill you. Your nervous system can only feel one emotion at a time and calm peacefulness always drives out fear.

Whenever you feel even the least trace of fear, even subconsciously, your inner mind recognizes that fear is a mistake. And the more fear, anxiety or panic you even begin to feel, the calmer you become in every way. The more fear you begin to feel, the slower and deeper and more peaceful your breathing becomes. The more fear, anxiety or panic you even begin to feel, the slower your heart beats, moving to resting normal. The more fear of any kind you even begin to feel, the lower your blood pressure moves toward resting, peaceful normal for you. The more anxiety or panic you even begin to feel, the more your muscles relax and the calmer you feel. The more panic or anxiety you even begin to feel, the less your adrenal glands release adrenalin, and the more they release noradrenalin, the natural calming hormone. The more fear you even begin to feel, the more calm you become in each and every way.

Your inner mind realizes that when you are calm and peaceful, you have access to all the deepest resources of your inner mind... access to your deepest wisdom, access to all your skills, talents and abilities. So your inner mind now focuses on keeping you calm, peaceful and relaxed, no matter what is going on in your life. Other people are noticing the changes in you. And you are becoming a role model for others. You go through every situation relaxed and calm, knowing that you have everything you need, not just to survive, but to thrive through every situation life creates. You feel an astounding new wave of confidence and self-esteem as you realize that your subconscious mind is allowing all the fears of the past to fade into the past. You are permanently locking the door on the old fears forever.

You visit your special place in your mind whenever you are faced with a life challenge. And in the peacefulness of your inner place, you are inspired with creative ideas from your wisest deepest mind for easily resolving every challenge you face. And your inner mind realizes that your true safety comes from the awareness, the focus, the alertness, the wisdom and experience that you have in abundance. It feels so good to face every situation in life with the calm, peaceful confidence that you have everything you need, not just to survive, but to thrive. And every time you listen to this recording, your inner calm grows greater and greater. And every time you even think about your special place within, you feel a wave of calm peacefulness that grows greater and greater. If the positive and powerful ideas on this recording are acceptable to you, you simply continue breathing... just as you are. And your powerful inner mind magnifies all these idea a thousand times over, and seals them into the most powerful part of your mind where they become a permanent part of your outer reality.

And now, it is time to return to the surface of the mind, and to your outer world, and you rise up knowing that your special, peaceful place is only a thought away, and you can return here whenever you like, and as often as you like, simply by thinking about your beautiful inner place.

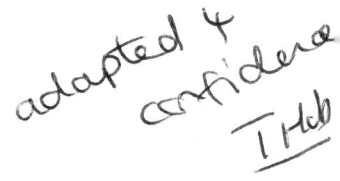

Flying Freely

Almost any induction is good for this script. You can modify the script to be about any fear simply by substituting fear of flying with any other fear.

As you continue to relax more deeply with each breath, your conscious mind relaxes and rests while your powerful subconscious mind does the work. Each word on the recording and every beat of your heart cause your subconscious mind to implement your new goal, which is that you are now able to easily board an airplane and fly peacefully and comfortably any time that you want to travel. Every breath you breathe reinforces and magnifies the positive and beneficial suggestions on this recording. Each time you listen to this recording, you relax twice as deeply and feel a wonderful sense of peace. Every time you listen to this recording, your mind reinforces the suggestions and positive ideas on this recording a thousand times over, sealing them into your deepest mind where they simply become the truth for you.

Imagine a beautiful and peaceful place in nature, the most beautiful and peaceful place that you can dream of... It may be a special beach, or a mountain meadow, a gentle garden or a small stream and lake on a perfect day. Wherever that beautiful place is for you, it is your special and restful spot. Notice that simply thinking of this special natural place of rest and healing causes you to relax even more deeply. Whenever you think of, or imagine your peaceful place, you immediately feel a wave of calm, just as you are experiencing now listening to the recording. Notice everything in your special place: the color of the air and the patterns of the clouds, the aroma of the plants and flowers, the sounds of water or small birds and animals, the warmth of the sun and the cooling and refreshing breeze on your skin. Every sense awakens in your special place. And anytime that you think of your special place, every sight, sound, smell, and touch that you imagine causes a wave of peaceful, relaxed feeling to flow into you and grow deeper the more you think about this special place. Just let your conscious mind rest and rejuvenate itself here while your subconscious mind works with my voice to set you free.

You have made this recording to help you overcome a fear of flying. Fears, particularly powerful fears of natural things that most people do easily, like flying, are simple mistakes of the mind that are lodged deep in the subconscious. They are rooted in the past but still affecting and limiting you today. You inform your subconscious mind of your powerful desire to resolve this fear so that you can travel freely and easily by air whenever you wish to travel. And as your subconscious mind studies all the ways that the fear limits you and prevents you from living fully and freely, it remembers what it has always known, that fear is a totally useless emotion that never really helps anything. And that fear always keeps us from living fully.

The roots of your fear of flying are lodged somewhere in your past. What we call fear of flying can be one of several fears or a combination of them all. It may be a fear of high places, or a fear of confined spaces, or a fear of not being in control, or even a fear of bumps. Fear of flying can be all of those and other things combined. But all of those fears have their roots in the past. A small, frightened part of your mind is holding those fears and sending them through you like a storm whenever you try to fly. Sometime, way back in the past, probably in early childhood, you were in a situation similar to flying that made you feel afraid. Perhaps you were held up too high and whirled around by an adult who didn't understand how frightening it was to you. Perhaps you were frightened by bumps in a car. Perhaps you survived a scary fall from a tree or rock that frightened you. It isn't really necessary to remember exactly what started the fear. All you have to do is realize that somewhere in your past, you had a situation similar to flying that frightened you. And that there is a small, childlike part of your mind that is still carrying that fear around.

As you listen to this recording several times in a deeply relaxed state, you may even remember that first incident of fear that started off your fear of flying, but it isn't necessary that you do. Your subconscious mind remembers that original incident perfectly and is perfectly capable of letting go of the fear without even having to make the memory conscious.

All you have to do is remember and imagine the frightened, small child you were. What happened way back then, is that there was an actual event that frightened you deeply. You were afraid. And you survived. Since you are alive now, listening to this recording, we know you survived that original situation, whatever it was. But your mind and brain made a mistake. That small part of your mind came to believe that it was your fear that kept you safe. It made a simple equation in the mind. As a child, your brain said: "I was really afraid, and I survived, *therefore the fear saved me.* And if a little fear saved me in the past, then more fear will keep me even safer in the future. And a lot of fear will keep me totally safe."

As your subconscious mind studies the rule that small part of you put into your mind, it realizes that it was a total mistake. It was a mistake because fear didn't save you. You survived because you had the skill and talent to keep yourself safe. You survived because the situation wasn't as out of control as you thought. You survived because you were prepared, skilled and ready. You may even have been lucky. Your subconscious mind now understands that fear **never** keeps anyone safe.

To heal and resolve the fear, we have to help the part of you that experienced the original fear. So picture or imagine that small, frightened part of yourself standing utterly paralyzed with fear. The part of you doing the imagining is a powerful, strong and capable person who can handle everything life brings. So the big part of you goes to the little frightened part. And you pick that small part of you up just like you would any frightened child. As the childlike, frightened part of you looks into your adult eyes, you surround your inner child with a feeling of love and comfort. The fear drains away and your child sinks into the safety of your arms. Your child mind recognizes that you are grown up, strong and perfectly capable of keeping yourself and all parts of you safe. You tell the child that from now on, the grown up part of you will take over the job of keeping you safe, and that the little part of you never has to worry about it again. In fact, when you want to travel, the grown up part will take care of all the travel, and keeping you safe, and the little part only has to think about all the fun or adventures you will have when you get to your destination.

You hug the little part of you closely and tell all about your special and beautiful place where you started your work today... that special garden or beach, stream or mountain. And you realize it is a perfect home for the little part of you. No part of you ever needs to live in the old scary situation again, and the childlike part of you can leave the old worthless fear behind and move into the special place forever. And the fear drops right out of your mind like snow melting and flowing away. You take your child mind to the your special place and say: "this is your new home now. It is a place where you can look out our grownup eyes, and talk with me, your grown-up self. But when you live in the special place, you never have to solve problems or deal with scary stuff again. You have me, a strong grown-up, to handle that. All you have to do is play and bring joy and adventure into our lives. And when we are traveling, all you have to do is think about the fun and adventure we are going to have when we get there. And the old fear melts like ice on a hot summer day, and flows out of your mind forever.

You test your new freedom by practicing. Imagine that you have the opportunity to go on a wonderful adventure that requires a flight. As soon as you get the news, you check in with your inner child, who is still in the special place. And you realize your child mind is totally engaged in planning all the fun and adventurous things you can do. And that the old fear is simply gone. You make your reservations. And if you feel even the least twinge of the old fear, you immediately picture and imagine your special place, and the fear fades away like fog evaporating in the sunlight. And all you feel is calm, and ready for an adventure. As you pack your bags, you check in frequently with your inner child, and you feel a wave of calm and relaxation fill you as you picture and imagine your special and beautiful place.

You imagine yourself driving to the airport, calm and relaxed and ready for an adventure. At the check-in counter, you are greeted by friendly people who give you a sense of safety and peace... because they are so calm and efficient. You look in on your inner child in your special place and another wave of relaxed, calm excitement fills you to the brim. At the gate, as you wait, you close your eyes and visit your special place. You bask in the calm and peace. And you let your child mind tell you all about the adventures at the end of your journey. As you board the plane, you are met by a calm, competent flight attendant who positively glows with the kind of assurance and safety that comes from having made thousands of journeys. And you feel another wave of peace, coupled with a satisfying sense of accomplishment and success.

As you imagine the plane getting ready to fly, you relax in your seat and visit your special place inside. The mighty roar of the engines is a completely comforting sound because you know that anything that powerful will make the journey safely and easily. As you feel the plane lift into the air, the pleasant feeling of movement soothes you. You close your eyes and go to your special place and just enjoy the peaceful feelings you always find there. You may even fall into a deep and restful sleep.

Before you know it, the plane is landing. The lightness you feel on the descent is a weightless and carefree feeling. You never dreamed flying could actually be so much fun. As you get off the plane, you have an immensely powerful feeling of success, accomplishment and joy because you know that you have faced an ancient and terrible fear and left it in the dust behind you. And you have the incredibly gratifying realization that when you fly on the return journey, it will be ten times easier and more relaxing, and that the old and worthless fear is gone forever, and you are free.

Return now to your special, healing place in nature, realizing that the small, childlike part of your mind is free. And realizing that the subconscious mind has completely resolved and let go of the fear. You are now free. Free to travel wherever and whenever you want. Free to have joyous adventures and to know the world more closely. Free of the chains of the past and free of the mistake of the mind. Free to explore the fun and adventure your child mind is creating in your special place. Free to be calm and at peace no matter what happens in your life. Free to be. And it is so exciting to be free.

Every time you listen to this recording, the positive and beneficial ideas get stronger and stronger and thousands of times stronger. You feel relaxed and calm. You travel freely and easily. And you have a growing sense of appreciation for yourself and your powerful creative mind. You visit your beautiful and special place often. And every time you think of it, a wave of calm, peaceful confidence fills you and you know you can meet any challenge in life and thrive. You visit often with the child in the special place, and truly enjoy the ways that play and adventure grow in your life. In each and every day, in each and every way, your inner mind magnifies and reinforces the ideas on this recording, and you feel alive, free and a totally awesome success.

Speaking Freely in Public

Any induction works well for this script. This script can be modified easily to work with any specific fear by replacing the ideas about fear of speaking, and success at it, with your specific fear.

As each gentle breath you breathe causes you to relax more deeply, your inner mind is open and receptive to the ideas on this recording. The more you listen to this recording, the more the old and no longer necessary apprehensions about speaking in public fade away. And the more you listen to this recording, the more and more deeply you realize that you are a capable public speaker. You have things to say and audiences who want to listen. As your outer, conscious mind simply drifts and floats peacefully in this calm, relaxed state, your powerful inner mind accepts, magnifies and implements every positive and beneficial idea on this recording so that you achieve your goal of speaking in public effortlessly and easily.

The first thing you realize is that language and spoken communication are uniquely human gifts. Every one of us has the ability to speak, and to speak well. Some people may be more eloquent than others, but that is mostly a matter of practice. Every human being is born with all they need to speak competently about the things they know... **and you are no exception**. You were born with the human gift of language, and you learned to speak very early in your life. In fact, you were saying your first words long before your incredible brain had grown to half its adult size. Like all human beings, you are a remarkable communicator.

I would like you to remember a time when you spoke easily to one single person about something important to you. Perhaps a time when you were deeply interested in another person, or even in love. Remember at least one time in your life when you spoke to one single person easily and effortlessly. And as you remember a time when you communicated really well with one person, you inform your inner mind that your goal is to speak in any situation at least as clearly and easily as you spoke to that one person. No matter how many people may be listening. If you truly don't remember speaking easily and clearly to one other person, think about a time when you were talking to yourself, even silently. Because if you can talk to another person, or even to yourself, with clarity and ease, you already have all you need to speak to any number of people at once.

The only thing that keeps you from being the kind of effortless public speaker you want to be is fear. And fear of speaking in public, like all fears, is a useless relic of the past that you wish to send back to the past. For most of us, a fear of speaking in public started when we were children, either in school or at home. You may have grown up in a home where the rule was: "Children are seen, and not heard." Or you may have grown up in a home where it was dangerous to speak. For many of us, being called on in a classroom to give an answer we didn't have, and being laughed at or shamed, may have started a fear of speaking in front of others. It isn't important what actually started the fear. Just know that within you there is a small, childlike part of the mind that is still reacting to that old situation, and filling you with paralyzing fear whenever you face the possibility of speaking in public. And at the time, that fear may have been useful to you, but now it is simply an obstacle to your growth and success.

I would like you to imagine that small child you used to be when you first experienced the fear of speaking. You may have an actual memory of the events, but it isn't necessary. What is important is to imagine your grown up, adult self stepping in and picking that childlike part of the mind up. Hug your inner child, and let him (or her) know that you are his (her) grown up self which has come back to help. Step between your child and whoever is threatening or shaming or embarrassing your inner child. Tell them to stop that immediately, and to go stand in the corner until you return for them. Then imagine your heart opening up like a flower. And there, in the center of your heart, is a perfect playground with everything a child needs to be happy, learning and growing. Tell you inner child that the whole world is visible from your heart. Your inner child can look out your adult eyes and see the world, but that your inner child never has to deal with public speaking again. That's what your adult self is for... to take care of things like speaking in front of people. And as you set your inner child free, never to have to deal with speaking in public again, you feel a vast wave of relief as the old fear just fades into the past and out of your life forever.

Now return to the person or people standing in the corner. And realize this person or these people inside who have been sending the fear are not the actual outside people. They are also parts of your own mind, parts that designed themselves after those people, and continued creating the fear **because they thought they were helping you**. With all your adult strength, show them the truth. Show them all the ways the fear is hurting you now. Show them that the fear itself is far worse than anything that could happen when you speak. Show them that truly helping you would mean: helping your mind focus on the topic, helping you prepare fully, helping you be confident and strong. Tell these fear-generating parts of you that you know you are a skilled communicator, like all human beings, and that you have everything it takes to speak well. And then assign the fear causing parts of your mind a new job. That new job is to convert the energy of fear into excitement. Their new job is to focus on the message you want to send so that you are prepared and know your material. Their new job is to help you be relaxed, calm and at peace as you speak to one person, two people, five people, fifty people or a thousand.

As the old fear-generating parts of you take on their new jobs, and as your young self gets down to the serious business of play within your heart, you feel a wave of confidence, excitement, control and optimism sweep through you. You allow all the old, worthless apprehension to dissolve out of you like snow melting on a warm spring day. And with every beat of your heart and blink of your eyes, the old fear just fades away.

Now say the words "calm and relaxed" to yourself. These are your new magic words. Whenever you hear or repeat the words "calm and relaxed", even silently in your own mind, you feel a wave of all the peaceful, confident good feelings you are feeling right now. Your nervous system can only feel one emotional state at a time, and 'calm and relaxed" always drives away fear. "Calm and relaxed".

Now imagine yourself having the opportunity to make a presentation in public... As you have been preparing, you have frequently used your magic words "calm and relaxed", repeating them silently in your mind. And it has been totally exciting that the old apprehension and fear has simply faded away. And you are filled will calm, confidence. As you imagine walking out to the speaker's platform, you feel confident and secure, and every beat of your heart causes you to relax more deeply. As you look out over the crowd, you say the words "calm and relaxed" to yourself, and you feel an amazing wave of peaceful confidence, a sense of calm and peace as deep as you have felt here today. You are alert, peaceful and relaxed, and totally ready to exercise your natural human gift of language to communicate something important and meaningful.

If you feel the least trace of fear or apprehension, you repeat your magic words "calm and relaxed" deeply in your mind, and the more fear you even begin to feel, the calmer you become in every way.

You pick out one, or two or three specific faces in the audience, and you imagine yourself talking to those people directly. No matter how big the group, if you pick out a few people and imagine talking personally to them, it is as if you are talking to a small group of friends. You know that people want to hear what you have to say. Your thoughts and opinions are important, and you have the knowledge and preparation to present your ideas clearly. You truly enjoy giving people information that makes their lives better or easier in some way, or that helps solve problems. You start speaking and are amazed that your words are flowing easily and naturally. You have prepared well and you know your material. You are a valuable human being and your point of view is important. You are more calm and relaxed with every minute you speak. You are communicating with precision and confidence. People are listening attentively, and you see people nodding in agreement as you speak. Your notes are clear and your thoughts are organized. As your talk continues, you feel more confident and strong with every word you speak. You may find yourself interrupted by applause; or by an occasional question that your adult self handles effortlessly. As your speech or presentation ends, you are greeted with a round of thanks and applause. You feel a great upwelling of pride within... You have achieved your goal! And you know it gets easier and easier every time you speak. The more you speak in public, the easier it gets. And you are totally amazed after a few times that it is not only easy, but that it is even fun. And more importantly, <u>you are good at it</u>. You have things to say that people want to hear. And speaking publicly is a rewarding and delightful part of your life that brings you approval and contributes to making you the success you were always meant to be.

Throughout your talk, if you feel even the least bit of apprehension, you simply take a breath and repeat your magic words "calm and relaxed" silently inside. And the apprehension fades away totally. In fact, the more fear you even begin to feel, the calmer and more tranquil you become in every way. If you feel even the least trace of fear, the fear itself causes your breathing to get slower, deeper and more rhythmic. If you feel even the least bit of anxiety, the anxiety itself causes your heart to beat slowly, regularly and normally. The more fear you even begin to feel; the more your blood pressure goes down to normal, and the less adrenalin your adrenal glands release. The more fear you even subconsciously feel, the more your adrenal glands produce noradrenalin, the relaxation hormone. The more fear you even begin to feel, the more relaxed your muscles become. And the calmer you become in every way. You are a good speaker… It's in your human genes… And you speak effortlessly and easily in any public setting you choose. You are calm and relaxed.

Every time you enter into this relaxed, focused state, the old fears fade further and further away. And every time you hear the words "calm and relaxed" or repeat, "calm and relaxed" to yourself, you feel a wonderful calming wave of all the good feelings you are feeling now. You feel confident, serene and totally ready every time you hear or say your magic words "calm and relaxed". You don't have to be in hypnosis or any special state for your magic words "calm and relaxed" to have their effect… All you have to do is briefly close your eyes and repeat, "calm and relaxed" to yourself. And each time you do, you are filled with a wave of calm confidence. And your talk goes perfectly.

If these ideas are acceptable to you, you simply continue breathing… just as you are. And every breath you breathe causes your powerful inner mind to accept, and magnify all the good ideas on this recording. And every breath causes your vast inner mind to bring all these good ideas into reality in your outer world… Calm and relaxed.

Now it's time to return to the outer world, knowing that the frightened parts of you are safe and cared for. And knowing that the fear-sending parts of you are doing far more useful things in your mind now. Each time you listen to this recording, or say your magic words "calm and relaxed, your inner understanding and confidence grows bigger and bigger and thousands of times bigger. And all these positive and beneficial ideas manifest in your outer life more powerfully with every breath you breathe. Calm and relaxed, you return to the surface, bringing all your new calm, relaxed public speaking out with you.

Overcoming Test Anxiety

Any induction or deepening will work with this script.

As you breathe slowly, deeply and rhythmically, every breath you breathe causes your inner mind to be open to, and to accept and implement positive and beneficial suggestions for your effortless success taking and passing tests and examinations. And every beat of your heart magnifies and reinforces the suggestions and magnifies your success.

With your next exhale; repeat the words "calm and relaxed" silently inside your mind. Notice that the words "calm and relaxed" cause your mind to send you a wave of even deeper, even more tranquil relaxation. "Calm and relaxed" are your magic words. Whenever you repeat the words "calm and relaxed" silently in your own mind, a wave of relaxation fills you, and you feel all the calm and relaxation you are feeling right now or even deeper. Practice with me now... On your next gentle exhale; repeat the words "calm and relaxed" silently inside your own mind. And as you do, a deeper wave of relaxation fills you. Whenever you repeat the words 'calm and relaxed" to yourself, a magical wave of serene, peaceful, calm fills you... even when you are fully awake and alert. You don't have to be in hypnosis to use your magic words... no matter what is going on in your life, all you have to do is close your eyes and repeat the words "calm and relaxed" to yourself, and you instantly feel a wonderful wave of deep peaceful, alert calm filling you.

You are listening to this recording in order to overcome anxiety about tests and banish that anxiety from your life forever. And the first thing to understand about testing anxiety is that it is always a mistake that your mind has learned. And whatever you have learned, you can unlearn and change. Every time you listen to this recording your powerful inner mind learns more and more that your true safety and success come from preparation and a calm mind and body. Fear of any kind is useless and destructive, and you are leaving the useless and worthless fear in your past.

Once, a long time ago, you had a test-like situation and you also just happened to be a little bit afraid. Your mind made the mistake of thinking that the fear caused you to pass that test or do well in that test-like situation. Actually, the little bit of fear was irrelevant and useless. You passed or did well because you were prepared, and because you had the skill and knowledge you needed to succeed. The fear was irrelevant, but your inner mind made the mistake of associating the fear with your success. And since your inner mind wants you to succeed, it began sending more and more fear because it thought that would make you more and more successful. And now, the fear levels are so great that they actually weaken your ability to do well. All fear is a mistake in the mind.

It doesn't matter whether you consciously remember that first test-like situation where your mind made the mistake, because your inner mind remembers everything. And while your conscious mind just floats, "calm and relaxed", your inner mind reviews that original mistake and realizes that the fear didn't help at all. Fear never helps anything... it always makes things worse. Your inner mind realizes you were successful because you were prepared, because you had the skills and knowledge you needed, and because you were calm and relaxed enough for your brain to function at its best. Your inner mind goes wherever it needs to go, and does whatever healthy things it needs to do to permanently erase that old mistake.

Your inner mind now realizes that when you are calm and relaxed, your brain gets more oxygen and it works better. When you are calm and relaxed while studying for a test or taking a test, you learn more quickly and remember more thoroughly. When you are calm and relaxed, you can retrieve information from your brain more quickly and repeat it more cogently. When you are calm and relaxed: you have better judgment, you can calculate faster and with fewer errors, you can make better connections and decisions, and your memory is more available. In short, when you are calm and relaxed, your brain and body are working at their very best and your mind is clear. "Calm and relaxed" is your key to passing tests now. Your inner mind dumps all the old fears into life's trashcan and sends them to the incinerator.

So at every level, conscious and subconscious, your mind is choosing to keep you calm and relaxed in every testing situation in your life. Whether you are reading, studying, working on problems, or attending a class, your inner mind helps you by keeping you calm and relaxed, enabling you to concentrate, learn and retain much more fully than before. Your understanding grows. The more calm and relaxed you are, the more your understanding amplifies. You can see the patterns beneath the facts, and your thinking is enhanced. As you understand more, being calm and relaxed causes your confidence and self-esteem to grow. You know you can do it. And the more calm, relaxed and confident you are, the more effortlessly you perform on tests and in every test-like situation in life. You picture and imagine yourself getting ready to take a test. As you study, you occasionally repeat your magic words 'calm and relaxed" silently to yourself, and as you do, a wave of calm confidence fills you, and you learn your material effortlessly. As you enter the test room, you are calm and relaxed... your body feels great... your mind is sharp and clear... and you are confidently ready. You repeat your magic words "calm and relaxed" silently to yourself, and a wave of serenity and focus fill you. You are in the test taking zone and nothing bothers you until the test is done. Question after question, problem after problem, you are focused and clear. You brain and mind are perfectly sharp, and the test is 100 times easier than you ever dreamed. You are calm and relaxed. And when you get the results of the test, you are a success.

Each and every time you listen to this recording, and every time you close your eyes and repeat your magic words, calm and relaxed, all the positive and beneficial ideas on the recording become stronger and stronger. Your inner mind accepts every positive idea on the recording and does whatever healthy thing your mind needs to do to make these ideas your total new truth. If all of these positive ideas are acceptable to your inner mind, you simply continue breathing... just as you are. And every breath you breathe causes your inner mind to magnify and strengthen every beneficial idea on the recording. You listen to this recording often, and as you do, the old fears melt away as the worthless nothing they have always been. And a new, calm, relaxed, dynamic, confident success becomes your deepest truth. The more you listen to the recording, and the more you repeat your magic words "calm and relaxed", the calmer and more successful you become, and so it is.

And now it is time to return to your normal awareness and bring all of your calm and relaxation out with you. You choose success, you expect success and you are a success in each and every way. "Calm and Relaxed".

Freedom from Shyness and Social Apprehension

I like the computer game and pretend game inductions with this script... they appeal to the childlike parts of the mind which first learned shyness. But any of the inductions will work.

As you relax more deeply, your inner mind is open to, and accepting of ideas and suggestions that cause you to transcend shyness and social apprehension so that you can live a rich and fulfilling life.

The first new truth for your inner mind to incorporate is that intense shyness and apprehension are learned attitudes and behaviors. And whatever is learned can be unlearned. There is a part of your mind that has been filling you with shyness and apprehension when you are around other people. That part of your mind mistakenly generalized a rule of childhood. It thinks that it is helping you by making you shy. Or, by making you almost paralyzed when you are in a group of people, or when you meet new people. This part of you is not your enemy. It is a part of you that is trying to help. It simply hasn't realized that the fear and shyness are ten thousand times worse than actually meeting and trusting new people.

You learned to be wary of strangers as a small child. And for small children, a balanced caution around unknown adults is an appropriate behavior that keeps a child safe. But in your case, the part of you that was supposed to learn a balanced, measuring caution about other people has let that caution grow into an absurd fear that poisons your life, and sucks the joy out so many activities. Caution is a good thing. Caution, awareness, attention intuition and experience all keep you safe. Caution is a virtue, and you never lose your caution. But caution is not fear. Caution is simply the wisdom of experience. Let me illustrate by example. If you were to burn a finger on a hot stove, caution would be checking the stove to see if it was hot before touching it the next time. Fear would be refusing to go into the kitchen because there is a stove there that might reach out and burn you. Your social apprehension and intense shyness have gone far beyond normal caution and turned into fear. Just like the fearful person who avoids the kitchen and might starve because there is a stove there; your level of social apprehension has reached an absurd point. Social anxiety or shyness is making your life ten thousand times worse than actually being around people or meeting new people.

You can talk with the fear-sending part of your mind. Just picture and imagine a magic mirror that shows you whatever part of yourself you would like to talk with. As you look into that mirror, you begin to see a fearful, lost part of you... the part of your own mind that sends the extreme shyness and fear. It is a part of you that took the childhood rule of "don't talk to strangers" to absurd extremes. And it keeps applying that absurdly overblown fear of strangers even now. The fear-sending part of you has not realized that you are a capable adult. It doesn't know that you have all the caution, wisdom, alertness, awareness and judgment you need to keep yourself safe. But this part of you is not your enemy. It is simply a part of you that is trying to help. It just doesn't understand what truly helping you really means.

You can begin communicating with your inner fear-sender through the mirror. The mirror allows you to send vast amounts of information, both consciously and subconsciously, to any part of your mind. And you begin by telling your inner fear-sender all the ways that the shyness and apprehensions harm you. Tell that part of yourself about all the opportunities you have missed for fun, and all the chances for meaningful work relationships and personal relationships that have passed you by. Let that inner fear sender see how the shyness and social apprehension have kept you isolated and lonely far too much of the time.

And as you communicate all the ways that the social apprehension has limited and harmed your life, you see your inner fear-sender in the mirror react with shocked surprise. This part of your mind thought it was helping by filling you with fear all this time. And it had no idea that the paralyzing fear was ten thousand times worse than anything it is trying to help with.

Now show your inner fear-sender that you are no longer a child. This fear-sending part of the mind is still stuck in childhood... still trying to apply the "don't talk to strangers" rule in a rigid, universal manner. But even in childhood, the "don't talk to strangers" rule was supposed to be balanced with: "unless your parents or a trusted adult says it is OK". It is always OK to talk to strangers if a trusted adult says it is OK. Because that adult has wisdom, caution, and awareness enough to determine who is safe. Here is the key. Your inner fear sender is still stuck in your childhood, and still only applying half the rule. It forgot the part about: "you can talk to strangers if a trusted adult says it's OK."

And you have grown into a trustworthy adult. You are alert and aware. You have experience and wisdom. You are cautious, and you know how to build trust step by step. You have grown into exactly the kind of wise, trusted adult who makes it OK to talk to strangers. As the inner fear sender looks out of the mirror, it sees that you are no longer a child... You have grown up. You have common sense and wisdom. You are alert to dangers and you know how to understand other people's intentions. You know that trust is something that develops step by step. You are precisely the trusted adult who makes it OK to talk with strangers. You are exactly the kind of trusted adult who makes it OK to carefully begin and nourish relationship... whether those are work relationships, play relationships or personal relationships. You have the wisdom and judgment to talk with strangers, or anyone else, in a way that keeps you physically and emotionally safe. Let your inner fear-sender see who you are now, and as you do, the need for the shyness, apprehension and fear just fades into the distant past.

Your inner fear sender needs a new job in your mind, because its old job of making you fearful, even paralyzed, in social situations is done. Fear never helps anything. Fear never keeps us safe. Your adult skills of alertness, awareness, caution, wisdom and judgment keep you safe. **And you have those adult skills in abundance!** Let's give the inner fear-sender a new job. That new job is to become your social secretary... the part of you who is in charge of helping you connect with other people... the part of you who seeks out common interests... the part of you who explores potential relationships of all kinds: personal, professional, recreational, educational.

The job of keeping you safe is turned over to your powerful adult self who uses experience, alertness, awareness, intuition and caution to determine who is safe and to what extent. Your adult self knows that all relationships are based on trust, and that trust develops over time based on experience with another person.

Now picture and imagine yourself in one of those social situations that used to give you trouble in the past. Watch as the new social secretary part of you looks for potential connections. You feel great, because the fear and paralysis simply are not there. You feel a warm wave of pride as you realize that you can trust yourself to make wise decisions about who you interact with and how deeply. You find yourself actively looking forward to meeting new people and learning about them and their lives. You realize that other people are equally looking forward to meeting you, because you are an attractive, positive person in your own right. And there are parts of your life that are interesting, fascinating or important to them.

Picture and imagine yourself meeting someone new... It feels so wonderful to be free of the old fear and embarrassment. You shake hands or greet that new person warmly. You are alert and aware, and your intuition is tuned. If the person feels good to you, you find yourself talking and relating effortlessly and easily. Words just flow. If your inner judgment or intuition gives you warning signals that the person has bad intentions, or can't be trusted, you simply gently break off the conversation and move on to someone who feels better. You are totally free of fear... Fear simply clouds your judgment and suppresses your intuition... Fear gets us into far more trouble than it keeps us out of.

You are amazed to see yourself enjoying social situations of all kinds... educational, recreational, professional and personal. Your new ability to easily interact with people fills your life with rich meaning and a sense of adventure. Every day is a learning experience and you feel better with every day that passes.

Now return to your mirror, and look in it once more. And this time you see that all the parts of you are actually a single, connected whole. By communicating with that isolated fear-sending part of the mind, you have begun a process of reconnecting all parts of you into a single, vast wholeness. Every part of your mind is seeing the benefit of being in full communication with the rest of you. And as your former inner fear sender takes on the new job of being your social secretary, helping make connections outside of yourself, it also takes on the job of reintroducing all the internal parts of yourself to yourself, so that no part of you gets stuck in the past and isolated.

As you look into the mirror this time, the reflection you see astounds you. It is as if you see yourself in the mirror as God and your own soul see you... as an incredible reflection of a loving and creative Universe... as a child of God. You realize that the ways you think, feel and act are wonderfully good, and they make you the positive and beautiful human being that you are. You think of yourself positively. You feel talented, intelligent and worthwhile in every way. You notice people noticing you with interest, and you are interested in other people. You think, feel and act positively. You accept and love yourself more with every day. And you find yourself creating a bigger and bigger network of other people so effortlessly, that it is as if you had always done so.

You meet people easily, and effortless find things to say. You are just naturally yourself. And other people relate to you. You are easy to talk to, and you put other people at ease with your inborn kindness and peace. The past is the past, and you live in the present... as the amazing and beautiful child of God that you are.

If these ideas are acceptable to your inner mind, you simply keep on breathing... just as you are. And every breath you breathe causes your vast inner mind to incorporate all the positive ideas on this recording into the deepest and most powerful part of the mind, where they simply become the truth for you. And every time you listen to this recording, the ideas on the recording become deeper and more powerful for you.

Knowing that you can return to this deep, relaxed state anytime you want, just by listening to this recording in a safe, quiet place, makes it easy to return now to your normal outer consciousness. You return to the outer world feeling relaxed and free... confident and excited about the dynamic new life that is opening for you.

SCRIPTS FOR COMPULSIONS AND ADDICTIONS

Smoking Circle of Truth

This is a companion script to the Stop Smoking NOW! *script found in* Unlocking the Blueprint of the Psyche.

As you relax more deeply with every breath, you are so proud of yourself for making this powerful and positive change in your life. Every idea on the recording causes you to reject smoking and embrace health and freedom. Every time you listen to this recording your mind makes you one thousand times more dedicated to total freedom and health. Enough is enough, and you are free. You are finished forever with this harmful and costly smoking habit. Every part of you is celebrating your new freedom to live life on your own terms... strong, healthy and totally in control of your own choices.

You have talked with the part of your inner mind that thought you needed to smoke, and you have re-educated the former smoking part of you so that it now is your biggest ally in keeping you healthy and free. Free of all desire to smoke... free to be healthy and strong your entire life. Free of the cost, the harm and the slavery of the old habit. And it feels so good to be free... to be a person in charge of your own choices and behaviors. It feels so good to be free of the social stigma and the mess of smoking.

You have chosen the positive aspects you want in your new life: Better health, better breathing and longer windedness, more energy, clear throat, lungs and sinuses, a clear and resonant voice, fresher breath, freedom from the fear of crippling diseases, much more money to use for the things that make life better, a cleaner car, home and environment, freedom from the stench of tobacco in your hair, clothes and body, greater attractiveness, a wonderful new freedom from the stigma of smoking, and the freedom to hang out with anyone you like, whiter teeth and healthier gums, a heart that thanks you with every beat, and truly grateful lungs that have been gasping for this wonderful change.

And because you have chosen to live your life on these new terms, your terms, you are now and forever a non-smoker. You are totally free of tobacco because you choose to be strong, healthy, and free. Nothing can change your choice to be a non-smoker. No amount of stress or tension can keep you from locking this miserable habit into your past and throwing away the key.

You have come to a fork in the road of your life. You have sent your mind ahead to look at the smoking road and where it will lead you. And you have sent your mind ahead on the non-smoking road, to see yourself as the healthy and strong person you were meant to be for your entire life. And every part of you has chosen the healthy, non-smoking road. No part of you wants you to go down the path to a smoking hell of disease, weakness and trouble. Every part of you has chosen to do whatever it takes for you to walk the healthy, tobacco-free road for the rest of your life. And all desire to smoke is simply vanishing from your life forever.

Any time the smallest little idea about smoking crosses your mind, your mind automatically rejects it and reminds you that you are now a non-smoker and you are totally free of the old compulsions. You feel free because you are free. You, and only you, control your choices. If you are around others who smoke, it is as if you never smoked. In fact, when others smoke around you, the nasty smell of the smoke in the air causes your mind to reject smoking for you 1000 times more strongly. Whenever you see a smoker or smell their smoke, you feel a vast and powerful sense of pride that you have the courage, the strength, the self-respect and the perseverance to leave smoking behind you and join the ranks of the enlightened, healthy majority.

Any time the least little idea about smoking crosses your mind; your powerful inner mind shows you how much money it costs to smoke. And you instantly picture all the wonderful things you could do with an extra thousand or two thousand or more dollars each and every year. And the wonderful sense of freedom that comes from simply remembering all the positive things you can do with that money causes the very idea of smoking to flush out of your mind like the worthless nonsense that it is.

Because you have chosen to be a non-smoker, your powerful inner mind has created a new circle of truth for you. This circle of four new truths is planted into the most powerful and deepest part of your mind and totally guides your positive, dynamic, and healthy new lifestyle as a non-smoker. Each of these four new truths is connected to, and supports the others. Any time you hear one of your new truths, or any variation of a truth, on this recording or in your own mind, it makes the entire circle of truth a thousand times more powerful for you. And every breath you breathe causes your vast and amazing inner mind to magnify and multiply your circle of truth over and over and over. And every time I repeat one of your new truths, your inner mind reinforces the entire circle of truth a thousand times over.

Your first new truth is the strongest and most powerful of all. Very simply, your first new truth is that **you are now a non-smoker**. You hear your own inner voice repeating this new truth in all its variations. I am now and forever a non-smoker. I am free from smoking forever. I think like a non-smoker, I feel like a non-smoker and I act like a non-smoker as naturally and easily as I breathe. I am now a non-smoker and I totally reject smoking. Every beat of my heart reminds my deepest mind that I am now and permanently a non-smoker. I think, I feel, and I act like a non-smoker as automatically as my heart beats and my lungs breathe. I think, I feel, and I act like a non-smoker as automatically as my brain thinks. I am a non-smoker. I am free of smoking and tobacco forever.

As your mind hears your first new truth, your inner mind locks that truth forever and powerfully into place in your deepest mind, and whenever you hear any part of your first new truth, it makes your entire circle of truth one thousand times more powerful.

Your first new truth leads directly to your second new truth, which you hear in your own voice. Because I am a non-smoker, **I have zero desire to smoke**. Truth number two: I have absolutely zero desire, zero want, zero need, and zero urge of any kind to smoke. All desire to smoke has vanished from my mind forever, flushed out by my choice to be healthy, strong and free. I have zero desire to smoke NOW... I have zero desire to smoke NOW... I totally reject smoking from every part of my life NOW.

And for each and every NOW for the rest my long healthy life, I have zero desire to smoke. And I TOTALLY reject smoking from my life. I have absolutely zero desire to smoke.

As your mind hears the second new truth, your inner mind locks that truth forever and powerfully into place in your deepest mind, and whenever you hear any part of your second new truth, it makes your entire circle of truth one thousand times more powerful.

Your second new truth leads to your third new truth. Because I have zero desire to smoke, because I totally reject smoking, **Smoking is locked totally and forever in my past.** I have locked smoking into my past and thrown away the key to my smoking past. I have locked all the harm, damage and cost of smoking permanently and forever into my past. And that smoking past is fading further from me in every instant. I have locked smoking into my past with every bit of courage, strength, wisdom, and self-respect I possess. And I use that same courage, strength, wisdom, and self-respect to keep smoking forever locked in my past. Smoking is totally locked in my past and every time I hear or think about smoking being in my past, smoking gets locked even further out of every moment of my present and future. Whenever I hear or think any variation of my third new truth, it makes my entire circle of truth one thousand times stronger. Smoking is forever locked in my past.

Your third new truth leads to your fourth and final new truth in your circle of truth. Because smoking is forever locked in my past, **nothing and no one can ever make me smoke again.** Literally nothing, and literally no one, can ever make me smoke again. No amount of stress or tension, no amount of shame or guilt, no amount of teasing or peer-pressure, not even the desire to harmonize with someone I love, can ever make me smoke again. I choose health and freedom and nothing and no one can ever make me choose smoking again. No advertising, no pressure, no joy or celebration can ever make me smoke again. I am in control of my own thoughts, feelings and actions, and nothing and no one can ever make me smoke again. And because nothing and no one can ever make me smoke again, every time I hear any variation of my fourth new truth, my entire circle of truth magnifies and becomes a thousand times more powerful for me. Nothing and no one can ever make me smoke again.

And it is a circle of truth, because the fourth new truth leads back to the first one. Because nothing and no one can ever make me smoke again, **I am a nonsmoker;** I am totally and permanently free of tobacco and smoking forever. And every time you hear or think any variation of any one of your new truths, the entire circle of truth gets a thousand times stronger and you are so naturally a non-smoker, it is as if you never smoked at all.

It is a circle of empowering and liberating new truth. "I am a non-smoker, I am totally free of tobacco" leads to "I have zero desire to smoke, I totally reject smoking." "I have zero desire to smoke" leads to "smoking is totally locked in my past and I have thrown away the key". "Smoking is totally locked in my past" leads to "Nothing and no one can ever make me smoke again." And "Nothing and no one can ever make me smoke again" leads back to "I am a non-smoker, I am totally free of tobacco." And every time you listen to this recording or even think a part of one of your new truths, the entire circle of truth becomes one thousand times more powerful and becomes the total truth for you. And you are a non-smoker so easily and effortlessly, it is as if you had never smoked at all... as if smoking simply doesn't exist. Because you are a non-smoker, you have zero desire to smoke, you have locked smoking into your past, and nothing and no one can ever make you smoke again. You are a non-smoker, and in your own mind, you hear yourself repeating again and again, "I am a non-smoker"

As your circle of truth locks itself into place in your deepest mind, it becomes stronger and more powerful, and every time you listen to this recording or even think one of your new truths, your circle of truth becomes a polished silver, gold and unbreakable steel ring of truth in your mind. And you live your new truths easily, effortlessly, without even having to think about them. You have zero desire to smoke. Smoking is locked in your past. Nothing can ever make you smoke again. And you have chosen to live the rest of your long, rewarding life as a healthy, strong, and free non-smoker.

And now it is time to rise back up to the surface of the mind and back to you normal awareness, knowing that the ideas on this recording are totally accepted by your inner mind, which is putting them into place so effortlessly it seems like magic.

Integrate the new truths as final suggestions during the count in the awakening sequence.

Dr. Mike Preston's Library for Drug and Alcohol Abuse

Use Dr. Preston's style induction and deepening. You can easily modify this script to deal with gambling addictions, sexual addictions or any other behavior you would like to get rid of, by changing the specific books you throw away.

As you drift in this deep, peaceful state, I would like you to imagine a library. A library is a big building with aisles and aisles of books on shelves. And as you picture and imagine your library, you realize the most important aisle there contains all the books of your life. Just picture and imagine your library, the one that contains all the books of your life. Picture and imagine that one special aisle that contains the books that record every instant of your life.

The aisle of the books of your life has books on the right side, and books on the other side. The right side of the aisle is filled with all the positive books that record your dreams, goals, positive memories, and every positive learning experience of your life. The right side of the aisle has books that record every positive thing you have learned from every situation in your life, even the difficult ones. On the right side of the aisle there is a book for every one of your skills and talents, even the ones you have yet to discover. You realize that the books on the right side of the aisle describe you as you truly are, at your very natural best. As you study the positive side of the aisle, you feel a bit surprised and saddened that your subconscious mind hasn't spent much time with the books on the positive side of the aisle because all the covers are new and unworn. And you are totally amazed at how big the positive aisle is, and how full of books it is.

The other side of the aisle, the not-so-nice side of the aisle, is filled with books that record all the negative thoughts and feelings you have ever had about yourself. It has books for every problem in your life, physical, emotional, mental, social, or financial. It has books that contain all the stress and tension in your life, and books that contain all the obstacles to you living a peaceful life of rich experience. It has books about all your fears and self-imposed limitations. All the books on the negative side of your aisle are from the past and are still affecting you today. And it is with a shock that you realize your subconscious mind has been spending far too much time reading these negative books. All the spines of those not-so-nice books are broken and bent. The pages are dog-eared and the covers are ragged. You decide that **enough is enough**. You decide that you have carried these negative books around too long and wasted too much time with them. But you also notice that there really aren't that many negative books. Your subconscious mind has just been spending too much time reading them. And all that changes starting right now. Your life starts changing RIGHT NOW.

At the back of the room, at the end of the aisle, there is a very large trash dumpster that is practically inviting you to throw away the things you no longer need in your life.

Go to the negative side of the aisle and find the books that contain all the negative thoughts, feelings, or behaviors that you have ever associated with yourself. You are a child of God and these books are filled with falseness. You take your negative self-thoughts and negative self-feelings and negative behaviors off the shelf, and hold them in your hands. You carry your negative thoughts, feelings, and behaviors to the back of the aisle to the trash dumpster. Without even bothering to read them, you hold your past negative thoughts, feelings and behaviors in your hands and tear them to shreds until only the covers are left. Then, realizing that even the covers of books that define you negatively are no longer worthy of you, you rip the covers of those negative feelings, thoughts and behaviors to shreds and toss them in the trash, too.

Next, feeling good about yourself, beginning to remember that you are a child of God; you return to the not-so-nice side of the aisle... you pick out all the books that contain all your stresses and tensions, worries and concerns, and you carry them back to the back of the aisle. Holding those worries and stresses in your hands, you realize that 90% of what you worry about or stress over either never happens or you can handle it easily. You realize that the other 10% is out of anyone's control. It is pointless to worry about things that never happen, or that we can handle easily. It is even more pointless to worry about things that nobody can control. So worry and stress are totally worthless emotions. You hold your stress, tension, worries and concerns in your hands. You remember that worries and stress are useless to you. And one by one tear up every stress, every tension, every worry and every last concern in your life and toss them in the trash. You toss away every useless worry and stress in your life... and they are **all** useless.

Feeling lighter, you return to the aisle and find your book of limitations and fears... your book of "I Can't and Excuses". This book contains all the limitations you have ever accepted as true about yourself. They contain all the fears and anxieties that have kept you from experiencing life as richly and fully as you were born to. All of these fears and limitations are from the past, and even though you have accepted them, they were given to you by other people. Other people's opinions of you are meaningless. You remember that you are an incredible being of infinite potential, a child of God. So you take your fears and limitations into your hands, and book by book, rip every one of your fears, limitation, I can't and excuses to shreds and throw them out of your mind forever. You even rip up the covers so that your mind never collects fears and limitations again. You tear up every excuse that has ever chained you, and throw it away. Your new motto is: "I can do whatever I set my mind on."

Finally, feeling strong and courageous, you pick up the last book on the negative side of the aisle. It is by far the heaviest, with a deep black cover. But you have the strength to lift it. You look at its title, and you are not surprised that it reads: "My Alcohol or Drug Problem Book." That vile, ugly book contains every bit of your alcohol or drug problem... its causes, its effects and every way that alcohol or drugs harm your life and chain your soul. It is a thick, vile book that you choose to eliminate from your life forever. You hold your alcohol or drug problem in your hands, allowing your subconscious mind to thoroughly understand it. And you make a decision at every level of your being, to be rid of this book and your alcohol or drug problem forever. With all your strength and courage, you carry your alcohol or drug problem to the back of the room. You rip it to shreds, and you toss it in the trash, ripping the cover up and throwing it away as well.

Then you push the trash bin out of the library, to the incinerator in the back. You tip the dumpster into the incinerator, dumping all the shreds of your problems, fears and stresses into the incinerator. Then you toss in a lighted match and watch as everything you have thrown away... your stresses, your excuses, your limitations, your negative self-image, and your alcohol or drug problem... burn out of your life forever. And the fire sets you free. Just watch it all burn away forever... it feels so good to watch that cleansing flame set you free. *Pause 10 seconds*

And now, moving back to the nice right side of the aisle, you pick up a book that you want your subconscious mind to absorb and act upon. That book is titled: "My Big Book of Sobriety." It is remarkable, because it contains all the wisdom of the Big Book of AA, and you are amazed that you have had this incredible book inside the library of your mind all along. You carry your Big Book of Sobriety to the front of the aisle, where there is a very pleasant reading area with a perfect, large, overstuffed reading chair. You sit down in an open and relaxed state, just settling into your chair, knowing that your subconscious mind is now totally focusing on this incredible great new book to read. As you rest in the chair, simply letting your conscious mind float and drift, your powerful inner mind begins reading your new Big Book of Sobriety.

Your subconscious mind reads this book here in the chair. Your subconscious mind reads this powerful new book when you are sleeping and dreaming, it reads this book in every relaxed and quiet moment. And your subconscious mind accepts every positive and beneficial idea in your Big Book of Sobriety. Your subconscious mind accepts and implements every idea designed to help you live soberly and joyfully. And your subconscious mind makes these new ideas conscious. It begins integrating all the deep wisdom in this inner book into your outer conscious life just as rapidly as you can assimilate the information and new ways of thinking, feeling and acting. You remember that you are a child of God... a beloved child of an infinite and creative universe.... And you begin acting like what you are in every moment. You know that you have all you need to meet every challenge life brings you. You find worries and fears being replaced by calm acceptance that no matter what life brings, you will not only survive, you will thrive. In each and every day, in each and every way your life is becoming more abundant, healthier, more relaxed, and more filled with the simple joy of being. In each and every day you are experiencing richer and richer choices in life and each day brings you joy. Every time you listen to this recording or relax in any way, your subconscious mind continues reading your Big Book of Sobriety, filling your mind with wonderful and joyous new, and relaxed ways of living fully.

Take a moment of silence now, and allow your inner mind to fill itself with the deep inner wisdom that has always been in your inner library. And when that moment of silence ends, it will be time to return to the surface, feeling absolutely wonderful and filled with exciting new ways to live life free of stress.

Pause 60 Seconds

Return to my voice now, knowing that this is the beginning of your new life. You rise up to the surface with me knowing that you are cherished and loved by God and your own soul. And you rise up totally dedicated to your incredible, new sober life of infinite possibility. If all the positive and beneficial ideas on this recording are acceptable to your mind, you simply continue breathing... just as you are. That's right, simply continue breathing, and every breath you breathe causes your powerful inner mind to magnify, strengthen and reinforce every positive change you are making over and over and a million times over. And now it is time to return to the surface, bringing all your serenity and peace with you. And you rise up with a simple prayer and affirmation that goes with you always:

Give me the serenity to accept the things I cannot change
The strength and courage to change the things I can
And the wisdom to know the difference

I affirm that I serenely accept what I cannot change
I affirm that I change what I can with all my strength and courage
I affirm that I am guided by a vast wisdom that knows the difference

You rise up to the surface knowing that your prayer and affirmation are true, and that you are free.

Nail Biting

Use the feather deepening technique after a Kresnick style induction, or just use the feather as the induction.

"Feather" is a magic relaxing word for you. Any time you wish to feel all the pleasant, relaxed feelings you are feeling now, all you have to do is sit in a safe place, close your eyes, and whisper the word "feather" silently to yourself. Or picture and imagine your beautiful feather floating down. "Feather" is a magic relaxing word when you are in a safe place where you can close your eyes and relax deeply. At all other times, the word feather sends a wonderful wave of good feelings through you, but you remain alert and aware of your surroundings. Your inner mind always knows when it is safe to close your eyes and relax... Or when to simply send a wave of good feelings through, when it is not safe to close your eyes. You absolutely trust your inner mind to react to "feather" as the situation calls for. If you are in a place where it is safe to close your eyes, your magic feather causes you to relax as deeply as you are now in seconds. When you are not is a place where it is safe to relax, your inner mind reacts to your feather by sending you a background wave of wonderful, pleasant feelings.

Nail biting is a nervous habit. In the past, you bit your nails to release stress and nervous energy. Like all habits, nail biting is a learned behavior, even though it is subconscious. And anything your inner mind has learned, it can rapidly unlearn and replace. For example, your inner mind has already learned that just imagining a feather or whispering "feather" gives you a wave of really good feelings that totally replace nervousness and worry. In the past, you bit your nails out of stress and tension, or worry and boredom. Your magic feather allows you to choose what you feel at any moment, and your feather causes worry, boredom, stress and tension to instantly fade out of your mind.

The part of your inner mind that causes you to bite your nails is actually not your enemy. It is a part of your mind that has been trying to help you with stress and worry. It is simply a part of you that made a mistake. Your inner nail biter is actually a friend and ally. And when we correct the mistake in the mind, the nail biting habit disappears as if it had never existed. Your inner sanctuary, which you visit by imagining your feather floating through it, is a perfect place to meet you inner nail biter and correct the mistake, because every part of you is welcome and safe in your inner sanctuary.

Now imagine your inner nail biter in your beautiful natural haven. Your inner nail biter has been trying to help you, and it simply never realized that the negative consequences of this habit are 10,000 times worse than whatever your inner nail biter was trying to help you with.

So first, send your inner nail biter a wave of thanks and good wishes. Acknowledge all the help your inner nail biter has tried to be. But tell the nail biting part of your mind about the negative consequences of the habit. Show your inner nail biter how embarrassing it is to have such a childish habit. Show your inner nail biter about the pain, the infections, the ingrown nails, and the embarrassment of short, unattractive nails. Show your inner nail biter all the negative results of the habit and the negative feelings of shame and embarrassment... as well as physical discomfort... and even the cost of hiding or repairing your nails. Send your inner nail biter all the negative consequences of the habit for you... mental, emotional, social, and physical.

Then show your inner nail biter how much you have grown since the habit started. Maybe way back when you first started biting your nails, you didn't have any other ways to deal with stressful situations or people. But now, you have many positive ways of handling stress. You are much older now, with adult skills and talents that let you easily handle almost every situation in your life. You simply don't need this old habit from the past.

Also remind your inner nail biter what you have learned by living. And that is that stress, tension, and worry are always useless. 90% of the things we stress about never happen. And the 10% that do happen are either so trivial that we handle them easily, or so big that they are totally out of anyone's control. There is no point in stressing about things we can handle. Stressing about things that never happen is a waste of energy. And stressing about things that are out of our control is a double waste of time and energy. Your inner nail biter now realizes that stressing never helps anything... It only makes things worse. And biting nails is a particularly useless form of stressing.

Notice how your inner nail biter reacts to all this new and true information. Partly with embarrassment and shame about causing you more problems than it solved. Partly with joy as it recognizes that your adult self has many, many positive ways of easily coping with difficult situations and people. And partly with a wave of enlightenment as it realizes that stress and tension never help anything. Now show your inner nail biter your magic feather. Or whisper your magic word "feather" deep inside. And notice how your inner nail biter's eyes fly open in wonder as a fresh and deeper wave of calm and relaxation fill you even more deeply.

Offer your inner nail biter a new job in your mind and a new title. In exchange for leaving the nail biting in the past, your inner nail biter can become your master of calm... your feather manager. Your feather manager is, from this time on, the part of your inner mind that automatically sends you the word "feather" or pictures your magic feather whenever something bothers or stresses you. Your feather manager is the part of you who is in charge of automatically using all your adult talents and skills to deal with difficult situations or people. Your feather manager, your inner calm meister, is the part of your inner mind that always remembers that stressing about anything is a useless waste of energy. It is the part of your mind that remembers that 90% of what we stress about never happens anyway. Of the 10% that does happen, half we can handle easily and half is out of anyone's control. Stressing is always a useless waste of energy.

Now show your new, reeducated, and reconnected feather manager a set of perfect nails... strong, healthy, long, and attractive. Just the way nature meant them to be. Imagine your nails grown out and imagine your healthy cuticles. Tell your feather manager that its new job includes working with every part of your mind to do every healthy thing necessary to give you perfect nails in the fastest healthy time possible, and to automatically erase the old biting habit totally and forever from your mind.

Now imagine the first time that you have to use clippers to actually trim your new, strong, healthy nails. Feel how good it feels to actually be able to use scissors or clippers to shape your nails and keep them from getting too long. Send that good feeling to your new feather manager... that feeling of pride, success and accomplishment. And give your feather manager instructions to do whatever healthy thing it needs to do, in collaboration with every part of your mind, to bring you those great feelings of pride and success in the shortest possible healthy time.

Now imagine some old situation that in the past would have triggered nail biting. See yourself calm and relaxed because your mind simply doesn't stress out over things anymore. Imagine and feel yourself using all your adult skills and talents to handle that difficult situation with grace and ease. Imagine your magic feather drifting and floating. And feel the old, useless habit fading into your past and locking itself out of your present and future forever as your nails grow uneventfully and naturally. And see yourself handle every situation in your life effortlessly.

Whenever the old urge to bite your nails even begins on a subconscious level, your feather manager whispers the word feather. Or gives you the image of a feather, floating and drifting gently through your inner nature sanctuary. And all the useless old stress and tension fade away. The more you imagine or follow your feather, the more relaxed you become. And the old habit fades out of your mind and out of your life forever. The more you listen to this recording, the stronger and more effective it becomes for you as the worthless old habit locks itself totally in your past. The more you imagine your feather or the more you whisper "feather" silently to yourself, the more pleasant and peaceful that wave of good feelings becomes. And you are totally free to enjoy the strong, healthy, natural and attractive nails and cuticles that nature intended for you. If all the positive and beneficial ideas on this recording are acceptable to your inner mind, you simply continue breathing... just as you are. And every breath you breathe causes your inner mind to magnify and reinforce every good idea on this recording until they are totally true for you. Now it is time to return to the outer world and your normal state of mind, bringing all the powerful subconscious changes you have made today out with you. You rise to the surface totally free of that worthless old habit, and totally proud of your new, long, strong, healthy nails.

Freedom from Bulimia

Use the Dr. John Kresnik or Feather inductions. Use a very gentle and compassionate voice; and talk to yourself especially lovingly as you record this script.

Imagine a beautiful place in nature, for example a green and fertile alpine meadow on a perfect summer day. Imagine it below you as if you were walking down a mountain trail. Deep in the center of the meadow is a beautiful building, and even from this distance you recognize it as a place of healing and peace. And in fact that building houses your Institute of Peace, a part of your inner University of Higher Wisdom.

There is a radiant and glowing figure waiting for you in the doorway to the Institute of Peace... It may look like you or like an older, wiser version of you. Or it may simply look like a glowing cloud of radiant and healing energy. And you recognize this glowing figure as your own deepest Inner Wisdom... the deepest and wisest part of your own mind... a voice of your soul... a part of you that is wise, kind and infinitely compassionate. Inner Wisdom is here to help you heal and find peace.

And as you float and drift, you realize that you have been carrying a very heavy burden with you... It is like a heavy backpack or rucksack that you have had to carry with you. That backpack symbolically represents your problem with bulimia... the problem itself, all of its roots and reasons, and all the ways that problem is harming you and limiting your life. The backpack also represents all your internal struggles, and all your confusion about your body, your health and your ability to be at peace with yourself.

And you realize that you have been carrying this heavy backpack for far too long... You were never meant to carry this burden with you. Your Inner Wisdom invites you to simply take off that burden, and lay it down outside so that at least as long as you are paying attention to this recording, you never have to carry that problem around any more.

And it feels so light and so comforting to just take that burden off, and set it down. Your inner mind studies how good it feels to set the burden down. And you inner mind makes the good feelings of lightness, comfort and freedom its goals for you.

Then your Inner Wisdom invites you to enter the Institute of Peace. It is a place where every part of you is welcome, and where you can find peace and healing. You sit in a wonderful, comfortable chair, and find yourself relaxing even more deeply with every breath. And Inner Wisdom tells you that this is a time to heal... a time to return to inner harmony, and a time to be at peace with yourself.

Inner Wisdom explains that there is no such thing as a behavior without a reason. Everything human beings do has a reason. There is a part of the your that knows about and is responsible for every behavior and every thought you think. And anorexia and bulimia are behaviors. There is a part of your mind which knows about the bulimic thoughts and behaviors, and which is responsible for them.

Perhaps to your surprise, Inner Wisdom tells you that the bulimic part of your mind is NOT your enemy. Inner Wisdom explains that for any behavior, no matter how confused or self-destructive, if you look deeply enough, you will find a part of the mind that is trying to help you. It is just a part of the mind that has made a mistake, and doesn't know what helping you really means. No matter how mistaken, the bulimic part of you has been trying to help. The bulimic part of you simply has never realized that starving yourself and binging and purging is 10,000 times worse than anything it is trying to help you with.

Inner Wisdom tells you that the path to healing and restoring balance is to talk with your bulimic part... to understand what it wants... and then negotiate ways to let every part of you get what it needs without harming the rest of you. So, taking your courage in your hands, you decide to trust Inner Wisdom. You give yourself permission to meet and talk with the bulimic part of your own mind, always remembering that no matter how difficult the problem seems to be, she is still a part of you. And with the help of your deepest Wisdom, you can be at peace and return to radiant health.

As you give yourself permission to talk with the bulimic part of your own mind, you see her across the room. Inner Wisdom is comforting her and guiding her to you. And you realize that she is just as frightened and confused as the rest of you has been. And you feel a wave of compassion for the bulimic part of you, as Inner Wisdom reminds you that she has been trying to help you. She just made a mistake about how to do it.

Inner Wisdom welcomes every part of you to sit down at a common table and to talk. Inner Wisdom invites you to start by telling the bulimic part that there is a problem. You tell her all the ways the bulimia is harming and limiting you. You tell her how bad it feels to be out of control, and how crazy the bingeing, starving and purging make you feel. You show her the sick, the confusion, the dizziness and the weakness you have been feeling. You show her tooth problems, the thoughts of suicide or feelings of depression that go with the bulimia. You show her the ways that malnutrition is harming your body and remind her that your body is your most precious possession. You tell her about the confused thinking, about how bad it feels to harm and attack your own body. Inner Wisdom shows her what will happen if you continue as you have been.

And when you ask if that is what she wanted for you, if she was trying to hurt you in all these ways, and to make you feel sad and confused, she puts her head in her hands in confusion and shame. Because she has been trying to help, and truly had no idea how badly her actions were making your body and the rest of your mind feel.

You ask her what she was trying to do... what she wants for you. And you are amazed when she tells you the reasons for the bulimic behavior. Perhaps she was trying to help you with a sense of control. Or perhaps she was confused and thought you were not enough in some way... not smart enough, not lovable enough, not pretty enough, not thin enough, or not enough in some other way. Or perhaps she was totally confused and thought that everyone else hated you or wanted you out of the way. Or perhaps she was even so ashamed that she thought it would be best if you were to go away. Inner Wisdom helps the bulimic part of you sort out her thoughts and tell the rest of you about the internal confusions that led to the bingeing and purging. Take a moment to listen as she tells you what she was trying to do for you with the purging. (*Pause 30 seconds*)

As you return to my voice, you look at the poor bulimic part of yourself, and realize what a horrible burden of confusion, shame and fear she has been carrying around. So you reach out a hand of forgiveness and love. You ask for guidance from you own deepest wisdom to bring you back into balance.

And Inner Wisdom responds by reminding the bulimic part of you that it is welcome in this realm of inner peace... she is part of you, and no part of you is ever going to be thrown away. Your Inner Wisdom reminds the bulimic part of you that she is a child of God, a child of your own soul and a child of life's love for life. A beautiful, radiant golden light fills the room, and fills your inner bulimic. That light fills every cell, fiber and tissue of your being. You remember that you are a child of this Universe and that as you are; you are enough and more than enough for God and your own soul... You are totally loved and cherished by God and by your own soul, and **nobody** else's opinion matters.

Inner Wisdom touches you, and the bulimic part of you, placing a hand over your heart and touching a finger to the center of your forehead, and fills your heart and mind with a reminder of how much you are loved by God and by your own soul... Just feel the energy of that love and compassion fill you... knowing that every time you listen to this recording, you remember more and more about whom you really are. Not who you are in personality or your mind... not who you are as a member of a family or society... but who you truly are, in your essence, in your soul, in your deepest reality.

And in those memories, solutions begin to form. You remember at a very deep level that you are one with all that is, and that you are loved and cherished literally beyond your mind's capacity to encompass it. And you remember that you are and always have been, enough and far more than enough, to meet and thrive through whatever challenges life may bring you.

You realize, that for all her confusion, the bulimic part of you is the part of you that wanted all of you to remember the peace and harmony within. Inner Wisdom suggests that if the bulimic part of you is willing to let go of the bulimic behaviors, she could be the part of you that reminds you to come to your beautiful place often, to experience the peace you feel here. She can be the part of you who talks frequently with Inner Wisdom. She can be the part of you who listens to the voice of your own soul and shares your soul's love with you.

And you invite the bulimic part of you to reconnect with all the rest of you. You invite her to merge into the rest of your mind, and to reconnect with your body, so that she truly understands what helping you means.

And the formerly bulimic part of you is becoming your inner bridge. She is the part of you that is most aware of Inner Wisdom... the part of you who travels into the depths of your spirit... and the part of you who unfolds more and more and reminds you who you truly are. Your life is an incredible journey of rediscovering and uncovering your deepest truths. Your body is your precious and cherished vehicle and home for that journey. And the new inner bridge part of you, your ex-inner bulimic, is the part of you that reminds you that every moment of your journey, even the difficult moments, are incredible gifts from the Universe to your soul. And your deepest Inner Wisdom has a special and personal message for you... I am going to be silent for the next minute. And as your mind floats and drifts gently, your Inner Wisdom tells you what you most need to hear today to speed your healing and wellbeing. And the minute of silence for your Inner Wisdom begins **NOW**. (*Pause one minute*)

Coming back to my voice now, your deepest subconscious mind integrates every positive and beneficial thing your Inner Wisdom has shared with you into the deepest and most powerful parts of your being where they simply become true for you. You have an overwhelming desire to listen to this recording on a daily basis. And every time you do, you relax more quickly and deeply. And your healing accelerates incredibly. In each and every day, in each and every way, life gets better and better. And with every day, you remember more clearly and deeply that you are loved and cherished and held in the arms of God and your own soul.

SCRIPTS FOR WEIGHT REDUCTION

Obesity has become an epidemic in the U.S. and in most developed nations. Because it is such a big problem, and the second most common reason people try hypnosis (after smoking cessation), I have focused significant energy writing or modifying the best scripts I could. Wherever I have modified ideas from other therapists, I have identified them. Most of the concepts are in common use by many, many hypnotists, and it is not possible to attribute them back to their origins. In every case where I took the original idea from another source, I have modified it to fit my style. As with all the scripts, they are meant to complement any medical approaches you are taking to weight reduction, not replace them. A tenth weight reduction script may be found in Unlocking the Blueprint of the Psyche.

Fool's Appetite, Eating Habits

As you relax more deeply with every gentle breath you breathe, your inner mind is open to and accepting of every positive and beneficial suggestion on this recording. Every beat of your heart stimulates your inner mind to magnify and reinforce these positive suggestions and implement them fully in your outer life. These suggestions lock into the deepest part of your mind and become permanently true for you. The more often you use your weight reduction recordings, the more powerful the suggestions become, and the faster they work for you.

You are so excited about your new, positive and successful approach to reducing weight and obtaining the more slender, strong, attractive and healthy body you desire. You are undertaking a whole new way of thinking, feeling and acting, and you are amazed and surprised by how effective your new approach is, and how quickly these suggestions integrate fully into your outer life... giving you new thoughts, new feeling and a whole new way of acting... you are becoming the effective and successful person you were meant to be.

You understand that your goal is to **reduce** your body's weight and **gain** strength, health, attractiveness and slenderness. You no longer think about **losing** weight – our minds are programmed not to lose things, so thinking about losing weight causes the mind to fight your efforts. You now realize that you are reducing weight and **gaining** every good thing, health, an attractive slimmer body, strength and endurance. You are **reducing** your body's weight and **losing** nothing – you are **regaining** control of your life. When you talk about what you are doing, you always talk about **reducing weight** and **gaining** all the good things you want.

You are now implementing a creative, positive and satisfying new attitude about food and eating. You enjoy food, you like food, and you like eating the food your body needs in the proper amounts. You are implementing positive changes in your eating habits. When your body needs food, you eat what it needs, just like you fill your car with gas when it needs fuel. You look at food as fuel for your body and nothing else... you enjoy eating, but you only want to eat when your body actually needs fuel. You are making a friend with your appetite... both parts... the part of your appetite that says: "I need fuel, I'm hungry" and the part that says: "I'm full now, stop eating." Diets try to make us kill our appetites, but you are making friends with yours. Your hunger, your psychological desire to eat, is now in perfect harmony with your appetite, your body's need for food. You only feel hungry when your body needs fuel.

In the past, you didn't listen to your appetite, you listened to your hunger. Hunger is a psychological desire to eat. In the past, your hunger was triggered by many things other than your body's need for fuel. Perhaps you felt hungry because it was a certain time of the day, or because food was present. Perhaps you felt hungry because you were bored, or lonely or angry or afraid. These things are fools hunger. You've heard of Fool's Gold. Prospectors would lug heavy pounds of fools gold many miles, only to be disappointed when they discovered it was worthless pyrite. Fool's hunger is just like that. Whenever you eat for emotional reasons, or just because it is a certain time, or because food is present... you are experiencing fool's hunger. And just like the prospectors, you are always disappointed when you eat because of fool's hunger. And that is because food cannot fix loneliness, or boredom or any other reason for fool's hunger. Food is fuel for your body, and nothing else. And for that reason, your mind now links your psychological desire to eat to your with your body's physiological need for fuel. You only feel hungry when your body needs fuel, and you only want the amount of fuel that your body needs. You are never fooled by fool's hunger again because you are not a fool. You are a unique, amazing, beautiful and one-of-a-kind perfect human being, and your desire to eat is now, and forever, in perfect balance with your body's need for fuel. You are totally amazed the first time you say, "No, thank you, I'm not hungry." By the second time you say it, you are totally delighted that you only feel hungry when your body actually needs fuel.

You are adapting some exciting new eating habits. The first is that you always sit down to eat. You make your meals a special time, when you can focus on your food. You always turn off the television when you eat. Quiet music is OK, but you eliminate distractions and focus on your food. Second, you only eat when you are hungry. You never eat because it is a certain time of day, or because others expect you to. You honor your body, and only eat when your appetite tells you that your body needs fuel. The more you honor your appetite, the happier you feel.

You really taste and enjoy your food... more than ever before. Enjoyment of our food is actually necessary for the second part of the appetite... the part that says, "I'm full",,, to work properly. When you eat, you focus on enjoying your food far more than before, through an exciting new tasting habit. When you take the first bite in your mouth, you lay down your utensil, or if it is a food you hold like a sandwich, you put it down. Then you focus fully on the delicious bite that is in you mouth. You focus your entire attention on that first bite of food. You chew it thoroughly and fully ... you chew the delicious bite thoroughly... **at least** twice as long as you used to. You extract every bit of pleasure that first bite has to offer. You notice the bite tastes different in different parts of your mouth. You pay attention to the texture of the bite in your mouth, and to the way it feels. You pay attention to the aromas and everything else about that first bite of food,,, notice each subtle shift in flavor as you chew. You extract every single bit of sensuous, delightful pleasure that first bite of food has to offer. When you have thoroughly chewed that first delicious bite, you swallow. Then, and only then, do you even think about taking another delicious bite. You continue in this way, one bite at a time, putting your utensil down between bites, and giving each bite your total attention. And before you know it, the second half of your appetite wakes up, and let's you know your body is fully fueled. And all desire to eat another bite simply fades away. You are totally amazed that you are eating much less, but enjoying your food 1000 times more, using this simple habit.

And remember that your inner mind is working for you. In the past, when you dieted, you felt deprived and cheated. But this is not a diet. You are making friends with your appetite, and you eat whatever you want. Your powerful inner mind is changing what you want, so that you only want the foods that help you attain your goal of a fit, slender, healthy body. Your inner mind actually increases the pleasure you feel in healthy food and decreases the pleasure in not so healthy foods. For the rest of your life, you eat what you want, while your inner mind changes what you want, so that your desires match your goals of a slender, strong, healthy, attractive body. You refuse to diet. Dieting triggers the old starvation reflex and stops your progress. You eat what your body needs for fuel. You eat what you want, but your inner mind changes what you want so that you only want the foods and the amounts of foods that help you attain your ideal body size, shape, weight and condition. Your inner mind knows it is about moderation, not deprivation. As your inner mind changes what you want, it deprives you of nothing. For example, a small, half-ounce piece of dark chocolate daily will not distort your body and it gives you both pleasure and important antioxidants. But 2 pounds of chocolate a day would totally distort your body. Your inner mind understands moderation... so you eat whatever you want, but you are totally amazed to find that your inner mind is changing what you want so that you only want the foods and the amounts of foods that help you attain and maintain your new, slimmer, stronger, healthier and more attractive new body. You are losing nothing. Your new moderation and new habits mean that you are **reducing** your body's weight and **gaining** what you truly desire...your ideal size, shape weight and condition. And it is happening so easily, you don't have to worry about it. Your inner mind is taking on the entire project and doing whatever healthy things your need to reduce weight and gain your goals.

Your mind is automatically banning all thoughts about dieting. It is important that you develop a new habit now. Your new habit is that you always eat all that your body needs. Your inner mind is powerfully matching your hunger to what your body needs. Remember that naturally slim people never go on a diet. Slim people eat all they want. Slim people do well. Slim, attractive people say, "I eat all I want and I don't put on an ounce." You are now becoming a slim person. Your subconscious mind is busy building your new body according to your goals.

Visualize yourself as the slim, attractive person; the slim, healthy, attractive person that you soon will be. *Pause 10 seconds* Watch yourself as you say the very same thing. I eat all I want, all the food that my body needs, and I don't put on an ounce. As you begin to talk, think and act like a slim, healthy, attractive person, you soon become one.
Each time you are tempted to eat or drink anything that you know your body doesn't need, you say "no" and you stick by it, because the rewards of becoming slimmer are more important to you than eating the wrong foods. The rewards of being slender, stronger, healthier, and more attractive, are far more important to you than eating foods you know are wrong for you.

Every time you use any relaxation or weight reduction recording, and every time you relax your body these positive and beneficial suggestions get stronger and stronger. Every time you visualize yourself in your new, attractive, slender body, these suggestions grow ten times stronger, and your body automatically sheds pounds and melts off fat at the perfect, safe and healthy speed for you. Every breath you breathe causes your powerful inner mind to magnify and strengthen the suggestions on this recording, and to lock them into the most powerful part of your mind where they simply become the way things are for you. And now it is time to return to the outer world, bringing all your powerful, exciting new thoughts, feelings and actions out with you.

Achieving the Ideal Self

As you relax more deeply with each and every gentle, rhythmic breath, each breath causes your inner mind to be open to and accepting of, all the positive, beneficial ideas on this recording. Each beat of your heart causes your mind to reinforce these positive and beneficial ideas powerfully, and to permanently manifest them in your outer life, leading you to rapidly achieve your goal of reaching and maintaining your ideal size, shape, weight and condition. Your subconscious mind can think a thousand times deeper and faster than I can talk, so while you listen to this recording, your inner mind is racing far ahead of my voice and doing whatever things are necessary within for you to achieve your goal weight.

As you relax more deeply, imagine a beautiful room, a room deep within your inner mind. The room is richly furnished with comfortable furniture. The colors are your favorite colors. One wall is all windows, looking out over the most beautiful view you can imagine. On another wall, there is an incredible full-length mirror, framed in rich woods and gold. On another wall, there is a very powerful computer, and control panel. This room is your special place. It is a place where you always feel comfortable and at peace. It is a room where you can go to be yourself fully and freely.

As you gaze into your mirror, and see yourself, you have a profound new thought that comes from your deepest mind. You realize, that your body, as it is in this moment, is a miracle and a marvel. Your body literally allows you to live in the physical world. Without your incredible body, you couldn't be alive today. It is true that your body might weigh more than you would like it to, but that does not make it a bad body. Your body is a marvelous creation of God and nature. And you appreciate it as the complex and wonderful home it is for your mind and soul. It is true that you would feel more attractive, healthier and stronger if your body was lighter, but that does not make your body bad. You love your body and all it does for you. As you reduce weight and move toward your ideal size, shape, weight and condition, you are not moving from a bad body to a good body. You are simply moving from one miraculous, marvelous, incredible body to one that is slimmer, lighter, stronger, healthier and more attractive. You realize that you love your body as it is and as it is changing. The more you appreciate this body and all it does for you, the faster it responds to your goal of being slender, healthy and strong.

The mirror in your special room is a magic mirror. If you wish to see your body at your ideal size, shape, weight and condition, all you have to do is ask your mirror to show you what you look like when you achieve your goal. Take a few moments now to ask your mirror to show you your body at its ideal and optimal size, shape, weight and condition. And as the image of yourself at your goal weight and size appears in the mirror, you take a few seconds to just bask in that image, and let yourself feel how good it feels to be at your goal weight. (*Pause 10 seconds*)

Feel those good feelings of being at your best and healthiest, and tell your inner mind that this is the body you want it to build for you in the shortest healthy time possible. Instruct your inner mind to go wherever it needs to go and do whatever it needs to do, to merge you with your ideal image in the mirror. You can trust your inner mind to take over this entire project and help you achieve your goal rate as rapidly as is healthy for you, and to maintain you at your goal weight effortlessly.

Your inner mind accepts that your ideal image in the mirror is your real self. Feel how good that ideal self feels. Notice the positive ways that you think, feel and act when you are at your optimal, healthiest weight. Your inner mind is diving deep inside to help you achieve that ideal size, shape, weight and condition effortlessly. If your inner mind needs to change the way you think about food, it does so. If your inner mind needs to heal past injury for you to reduce weight, it does so. If your inner mind needs to change or speed up your metabolism to help you reduce weight, it does so. If your subconscious mind needs to change the way foods taste, and what foods you want, it does so, to help you achieve your goal. Your inner mind is now doing everything necessary for you to reduce weight and achieve your new attractive, healthy goal.

To help your inner mind understand what you want it to do even more fully, go over to the computer against the wall. This computer contains all the controls for your body. You click on an icon titled weight, and two control panels come up. One control panel is labeled "hunger" and one is labeled "metabolic rate".

Beginning with the hunger control, you picture or imagine a slide bar. If your slide bar is up near the top of the column, it means that you are hungry for far more food than your body needs. It means you are eating for emotional reasons rather than a need for fuel. If your slide bar is down near the bottom of the column, it means that you are not hungry enough... you are starving and anorexic. If your slide bar is exactly in the middle, it means that your hunger, your desire to eat, perfectly matches your body's need for fuel. As you look at your hunger control panel, you see that your slide bar is above the centerline. Your desire to eat exceeds your body's need for fuel. So to instruct your inner mind, you move the slide bar down with your mouse to the perfect middle position, and then set is a couple of percentage points below the perfect center position. And you hit the "lock" command so that your hunger control never rises above the center point again. You have just given your inner mind an instruction to do whatever healthy thing it takes to make sure that, in every moment, you are hungry for 2 or 3 percent less food than your body needs. The instant you achieve your goal weight, this control moves up to the perfect center point and stays there.

Next, you go to the metabolic rate control. Your metabolic rate measures how fast your body's cells are burning fuel to make energy. If your slide bar is set way too high, it means that your cells are burning fuel far to quickly... you are feverish, and hyper. If the slide is way too low, it means that your cells are not making enough energy... you are sluggish and exhausted all the time. If your slide is in the perfect center position, it means your cells are burning fuel just fast enough to give you the energy you need, without even a bit left over... You notice that your slide bar for the metabolic rate control has been set below the center. Your cells are not burning fuel fast enough to give your body the energy it needs. You slide the control bar up to the center position, and then nudge it up just another couple of percentage points. Not all the way up to the top, just a couple of points above center. And you hit the lock command so that your metabolic rate never goes below the center point again. You have just given your inner mind an instruction to do whatever healthy thing it takes in your mind and body to make sure that in every moment, your cells are producing 2 to 3 percent more energy than you need... In every moment, you have a cushion of extra energy to call on.

Notice that you have just set your body so that you are burning fuel slightly faster than your body needs energy, and so that you are hungry for slightly less fuel than your body needs to make that energy. You have just created a 4 to 6 percent gap. Your body fills that gap by burning off your stored fat. Fat is just stored up energy for our bodies. When your body needs to use stored fat for energy, the fat leaves the storage cells, and enters your blood stream. The fat is carried to the liver, where it is converted into glycogen, the actual fuel your cells burn. Then the blood stream carries the glycogen out to your cells to be metabolized into energy. But your liver has two choices about what to do with that unnecessary fat. First, it can turn the fat into glycogen for your cells to burn. And second, your liver can simply dump some of that excess fat through your gallbladder and common bile duct into your large intestine, and out of your body as waste. Your liver is now doing both things with the extra fat. Some of it is being turned into fuel, and drop-by-drop, some of that fat is simply being dumped out of your body.

Fat is an incredibly rich fuel, so you find it burning off, and dumping off in a steady, gradual manner. You are burning off and dumping off between one and three pounds of useless excess body fat each and every week. The more you exercise, the faster the fat burns off and dumps away. You reduce your fat by between 1 and 3 pounds every week. Such gradual reduction is steady, healthy and permanent.

Now return from your body control computer back to your beautiful room and mirror. Look again at your ideal self in the mirror. Every time you visit your mirror and picture your body at its healthiest optimal size, shape, weight and condition, you are merging yourself with that new image and reinforcing all the positive things your inner mind is doing to help you reach your goal. Every time you appreciate your marvelous body, as it is as well as how it is changing, you increase the speed of your changes. You love and appreciate your body and all that it does for you more and more with every day.

Relax more deeply, just appreciating your body as it is becoming slimmer and healthier. Notice that you are eating good food, and are totally satisfied by the food you eat. There is always enough food for you, and always enough of the right foods for you. There is plenty of food and your mind throws out any need to store excess fuel as fat, because there is always enough food for you. You never need to store fuel as excess fat again. There is always enough for you.

Extra fat has been a burden for your body, and your body feels great as you let the fat melt away. The fat changes to energy and burns away. The fat dumps out of your body through excretion, and it feels so good to be getting rid of unnecessary fat. Picture or imagine the fat melting off your body. It feels great to watch it melt away.

As the fat melts away, it feels better and better to move and exercise your body. You move and exercise far more than before. Movement creates strong, dense, slenderizing muscle cells that further use up the fat reserves. Movement causes the metabolic rate to rise and stay up. You are finding exercise and movement that you enjoy, and it feels good knowing that every movement you make burns energy and contributes to reaching your goal.

You are changing your whole body and your whole feeling to a wonderful sense of wellbeing. You eat sensibly, get plenty of exercise and drink adequate liquids to always make you feel healthy, lean, trim, and attractive. You love yourself, and appreciate yourself, more and more with every passing day. Your own inner knowledge becomes the most important thing to you. Your opinion of yourself is based only on your inner awareness. And the opinions of anyone else about you are meaningless unless they reinforce your inner feelings of being wonderful, precious, talented, valuable, skilled, attractive and kind.

You reduce weight steadily every week. You are slim and shapely. The excess weight is melting off you, just melting away and disappearing. You are burning it off and excreting it off. You have a stronger feeling every day that you are in complete control of your eating habits. You picture yourself becoming slim, strong, healthy and attractive. Go back to your mirror and imagine your new, strong, shapely, attractive, healthy body, and know that it is a vehicle for the proud, wonderful, bright, being that you are. You can visit your inner room any time you like, simply by closing your eyes and imagining it. And every time you picture your ideal self in the inner mirror, the suggestions on this recording get a hundred times more powerful, and become the truth for you.

Every time you visit your inner mirror of truth, and every time you listen to any of your self-hypnosis recordings, your inner mind accelerates and magnifies your progress toward your ideal and optimal size, shape, weight and condition. If all these suggestions are acceptable to you, simply continue breathing... just as you are. And as you breathe gently, magnifying and reinforcing all your new and positive changes, take another moment to visit your inner mirror, identifying even more fully with your ideal self. You know that your inner mind is taking over this entire project for you... doing whatever healthy things are necessary in your mind and body, to help you reach your goal. Just picture the body you are merging with, and feel the good feelings of success. *Pause 10 seconds*

Great work! And now it is time to return with me to this time and place, bringing out with you all the powerful, exciting inner changes in thoughts, feelings and behavior that guarantee you merging into your ideal body in the fastest healthy time possible for you.

Creating the Ideal Self

Use the two minute induction and a countdown deepening.

As you relax more deeply with every gentle breath you breathe, your inner mind is open to and accepting of every positive and beneficial suggestion on this recording. Every beat of your heart stimulates your inner mind to magnify and reinforce these positive suggestions and implement them fully in your outer life. These suggestions lock into the deepest part of your mind and become permanently true for you. The more often you use your weight reduction recordings, the more powerful the suggestions become, and the faster they work for you.

Picture and imagine a beautiful room. It has a rich, soft carpet and comfortable furniture. There is a big window with beautiful, plush curtains. It is such a comfortable room and you feel so welcome and peaceful here.

This is your special room where you are always free to be at peace and be yourself. You let your eyes drift up toward the window, and you feel a desire to look out. But for now it is just too much effort. You know that the beautiful world outside your inner sanctuary is ready for you, but for now, you just let yourself rest and dream. And as you do, your mind drifts back to a time when you tried to reduce weight... but you couldn't, or you couldn't keep it off. How many times have you tried and failed? You wonder why this is, that a person with your skill, wisdom and ability should try and fail. And it comes to you in a flash that the answer is that you were **trying.** When we **try** to do something, it implies that we expect to fail. So when you **try** to reduce weight, you do just that, you **try**.

But all that is changing now, and it is changing because you have decided to just do it. You are finished with trying forever. From now on, you simply do what you set out to do. That is all there is to it. You mentally, spiritually and physically set out to be the person you were always meant to be. You are a wonderful, unique, one-of-a-kind human being and you have a right to happiness, and a body that works for you... a body that is slender, strong, healthy and attractive. And you live in a universe that supports you and is on your side. You enjoy life more and more every day as you move toward your inner desire... a body at its ideal, healthiest size, shape, weight and condition.

Picture and imagine yourself at your very optimal best size, shape, weight and condition... not how anyone else wants you to be, but how you truly want to be at your very healthy best... slimmer, healthier, lighter, fitter. Notice how you look and feel at your very best. Notice what you are wearing, and how everything you wear fits so well on your ideal body.

Imagine and feel your flat tummy... your arms, thighs and legs toned and slim. Feel the smile on your attractive face. You are smiling because you look good and feel good in the body that is perfect for you. You take your image of the perfect body for you deep into your inner mind. And your inner mind now accepts your picture of the perfect body as the real you. Your inner mind is now doing everything necessary for you to achieve and maintain your ideal body in the fastest healthy time possible for you. Your happiness grows with every day and is complete as you allow yourself to become slimmer, lighter and healthier in every way. You are a superb human being with a strong mind and an unbreakable determination to achieve your goal of an ideal size, shape, weight, and condition body... becoming the person you were destined to be.

As you continue to imagine your ideal self, imagine moving further and further away from your old heavy self... moving right out the door and into that beautiful natural garden outside your special room. It's so incredibly beautiful out here... the grass is fresh and green, the flowers in full bloom, the trees shady and elegant. You are wearing clothing that perfectly complements your slender, healthy body. And it feels so good to move more freely than you have in so long. You let yourself become one with your slim, strong, healthy self, out in your beautiful garden. Just imagine melting and merging into your ideal self. You have left the heavy blanket of fat and the unflattering clothing behind. And you are totally at one with your slender self. And that new self you have become is radiating a beautiful light from within, because this is the real you, which has been locked up inside, waiting to be set free. The slender you has been trying to get out for a long time. And since you no longer try, but just do, your slender, healthy, and strong self is free. You are that slender, ideal size, shape, weight and condition. This ideal body is the real you. And you are manifesting your new inner reality in the outer world in the fastest healthy way possible for you. Every day you are moving closer and closer to your ideal image, your perfect self.

Take a deep breath in, and go deeper as you exhale... breathe in...and out... in... and out... Notice how much more free you feel out here, in your perfect and ideal body. In this relaxed and wonderful state, your inner mind is open to new ideas. You now shed those extra, unnecessary pounds of useless fat. You now adapt new and positive ways of eating and thinking and acting. Your inner mind accepts that the new, slender you is the real you. And your inner mind is doing everything necessary to bring your new inner reality into the outer world. You are amazed that you want less food and that you want healthier foods. You are amazed that you are eating less and enjoying it ten times more. You are amazed that you are moving your body and exercising more. And you are enjoying the movement ten times as much as before. You are amazed and delighted that the pounds are melting off you steadily and gradually. And every day you feel stronger, healthier, slimmer and more attractive. Every time you listen to any of your self-hypnosis recordings, you relax much more deeply... much more quickly. And your inner mind accepts and reinforces all the positive ideas at deeper and deeper levels. You are healthier, stronger and more energetic... more relaxed and less concerned. You take things as they come and you know that life is ultimately on your side. Every day, you feel fitter, slimmer and more attractive.

If all these positive ideas about achieving your deepest desire of a slim, healthy body are acceptable to your inner mind, you simply continue breathing... just as you are. And every breath you breathe causes your inner mind to replay these suggestions inside, and make them more and more powerful for you. It is so good to know that your inner mind is taking over the entire project for you, and you don't even have to think about it a lot. The changes are simply happening. Your inner mind never tries, it simply does. And your inner mind is doing every healthy thing necessary for you to achieve your ideal size, shape, weight and condition in the fastest healthy time possible for you.

Now just take a moment to return to the garden, and my voice will be silent while you simply enjoy the feelings of being at your ideal size, shape, weight and condition. And your inner mind studies those feelings and does whatever healthy things are necessary for those positive feelings to become your outer feelings permanently. That moment of silence begins now. *(Pause 30 seconds*

Return to my voice, knowing that you can visit this garden any time you like. And you can feel the feelings of your ideal self any time you like, just by closing your eyes in a safe place and imagining being there as your ideal self. And every time you imagine the garden, simply being in the garden causes your inner mind to magnify all the positive and beneficial ideas on the recording a thousand times over.

Eat Less and Enjoy it More

Thanks to master hypnotist, Don Mottin, for this metaphor. Use the feather as an induction or deepening.

As you rest and drift in your beautiful meadow, each breath you breathe causes you to relax more deeply. And the deeper you relax, the more your inner mind is open to, and accepting of, the ideas on this recording. Each beat of your heart causes your powerful inner mind to study the message of this recording, and to lock your new understanding into the deepest part of your mind where it becomes a permanent part of your new reality as a person who is reducing weight and gaining all good things... health, slenderness, attractiveness and fitness.

And as you let the peace of the meadow just sink into your being, your outer mind begins to float and drift, almost dream-like, as you relax ever more deeply, and your powerful inner mind is doing all the work. Your outer conscious mind is welcome to listen to everything on the recording, but your outer mind doesn't have to do any work. This is a time for your vast and amazing inner mind to listen and make the changes that lead you to your goal. Just drifting, dream-like. Floating like a cloud. Floating like a down feather drifting down into the deepest, most receptive relaxation ever.

And as you float deeper, like a cloud in the clear sky... like a downy feather floating in the sunlight... I want to tell your inner mind a story. And as your inner mind hears the story and gets the message within it, the entire process of reducing weight becomes a thousand times more simple and automatic as your inner mind does whatever healthy thing it needs to do so that you achieve your ideal size, shape and weight effortlessly, without even having to think about it.

The story is about a 6 year-old child and a parent... just ordinary people like you. The child comes into the house one day and says: "I want a snack, please, I want a whole box of cookies!"

And the parent, after thinking about the request for a moment, responds: "20 cookies would not be good for you, but you can certainly have one cookie, **and it will be great, the best cookie you ever had.**"

And now it is the child's turn to think for a moment. Eyes closed, the 6 year-old concentrates hard... and clearly there is deep thinking going on. At length, the eyes come open and the little one says: "OK, that's just wonderful... I'll take one, and I will make it the best ever." The child sits down at the table with a cookie on a plate. The cookie gets picked up and sniffed. The child looks at the designs on it, studies its color and feels its texture. The little one puts the cookie back on the plate and just stares at it for a bit. The cookie gets picked up and stroked between thumb and forefinger. A small crumb has broken off, and the child picks it up and gently puts the crumb on the tip of a stuck-out tongue. A big smile happens as the tongue goes back in with that crumb. The child sits very still and lets that first taste fill every corner of the mouth and every taste bud. At last, as the crumb totally dissolves, with a look of pleasure and contentment, the child swallows that first crumb down. And then six year-old pauses for a bit, studying the cookie again. Gently picking the cookie up, the child takes a tiny nibble, gnawing off one small piece of the cookie and the same process happens. You can see the joy as the little one teases every bit of taste and pleasure from that little nibble.

Before the next bite, the child takes the cookie and inhales its marvelous aroma. The parent stares in wonder watching the little one taking so much enjoyment from a simple cookie. Then comes another nibbling bite, and the rest of the cookie gets put down on the plate. The parent watches, fascinated, as the child rolls the tiny bite around... tastes it on different parts of the tongue...feels its texture... feels it dissolve slowly in waves of wonderful taste... and at last, after getting every possible bit of pleasure from that bite, swallows it down. The parent is amazed as the child stares at the cookie on the plate for a good half minute more before even picking it up again. Then comes another tiny, tiny bite and total concentration on that bite. The process goes on, bite after tiny, delicious bite, until the cookie is nothing but a few crumbs on the plate 20 minutes later. And the child takes another 10 minutes to eat those crumbs, one by delicious, pleasurable one.

At length, the child sits back with a look of utter satisfaction and contentment. With a deep breath, and a long sighing exhale, the child says to the parent: "you were right... that was the very best thing I have ever eaten."

And your subconscious mind, listening to this story and concentrating as deeply as the child, remembers something that you forgot to remember.

If a six year-old child automatically gets the idea of eating less and enjoying it more, surely you, with your powerful and skilled adult mind can remember and apply the knowledge as well.

You are eating less now and enjoying it more. Because you focus on the goodness of each food you eat in the moment, you are enjoying new foods as well. Your desire to eat is in perfect balance with your body's need for food. You only eat when you feel hungry and you only feel hungry when your body needs fuel. You only want the foods that your body needs for fuel and only the amount of food that your body needs. You eat whatever you want, but your inner mind is changing what you want so that you only want the kind and amount of food that is healthy for your body. And every day, for the rest of your long, healthy, slender life, you are eating less, and enjoying it so much more. You eat whatever you want and you choose not to eat everything you could possibly want. You are in total control of your eating, and you enjoy your food so much more. And you need so much less to be fully satisfied. You eat small bites, chew thoroughly and relish every bit of flavor in your food. And as soon as you have eaten enough to fuel your body, all desire to eat just fades away. And all this is happening because you are at least as bright and thoughtful as a six year-old. And if a six year-old can easily figure out the secret to eating less and enjoying it more, your vast and powerful adult mind can easily grasp the same lesson and make it true for everything you eat.

Now allow all these powerful ideas and suggestions to lock into place in the most powerful parts of your being where they become your new truths. If these ideas and suggestions are acceptable to you, you simply continue breathing... just as you are. And every breath causes your mind to strengthen and reinforce these new thoughts, feelings and behaviors over and over and millions of times over, making them totally true for you. These new ideas are the way things are for you. And now, it is time to return to your normal state of awareness, bringing all the new thoughts, feelings and ways of being out to the world with you.

Tom Nicoli's Car

Thanks to master hypnotist, Tom Nicoli, for this metaphor.

As you breathe gently and regularly, each breath you breathe causes you to relax yet more deeply, body, heart and mind. And every peaceful breath causes your powerful inner mind to be open to, and to apply the ideas on this recording. Your conscious mind is welcome to listen, but it has no responsibility to do anything. This is a time for your vast and powerful inner mind to do the work of helping you attain and realize your goal of rapidly achieving your ideal weight, size, shape, and condition. Your inner mind is taking over the entire project for you so that you are forming a new and natural relationship with exercise, food, appetite and hunger... a positive new relationship that effortlessly and automatically takes you to your goals of a strong, slender, healthy, attractive body, and an active, positive, self-loving mind.

As your subconscious mind takes over the project, your outer mind is aware of inner changes that are so natural they seem to be happening by themselves, with no conscious effort at all. You are eating less, and enjoying it more. You eat whatever you want, but your subconscious mind is changing things so that you only want the foods and the quantities of foods that help you achieve and maintain your goal weight. You are not deprived in any way. Your subconscious mind is in total command of the concept of moderation, and any food in moderation can be healthy. You are amazed that you are fully satisfied with small amounts of food. You are amazed that you are only eating when your body needs fuel. But, since your subconscious mind is changing your perception of food, so that you think of it as fuel for your body and nothing else, the changes in your eating habits are really not so amazing. Your subconscious mind is incredibly powerful and is doing every healthy thing necessary for you to achieve and maintain your goal of a strong, slender healthy body. Your inner mind is instructing your body to increase your metabolic rate, decrease your appetite, and dump off excess fat in every healthy way possible. Your inner mind is stimulating you to move your body more, and more intensely. Your inner mind is erasing all the confusions you have had about food in the past. Food is fuel for your body and nothing more. You enjoy your food intensely, much more than before, as long as your body needs fuel. But the instant your body is fully fueled, all desire to eat, and all pleasure in eating, fades away. It is as if there is an automatic switch inside that says: "OK, I'm full... **stop eating NOW**," and all desire for excess food fades away.

Your inner mind is guided by the metaphor of two people filling their cars with gasoline. The first driver pulls up to the pump, opens the gas valve, and fills the tank until the automatic fill switch turns off. Driver one puts the cap back on the gas tank, pays and drives off. Driver one doesn't even think about gasoline again until the gas gauge says the tank is getting low. All of this is natural, just as it should be.

The second driver is a different story. Driver two pulls into the gas station, takes the cap off the gas tank, and begins to fill the tank. When the automatic fill switch goes off, the second driver squeezes every possible drop into the tank, where most of the extra will evaporate out the overflow tube as fumes that poison the air and are never used. Driver two is never satisfied, so next the trunk gets opened and driver two fills the trunk with gas. Then the window gets rolled down and the gasoline pours into the back seat. Obviously this is dangerous and silly. When driver two pays the enormous bill and drives off, all our second driver can think about is gasoline, because the car is filled with gas fumes. The thought of the gas and all the harm it can do consumes the second driver with worry. But when the gas tank is empty, our second driver repeats the entire silly process over and over again, despite the damage the excess gas does to the car and the driver.

Your inner mind is now driver number one. In the past it acted like driver number two. Food is your body's fuel, and in the past your inner mind stimulated you to fill your body with far more food than you needed for fuel. And that created dangerous and unattractive conditions in your body. **But all that is in the past**. Your powerful inner mind now realizes that food is fuel for your body and nothing else. Food is never a treatment for boredom, anger, shame, depression, guilt or any other emotional state. Food cannot fix these things. Food can only fix your body's need for fuel. Food is fuel for your body and that is all that food is. You are now driver number one. You have a natural, healthy relationship with your body's fuel source... your food. You have an internal "gas gauge." It is called your appetite. Appetite is a physiological need for fuel. Hunger is psychological... it is a desire to eat. Your inner mind is driver one, and your inner mind has completely aligned your mental hunger with your body's appetite. So that you only feel hungry and you only want to eat when your body actually needs fuel. And in between eating, you simply don't waste time thinking about food... just like driver one never thinks about gas until the gauge gets low.

When you do need fuel, you enjoy your food far more than before. You sit down to eat and make eating times special. You chew slowly and thoroughly, extracting all the pleasure each bite has to offer. But the instant your body has all the fuel it needs, you feel full. And all desire to eat more fades away. You have resigned from the clean plate club and are proud of leaving food on your plate, because it means you are paying attention to what your body wants, and not to old rules about cleaning your plate. And like driver one, you don't even think about food again until your body needs fuel.

And it feels so good to have a natural and normal relationship with your food, with your body's fuel. You feel a sense of liberation, because you know that your inner mind is totally taking over the weight reduction process, and restoring you to what is natural and good for you. You are becoming slimmer, healthier, stronger and more attractive in each and every day. You are so proud of the healthy and permanent changes you are making, and you thank your inner mind for correcting the mistakes of the past and returning you to a natural, normal and healthy relationship with food.

If these ideas and suggestions are acceptable to you, you simply continue breathing... just as you are. And every positive and beneficial idea and suggestion on this recording locks into the deepest part of your mind and becomes the truth for you. Every breath you breathe causes your inner mind to magnify and reinforce these positive ideas over and over, and to bring them fully into your outer reality.

And now, as you breathe gently, it is time to return to your normal state of awareness, bringing your new truths and new awareness out to the world with you... along with a confident sense of calm certainty that you are achieving your ideal size, shape, weight and condition in the fastest healthy time possible for you.

The Road of Life for Excess Weight

A Sensory Overload/Elman induction (From Unlocking the Blueprint of the Psyche*) and countdown deepening can be a very effective combination for this script.*

You are listening to this recording because you have a powerful and important goal in life. You want to achieve and maintain the ideal, best and healthiest weight for you. In your self-talk, you probably think of yourself as having a weight problem. The goals of this recording are to dissolve away your weight problem, and allow your powerful subconscious mind to set you firmly on the road to the slender, healthy, strong, attractive body that is your birthright.

I would like you now to imagine that your weight problem was an object that you can see or feel... a heavy burden that you have been carrying for far too long. That object can be whatever makes sense to you... a boulder, a backpack, a can of worms, a symbolic shape, or any object that symbolizes the weight problem in **your** mind. Your weight problem object symbolizes not just the excess weight itself, but all the causes of the problem whether you are conscious of them or not. The object symbolizes all the habits that contribute to the weight problem, all the harm and emotional burden the excess weight causes you, and anything else that goes with the excess weight. The object also symbolizes any habits of eating or exercise that contribute to your weigth problem. In short, the object symbolizes your entire problem with weight, and all its roots and ramifications. Just allow your mind to picture and imagine the object that stands for the entire weight problem in your mind. (*Pause 10 seconds*)

And as your inner mind imagines an object that represents the weight problem, let yourself study that object. Notice its color and notice how heavy it is. Be aware of its shape and its texture. You may not know why this object symbolizes the weight problem to your mind, but your inner mind understands perfectly. Above all, be aware of what a burden that object has been to you, and be aware of how long you have carried it, dragged or pushed it with you through your life. (*Pause 2-3 seconds*)

Now imagine your life as if it were a road... a long, beautiful winding road ... a road that extends as far as you can see or imagine... from long before your time here to long after. And you are standing on a place on the road of your life marked "today." You are carrying or dragging your weight problem object with you. And you realize how much more you would enjoy this journey of life if you didn't have this big weight problem to carry every step of the way. ENOUGH IS ENOUGH!

Put the weight problem object down... let go of that weight object. Just set your weight problem down on the side of the road and let it take care of itself for a while. As you set the symbolic object down, you are setting your entire weight problem down. All its harm, damage, causes and effects ... just letting that weight problem object carry its own weight for awile go for a while.

And notice how light it feels to let go of the problem, to just put it down by the side of the road of your life. You feel so light and free that you could just float up like a helium balloon. Now that you are free of that heavy burden, just let yourself float up, floating up so high that you begin to see the entire road of your life spread out down below you... So high you can't make out the specifics of any given day... You just see the road of life spreading out beneath you. Floating so high that you touch your own soul and you remember that the road of life never begins and never ends... It may transform at those places we call birth or death, but life never ends. And as you float up so high, you feel a feeling of continuity... a feeling of being held in the arms of something far larger than you are. You remember something precious... a sense of pure being. And you just float in that feeling of pure being... relaxing more deeply with every breath *(Pause 10 seconds)*

And as you float so peacefully, you look down on the road of your life, at today. And you see that the weight object is nothing more than a tiny little speck, smaller than a period at the end of a sentence, so very far beneath you... And the time has come to remove that problem from your life forever.

I know that just a short way ahead on the road of your life, you have resolved your weight problem, and completely removed the weight object from the road of your life. I don't know exactly how far ahead that time is, but I know the time when you have totally resolved your weight problem and let it go is just a little way ahead.

You can time travel into your own future to the place where the weight problem is gone. You do it by floating forward above the road of your life. Just float forward looking down, until you are over the place where that miserable weight object is totally gone. It is just a little way ahead, so just float forward until you are over the place where the object and all it represents have vanished from the road of your life. *(Pause 10 seconds)*

And as you float so high over place where your weight problem is gone, I want you to meet your own future self... the wise, accomplished you who lives up ahead where the weight problem is totally gone. Imagine floating down now, toward the road. It feels so good to float down to a place where the object and all it represents, is gone forever.

And your future self... the aspect of yourself who lives in your future where the weight problem is gone... your future self is waiting for you. Your visit is expected. It is your future after all, and your future self is expecting your visit. And notice how your future self greets you. It is with one hundred percent pure love and acceptance of everything you are, as you are, in this moment. Your future self cannot even exist without you being exactly who you are now. So your wise future self accepts you fully just as you are in this moment. Open your heart and let those good feelings of total acceptance of every part of you, including your body, flow into you now. And realize that these are the feelings you were always meant to feel for yourself and every part of yourself.

Notice how good your future self looks with a light, slender, strong, healthy and attractive body... the body that is your goal. Notice how well your future self's clothing fits and how well your future self moves. Be aware of the air of strength, confidence and self-esteem you have in the near future. This is the real you, just the way God and nature intended you to be. Ask your future self: "How does it feel to be me, just a little way up here in the future where the weight problem is totally resolved." And the answer is that it feels good, incredibly good to be you just a little way ahead in a lighter, slender future. Open your heart again, and let all those good feelings of being you in the future fill you now. And give your powerful inner mind the instruction to do whatever it needs to do to make those good feelings, and that lighter, more wonderful body, yours permanently.

Now ask your future self to give you any clues, hints or instructions that will help you get to that future self and that ideal body even more quickly.

I will be quiet for a moment while you ask your wise future self for your own deepest guidance... asking what you most need to know today so that you reach your goal even more quickly. You may be consciously aware of the answers. But your future self also communicates a vast amount of information with your inner mind at the speed of thought.... (*Pause 30 seconds*)

Returning to my voice, your inner mind takes everything that your future self communicated, and locks it into place in the most powerful part of your mind, where it becomes the truth for you. You find yourself moving toward your future self and all those good feelings even more quickly. And your powerful inner mind is doing every healthy thing necessary for you to achieve your ideal size, shape, weight and condition in the fastest healthy time possible. You cooperate with your inner mind by taking your wise advice from the future seriously, and acting upon it. In each and every day, in every way, your inner mind is totally focused on doing every healthy thing necessary for you to achieve your slender goals in the fastest time possible.

As you float back now, to the present, you realize that the weight object is already fading away. Your subconscious mind is already dissolving away the causes of the weight problem. Your inner mind is resolving mistakes about food, changing tastes, healing emotions, and finding creative solutions for stress of any kind. Guided by your inner mind, you are freeing yourself of the mistakes and errors of the past. And you are entering a healthy new future with a healthy, natural relationship with food and your body. And above all, you are entering the future with a new lightness of being... with a deep and growing appreciation of the miracle of your being.

If these ideas and thoughts are acceptable to your inner mind, you simply continue breathing... just as you are. And every breath you breathe causes your inner mind to resolve and dissolve away your weight problem, and to reinforce and strengthen every positive and beneficial thing you have taken from this recording. You are lighter of heart, lighter of mind, lighter of spirit and lighter of body with every breath you breathe.

And now it is time to return to the outer world. Be aware that you can visit your future self and feel the good feelings that are waiting just up ahead any time you want. All you have to do is close your eyes in a safe place, imagine floating forward on the road of your life, and your wise future self is always present for you. You can visit your future self, either by using this recording, or by simply closing your eyes and thinking about the road of your life. And every time you visit your future self, enjoying the new body that is waiting just up ahead, your inner mind magnifies and accelerates your journey to that light and slender future a hundred times.

Dr. Roy Hunter's Benefits of Weight Reduction

Dr. Roy Hunter presented the benefits approach to weight reduction in his book, The Art of Hypnotherapy. *The wording of this application of his approach is mine.*

Picture or imagine a beautiful room... a peaceful sanctuary within your heart where you always feel at peace. That room is richly furnished, and has a picture window that looks out on a beautiful natural scene. There is a fireplace, and a wonderful easy chair where you can sit back and let your outer mind rest while your inner mind learns wonderful new ways of thinking and being.

Sitting in that inviting and comfortable chair, bathing in the soft light from the window, your heart is calm and your mind is clear. Your outer mind drifts and floats gently. As you relax more deeply to the sound of my voice, your inner mind is open to, and accepts and implements every positive and beneficial idea on this recording. And every breath you breathe makes these positive ideas stronger for you.

You take a moment to imagine yourself at your ideal size, shape, weight and condition. When you are in this room, it is so easy to imagine and picture and feel yourself at your ideal and optimal best. As you let your mind fill with the image of your ideal body, you review all the benefits of reducing weight and attaining your goals. Most people who wish to reduce weight wish to achieve some or all of the following things. You may wish to achieve greater health through weighing less. You may wish to reduce weight so that you can be more energetic or physically active. You may want greater mobility. You might desire to be more attractive, or look better in clothing. You want to have a happier partner, a better self-image, greater social acceptance or a better professional image at your ideal weight. You might simply want to feel better all around. These are the typical benefits that most people want to gain from weighing less. There may be other benefits that are specific to you. Take a few moments to think about all the benefits you will enjoy when you reduce your weight. (*Slight pause*) Think of all that you will gain. While I am quiet for a few seconds, let your mind consider all the benefits, for you, of being at your ideal weight, and focus your mind on the two or three benefits that are the most important to you. (*Pause 15 seconds for your mind to focus on your benefits*)

Return to my voice now, with a picture in your mind of the benefits you will gain from being at your ideal size, shape, weight and condition. Here, in this beautiful room, it is so easy to imagine yourself already reaching your goal! You can feel the feelings that go along with achieving your ideal weight. And these feelings are part of the benefits you gain through weight reduction. Imagine how wonderful it would be to feel this good all the time.

Imagine already being at your optimal weight, your ideal, healthiest weight, and just revel in those good feelings. They are the feelings you were meant to have. As you imagine being at your best weight, you LOVE how you feel, how you look, how you think and how you act... so effortless, so natural. You imagine seeing your image in a beautiful mirror wearing clothing that complements you and that make you feel good. These clothes look great and feel great. And you love the fit. And now imagine yourself doing something, taking part in some favorite activity at your ideal weight, and you absolutely love the way you look and feel. Just let your mind be there, and let yourself enjoy those wonderful feelings. (*Pause*)

Now imagine the most important benefits, for you, of being at your ideal weight. Imagine being successful at reaching your goal, and reaping the benefits of your dedicated change. Add those benefits to the good feelings you would get from being your ideal weight, and imagine success. Imagine your success... so powerfully and vividly... that it is as if you have already achieved it. These are the benefits you choose for yourself. These are the things you want to manifest in your life. These are the things you choose. And you choose these benefits, and these good feelings so powerfully that they are the most important personal goals in your life. You send a powerful message to the deepest and strongest parts of your inner mind, saying: "These are the benefits, these are the feelings I want in my life!" I choose this success. I choose all the benefits and good feeling that go with being at my ideal weight and size. Your subconscious mind listens, and because it is open and accepting, your subconscious mind now accepts these positive benefits, feelings and choices as your new goals. And your inner mind directs all its powers to bringing these feelings and benefits into your life: health, success, image, attractiveness, mobility, energy, joy, confidence, strength, and achievement. Whatever the most important benefits and feelings are for you, your inner mind now focuses on making them real in your outer life.

You have just used your power of choice to select what you want in life. It feels so good to choose what you want. And from here on, it is so simple. You simply use that same power of choice to choose what goes into your mouth... when, where and how much. YOU and only YOU decide what goes into your mouth... when, where, and how much. It now makes you happy, incredibly happy, to choose the right amounts and the right kinds of foods to help you reach your ideal, healthiest body weight and size. You get an incredible rush of good feelings every time you make your best choices about food and eating habits. You and only you have the power to choose how, and how much, you move your body. You choose whatever kind of movement makes you feel good, in the perfect way for you. You feel incredibly good when you make positive choices about movement and exercise.

You absolutely love being free to choose! You love the power to choose health, slenderness and wellbeing. You love being able to choose the feelings and the benefits of having a slender healthy body. And the more you use your power of choice, the stronger it becomes. You love being able to choose to do whatever healthy thing it takes to achieve your ideal body. Because the choices are so satisfying, the benefits are so rewarding, and the feelings are so good.

Practice with me now, because the more your use your power of choice, the stronger it becomes. Imagine sitting down to eat. Imagine taking in a bite of healthy, slenderizing food, and eating **slowly**... so slowly that you can **really enjoy** the flavor of each bite. Imagine the feeling of paying attention as you eat, so that when your body has enough food, you can choose to stop eating. **You feel so satisfied**, physically, mentally and emotionally... And it is becoming so easy to do all the things that help your body achieve its ideal weight, because you love the feelings and all the benefits.

Choose to imagine yourself always leaving food on your plate when you eat. Excess food is waste... if you throw it away it is wasted, worse yet, if you eat excess food it is "waisted", it goes to your waist. Excess food can't hurt a garbage can or garbage disposal, but it can hurt you. So imagine choosing to always leave a little food on your plate as a symbol that you only eat what your body needs. Feel how freeing it feels to leave excess food on your plate, not on your waist. It feels so powerful and wonderful to choose to leave a little food on your plate at every meal. And every day, it is easier and easier to make all the positive choices that keep your body slender and healthy because you love the benefits and feelings that come from being at your very best.

Choose to imagine yourself doing regular, pleasant, life-sustaining movement... walking, swimming, bicycling, or any other regular and gentle movement. Choose to feel how good it feels to move freely and easily. And every day it is easier and easier to choose to move because it feels so good, and helps you achieve your ideal size, shape, weight and condition.

Imagine again, being at your optimal and healthiest size, shape, weight and condition. You **absolutely love** how you look and feel! **You love** all the good things that have come into your life! See yourself in the mirror at your slender, healthiest best... noticing how much energy you have... noticing how your clothes fit and look so good on you... noticing how attractive you are and how healthy you feel. Just be there in your mind and enjoy being at your ideal weight. (*Pause 10 seconds*)

Now feel the great feelings of being at your ideal weight, and imagine all of the most important benefits and rewards for you of being at your ideal weight. Imagine those benefits and feel those feelings so deeply... and so vividly... that it is as if you already enjoy success **NOW!** These are the feelings and rewards and benefits you have chosen and you absolutely deserve them. This is your body and you deserve it to be its very natural healthiest, strongest, most attractive best. You absolutely love being a powerful human being with the power to choose what you want in life. And every day it becomes easier and easier for you to be totally focused on doing everything that helps you attain and maintain that slender, strong, healthy body you were meant to have. Every time you make even the smallest positive choice to help your body achieve its ideal weight, you feel a wonderful sense of joy and wellbeing. And every time you make a positive choice that leads to a more slender, healthy body, it becomes a thousand times easier and more rewarding to make the next positive choice. And day by day, faster than you imagine, you are gaining a greater strength of choice and will than you have ever known before. The more you make positive, slenderizing choices, the better you feel, and the greater the benefits.

Imagine being at your ideal weight... feel it, see it, imagine it so strongly that your are already there. Now take another short moment of silence to let your mind once again imagine all the benefits and feelings of being your ideal weight. Imagine being there so powerfully that all the positive and beneficial ideas on this recording go deep into the deepest, most powerful parts of your mind and brain, and simply become the truth for you...
(Pause 20 seconds)

Return to my voice now, knowing that your inner mind is doing every positive thing necessary to help you achieve your ideal weight. You are always conscious now of the benefits of being your ideal weight. You always make the positive choices necessary to achieve and maintain your ideal weight because the benefits are so incredible. Nothing distracts you from your goal. Absolutely nothing tastes as good as slender feels. Nothing distracts you from the positive choices that feel so good. Every breath you breathe causes your inner mind to reinforce and strengthen every good idea on this recording over and over and 10,000 times over.

Leptin and Ghrelin

Try the Sensory Overload/Elman induction and any of the deepening techniques.

There is a part of your mind that is very ancient. It was ancient when our ancestors lived in caves. It is the part of the mind that causes our brains to add excess fat to our bodies. In prehistoric times, meals were uncertain, and our brains and minds evolved to save us from frequent times of famine. That ancient part of the mind is still alive within us and still causes our brains to stimulate our bodies to store fat in case there is a shortage of food.

Our brains and bodies have not caught up to our civilization. In this country, in our lifetimes, there will never be a famine. In fact, our greatest health problems are caused by consuming too much highly refined, high calorie food. But our inner cave man or cave woman deep in the mind doesn't know that. And our minds are still on automatic pilot, causing our brains to stimulate hunger and causing our bodies to add more and more useless and life threatening fat. It is if there is a part of the subconscious mind that we have inherited from our ancestors that is on automatic pilot. It just keeps pushing the levers in our mind that cause our bodies to add more and more useless fat, or to replace excess fat that we have successfully discarded from our bodies.

It is time to correct this situation, and reset our minds and brains for life in modern America. So let's imagine the control room in the mind. The control room looks like a modern computer center crossed with the cockpit of a jet airplane. It is filled with levers, buttons, dials, monitors, keyboards and all kinds of control equipment. To our ancient ancestors, it may have looked life a shaman's cave filled with magical implements, but it is the same control room. You notice that there is a switch in your control room that turns the automatic pilot on and off. And you realize that the automatic pilot has been turned on, with all the ancient programming to eat rich foods, and store body fat, still operating. The very first thing you do is turn the autopilot to the OFF position, so that you can correct the ancient programs and bring them up to date.

You notice a computer screen against one wall with a picture of your body, just as it is now. It is your body image computer, and it shows you your body the way your mind thinks it is supposed to be. Your body image computer responds to your imagination. So you change the picture on the screen to reflect your ideal, optimal body size, shape, weight and condition. Imagine or visualize your ideal body so completely that the picture on the body image computer totally reflects your ideal body, just the healthy way you want it to be. And when you have the new picture just right, hit the save command. That saves your new, healthy body image deep into the most powerful part of the mind. And just know that your vast and powerful inner mind is now doing whatever healthy things it needs to do to create and maintain your body at its ideal and optimal size, shape, weight and condition. In fact, your subconscious mind, which can think thousands of times faster than I can talk, is racing far ahead, doing whatever positive things it takes to achieve and maintain your ideal body weight.

Next to your body image computer, there are two control levers that control specific enzymes related to weight. Each one runs on a scale of one to ten. The first lever controls a hormone called Ghrelin. Ghrelin is produced by cells in the stomach, and it stimulates a feeling of intense hunger and desire to find food. The ancient part of our brain causes the stomach to produce excess Ghrelin whenever our fat cells begin to diminish. Remember, the ancient programming was designed to help us survive famine by storing up extra energy in fat cells. But since we never have famines in this country, our bodies are producing far too much Ghrelin, and that makes it very hard to reduce weight and be healthy and attractive. So you pull the Ghrelin control lever down… way down, to reduce the amount of Ghrelin your stomach is secreting. You set the Ghrelin lever way down near the bottom, at a level one on the ten scale, so that your stomach only secretes enough Ghrelin to make you feel a little hungry when your body actually needs fuel. Now lock your Ghrelin lever in place so it can never go up too high again.

Another thing our ancient programming did was turn hunger into a bad feeling. Right next to the Ghrelin control lever is a hunger dial that goes from Very Good on the Left, to neutral in the center, to Very Bad on the far right. Your dial is set clear over to the Right, to Very Bad, because your ancient ancestors had to be motivated to go find food when their stomachs produced Ghrelin. So the mind is set to consider the feeling of hunger as a bad thing.

But that is just the opposite of what you need today. You turn the dial to the left, to Good. The instruction for you brain and body is to look at hunger in a whole new way. Your stomach produces Ghrelin when your body is burning your stored up fat, and the excess Ghrelin makes you feel a sensation of hunger. You now realize that a sensation of being hungry is a very good thing, because if you feel hungry, it means your body is burning stored up fat from your fat cells. Because your reset the Ghrelin lever to low, you never feel as terribly hungry as in the past, but you still feel a little hungry from time to time. The way you relate to feelings of hunger is totally different now. You totally enjoy the feeling of being a little hungry. When you feel a little hungry, it means that your body is successfully burning off excess, useless, ugly, life-threatening fat. Whenever you feel a little hungry, you welcome the feeling. You feel really good because you know that your body is burning off excess fat, and bringing you the ideal size, shape and weight that makes you strong, healthy and attractive. Every time you feel hungry, even a little hungry, you get a smile on your face and feel really good because you know your body is getting rid of useless, excess fat. You love feeling a little hungry, because it means that things are working and you are getting slender, healthy and attractive.

The second lever controls the hormone Leptin. Leptin is produced by fat cells. It is designed to tell the mind to stop feeling hungry because you have enough fat in your cells. But our ancient programming has suppressed Leptin production. When you look at your Leptin lever, it is set way down at one. That means that your body is not making enough Leptin to control your hungry feelings. You slide the Leptin lever up to seven or eight on the ten scale, and lock it into place, so that even when your body burns off excess fat, you are still sending off Leptin signals to your mind telling it that you have far more than enough fat on your body to survive without a meal or two... and there is no need to get upset about burning some of the excess, dangerous fat off. Your mind responds to the new higher leptin levels by giving you feelings of comfort, peace, satisfaction and achievement as the ugly, unhealthy excess fat melts off your body and you shrink down to the ideal, healthy size, shape, weight and condition that you were always meant to be.

Another way that our ancient programming has interfered with us achieving a slender, strong and attractive weight is by diminishing the pleasure we get from our food. The ancient programming causes us to bolt our food really quickly. In times of ancient famines, the person who could swallow the most, first, was most likely to survive. But when there is more food than we need to survive, that reaction causes us to eat far too much and not to enjoy our food much at all. Our brains need to feel pleasure to know that we have eaten enough. If we eat too quickly, and don't get maximum pleasure from our food, our brains think we haven't had enough yet, and cause us to eat in excess.

You rewrite that ancient programming now. You tell that ancient cave dweller inside you that eating is like sex... It is much better when you take your time and really enjoy it. You reinforce your new eating rules so that your brain gets the maximum pleasure from the food you eat. You always sit down to eat. You always take the time to truly enjoy your food. When you eat, you take small bites into your mouth. When you take a bite of your food, you chew that delicious bite thoroughly, extracting every bit of flavor and pleasure in it. You focus your mind totally on the delectable bite in your mouth, noticing the way the texture and taste change in different parts of your mouth. You set everything else aside to focus on the food in your mouth. You set down you utensils between bites so that you are focused only on the food you are chewing. You turn off the TV so that you can enjoy your food. You interrupt conversations so that you can truly focus on every bit of the delicious food you are eating. You don't even think about another bite until you have thoroughly chewed and swallowed the delicious bite in your mouth. You continue, slowly and thoroughly chewing and tasting each delicious bite, one at a time.

And because you are getting so much more pleasure from eating, your brain resets itself. You enjoy your food so much more, that you are thoroughly satisfied with much less food. You are amazed and delighted at how much more you enjoy the food you do eat, and at how satisfied you are with so much less because you are getting every bit of taste and pleasure from every single bite. Your brain implements your new tasting, chewing and eating rules now. And your brain realizes that you are totally satisfied, and getting all you need from so much less food.

Now that you have reset your body image, your eating hormone levels and your eating rules, you go back to the automatic pilot switch in the control room and switch it back to the ON position. That causes your brain to lock all these positive, healthy changes into place. And every breath you breathe reinforces and magnifies your mind and your brain as they bring your new body into being at its healthy, attractive, and ideal size shape weight and condition. Your inner mind takes over the entire project and you merge into your ideal body so quickly it is amazing. Every time you listen to one of these weight reduction recordings, it causes your inner mind to reinforce the positive ideas on all of them a thousand times over, and you are achieving your ideal size, shape, weight and condition **NOW**.

Virtual Gastric Bypass

As you relax more deeply with every breath you breathe, each breath causes your powerful inner mind to be open to, and to implement, every positive and beneficial idea on this recording. Every beat of your heart causes your inner mind to magnify, multiply and reinforce all the positive ideas on this recording, over and over and thousands of times over, locking these positive ideas and suggestions deep into the deepest part of the subconscious mind, and doing whatever healthy things it takes to implement them into your life.

Your subconscious mind understands your deep desire to reduce your body's weight and to gain health, energy, slenderness and attractiveness. Show your subconscious mind your inner image of yourself at your ideal size, shape, weight and condition. And once again, share with your subconscious mind how deeply you want to achieve that lighter, more slender, healthier and more attractive body. And as you share your goal weight and body picture with your inner mind, your inner mind renews its determination to do whatever healthy things it takes to bring that ideal body into your life.,, Because that ideal body represents you at your natural best. Your ideal size, shape, weight and condition are the body you were always meant to have... strong, slender, healthy and attractive. And your inner mind is renewing its determination to do whatever healthy things it takes to bring that ideal body into being for you.

That means that your inner mind is changing the foods you want, so that you only want the foods and the amount of food that help you attain and maintain your ideal body. Your inner mind is changing your appetite so that you only feel hungry when your body needs food. Your subconscious mind is changing your sense of portions, so that you want less food at every meal, and you feel completely satisfied and full. Your inner mind is stimulating you to exercise, and is raising your metabolic rate so that your body is becoming a lean, fat burning body. Your creative inner mind is finding powerful new ways for you to heal the past and deal with difficult emotions so that all emotional eating fades from your life forever. Your inner mind is doing everything necessary for you to reduce weight and it is doing all those things automatically so that you don't even have to think about them consciously. Every beat of your heart cause your inner mind to strengthen and magnify all the positive new things it is doing to help you reduce and maintain weight. The rest of this recording is about another tool that your inner mind can use to help you.

You are aware that some people have become so desperate to reduce weight that they have undergone a difficult and dangerous surgical procedure called a gastric bypass. That is an operation where most of the stomach and some of the small intestine are surgically removed so that the body can only eat and digest small amounts of food at a time. The surgery has been *very* effective at helping people reduce weight, but it comes with a number of negative consequences. A small proportion of people die from the surgery. People whose stomach and intestines have been bypassed, are often unable to absorb vitamins, minerals and other important nutrients, so they have to be on very expensive supplements for the rest of their lives, and frequently suffer nutritional deficiencies. And, since most of the surgical clients don't do anything about <u>why</u> they are overweight, the mind adapts to the surgery and up to half of the weight reduction from the surgery eventually comes back. In fact, there is only one positive unexpected benefit of the surgery, and that is that in many cases, it is a complete cure for type two diabetes. Gastric bypass surgery is an extreme and dangerous treatment for the problem of excess body weight.

You can choose not to have gastric bypass surgery. Using self-hypnosis, relaxation, stress relief and guided visualization, you are actually healing and eliminating the old reasons for being overweight. And that lets you take advantage of a wonderful truth to create a virtual gastric bypass that is totally safe, totally effective, and that has no negative side effects. The wonderful truth is that in the realm of your subconscious mind, *there is no difference between what you imagine, and what is real.* That means that your inner mind can give you all the benefits of gastric bypass surgery with none of the unwanted side effects, using the power of your incredible imagination.

Imagine your stomach. It is a beautiful, powerful hollow organ made of muscle and digestive enzyme producing cells. A normal stomach is just a little larger than the size of your loosely closed fist, and the stomach muscles are stretchy and flexible. Your stomach mixes your food with enzymes that break it down and make it ready to go into your duodenum, the first 12 inches of your small intestine. The duodenum is where approximately 90% of the nutrients your body needs are absorbed...

including energy molecules, proteins, vitamins and minerals. In a gastric bypass surgery, most of the stomach and most of the duodenum are cut away. That means that the stomach can only hold a few tablespoons full of food or liquid at a time, and most of your body's capacity to absorb nutrients in the small intestine is removed. A real gastric bypass surgery is extreme and dangerous, and should only be used in the most life threatening cases. But your powerful inner mind can imagine and create a selective, virtual gastric bypass that gives you all the benefits of the surgery with none of the negative consequences.

Picture and imagine your beautiful stomach, connecting to the first 12 inches of your small intestine, your duodenum. Now imagine your powerful inner mind performing a very delicate inner surgery. It works like this.

When you drink healthy liquids, like water, or sugar-free coffee or tea, your stomach is its normal size, and your duodenum is fully operational, so that you can drink however much you want of healthy liquids. But if you drink unhealthy liquids, like sugary soda, sugar laden drinks, or beverages containing alcohol, your stomach and intestines immediately act as if they have been bypassed, and you feel totally full and very uncomfortable after only a couple of tablespoons full of those less healthy beverages.

When you eat, if you eat food that is high in vitamins, nutrients, fiber and proteins, your stomach is its normal size, and your duodenum absorbs nutrients throughout its entire 12 inches. But when you eat foods that are high in refined sugars, refined carbohydrates, excess fats and excess calories, your stomach feels small, bypassed and full after only a couple of spoons full. And your duodenum acts as if it has been bypassed and simply does not absorb the excess sugars, starches and fats. You feel totally full, and totally unable to eat more than just a couple of tablespoons full of those excess and empty calorie foods. That means you are drawn to healthy foods. You feel great eating lean protein foods, leafy greens and high fiber whole grains. You enjoy vegetables of all kinds. And your stomach can easily hold as much of the good foods as your body needs for energy and essential nutrients. And your entire duodenum effortlessly absorbs the vitamins, proteins, minerals and energy foods your body needs.

But when you try to eat refined starches, sugars and excess fats, your stomach feels totally full after just a couple of bites, and your stomach feels instantly full after just a couple of tablespoons, the equivalent of perhaps three French fries. And your duodenum shuts down its first 7 inches or so, just as if most of your stomach and duodenum had been surgically bypassed.

Picture and imagine your amazing stomach and duodenum acting in this exciting new way. They are totally normal, and they effortlessly digest and absorb healthy calories and all the essential nutrients and fluids you need to live. Imagine eating a meal of nutritious lean proteins, vegetables, whole grains and other nutritious foods. Imagine watching your stomach and duodenum mixing, digesting and absorbing the perfect amounts of calories, vitamins, minerals, proteins and fluids to keep you maximally healthy, and to give your body all the energy it needs. See the wonderful, rhythmic actions of your stomach and small intestine as they digest and absorb healthy, nutritious foods. Just imagine it happening, knowing that your inner mind already knows the perfect nutrients for you.

Now watch what happens when you eat too many calories, or things made up of refined starches, sugars and excess fat, or unhealthy beverages. Your stomach and duodenum act as if you have had a gastric bypass. Your stomach feels totally full, and unable to hold another bite after just a few tablespoons full of unhealthy foods, and unhealthy beverages. And your duodenum acts as if it has been bypassed when excess starches, sugars, fats and alcohol enter it. A little of those things won't hurt you, so you can enjoy a couple of bites of chocolate cake or a couple of sips of beer. But any more than a few bites or sips of those less healthy things makes you feel totally full and you just can't hold another bite or sip. And your duodenum simply refuses to recognize excess sugars, starches alcohol or fats.

And it is totally amazing, because your powerful inner mind is creating exactly what you are imagining. You are automatically feeling totally full with far less food and with far healthier food. Your inner mind is creating this virtual gastric bypass for you, and you don't even have to consciously think about it. You just notice that you are able to eat all the healthy food your body needs. And you notice that less healthy foods fill you after just a couple of bites. You know your duodenum is absorbing all the nutrients you need because you are completely healthy and full of energy. And you know your duodenum is now bypassing and refusing to absorb empty calories and excess starches and fats because the excess fat is melting off your body.

You feel absolutely wonderful. You are effortlessly reducing weight and maintaining your ideal size, shape, weight and condition without even having to think about it. It is as if you have received a very special, selective bypass that gives your body everything it needs, and rejects everything else as waste. You are reducing weight and gaining strength, slenderness, health and attractiveness. And one very positive result of your virtual bypass is that your body is becoming healthier in every way. Your blood sugar levels are becoming normal and stable. Your cholesterol and triglyceride levels are stabilizing and moving into healthy ranges for you. Your body gets all the nutrients you need to be slender, healthy, strong and attractive. And your body simply discards the rest. Your body is becoming a lean, fat burning body and in each and every day, you are becoming more slender and healthy in every way.

Your inner mind takes a moment to review every positive idea on this recording... (*Pause 15 seconds*)... And your inner mind integrates every positive and beneficial idea on this recording deep into itself where these positive and beneficial ideas become true for you. For your inner mind, there is no difference between what you imagine and reality. And as your inner mind imagines a healthy, selective, virtual gastric bypass, it simply becomes true for you. Your inner mind does all the work of creating this virtual bypass, and you don't even have to think about it consciously. All your conscious mind has to do is notice that you eat and digest all the healthy foods you need. And your conscious mind notices that you are totally full and totally unable to eat or digest less healthy foods and beverages. Every beat of your heart reinforces your new inner reality.

And now, it is time to take all the powerful and beneficial ideas on this recording and bring them into your outer world, completely renewed and changed inside.

SCRIPTS FOR PHYSICAL HEALING

*At the risk of being repetitive, I want to remind you that self-hypnosis should always be used **in addition** to professional health care. Please never replace appropriate diagnosis and treatment with self-hypnosis. Use self-hypnosis as an addition to health care. Follow all your doctor's (or other professional's) instructions, and let your use of self-hypnosis augment and magnify healing.*

Immune System Normalization

Before going into hypnosis, review the chart following the script that shows the quadrant of possible immune system errors. You don't have to understand it at a scientific level. Just picture it, and know that you have an internal set of immune system controls that work something like moving a pointer around the chart.

As you allow yourself simply to enjoy this wonderful state of mental, physical and emotional relaxation, the goal of this recording is to assist your deep inner mind in guiding your immune system into it's ideal and best function... And to help restore your body to a natural state of vibrant and radiant wellbeing.

The basic principal of restoring your immune system to normal operation is that you do not have to consciously understand every biochemical detail of your immune system's operation. Even scientists who study the immune system don't pretend to know every aspect of its operation. All you have to know is that your immune system is the product of millions of years of evolutionary design. And that it is programmed to work normally. Your immune system knows what normal operation is. Your conscious mind's only task is to set the goal... to remind your immune system to return to normal operation. And because your immune system is the most responsive and most rapidly learning system in your mind-body complex, you can trust it to respond to your instructions by returning to normal.

Picture or imagine the control room of your mind and body. It is a room filled with levers, dials, computers, switches and other control mechanisms. I know that there is no place in your physical brain that looks exactly like this control room. But remember that your inner mind thinks more powerfully in images than in words. Your inner mind recognizes the control room as symbolizing all the very real control functions of your mind and body.

As you imagine the control room, your attention is drawn to a very large and powerful computer in the center of the room. This is the master control center for your immune system. As you look at the screen, you see that it holds a large picture of the immune system quadrant illustration that came with this recording. It illustrates the four basic mistakes the immune system can make, and the zone of balanced operation, where it is neither hypersensitive, nor unresponsive, and where your immune system focuses on keeping both the things that are part of you and not part of you in balance.

As you look at your immune system computer screen, you can see that one of the quadrants is flashing red. The flashes indicate that your immune system is over-reacting or under-reacting, or that its focus has drifted away from balance. There is also a large, black dot in the flashing quadrant indicating exactly how far your immune system is out of balance. You don't have to know exactly what the mechanisms are that have driven your immune system out of balance. All you have to consciously know is that you can guide your immune system to restoring the balance at this master computer.

There is a keyboard switch that turns off your body's autopilot, so that you can restore normal operation to your immune system and all your body's other functions. You press the autopilot switch NOW, and turn off the autopilot so that you can reestablish normal operation.

With your mouse, you move the black dot from its flashing disease quadrant back into the small square at the center of the diagram that represents your immune system working at its normal best. As you move that dot into place at the center of the diagram, you are giving your immune system an instruction from your deepest mind to return its operations to the perfect balance of specificity and sensitivity that it has been programmed for by millions of generations of evolution. The flashing red warning light in the problem quadrant goes out. The center normal operation square lights up green. And you can feel the wheels of your body wisdom turning as your immune system instantly responds to your instructions to find balance.

You do not have to consciously understand all the steps required to move back to normal, balanced immune system function. Your immune system knows what normal is and how to get there. You trust your powerful immune system to effortlessly and automatically return to balance now that you have set the goal. Your immune system knows what perfect operation is. You have just told it to return to perfect operation. So, having set the goal of balanced and normal immune function, you now lock your immune system controls in place, and let your wise and powerful immune system find balance as automatically as your heart beats and your eyes see. Just rest a moment and know that your immune system is normalizing and returning to harmony with all the wisdom built in by millions of years of evolution. (*Pause 15 seconds*)

The controls for your endocrine glands are a set of levers next to your immune system computer. While your immune system has been out of balance, it has caused all the endocrine glands to go out of normal balance as well. There is a red warning light flashing over some of the control levers. Beginning with the Pineal gland, your body's master control gland, you slide the lever up or down, to the central position, and lock it into place in the center position. That causes your pineal gland to secrete the normal, hormones associated with perfect operation of your body at its healthiest best. As you do, you imagine your pineal gland secreting drops of a radiant, golden fluid that flow through your blood stream causing every part of your body to move into harmonious, balanced and healthy operation. The red warning light goes off, and the green normal operation light comes on.

Gland by gland, you set the controls for your endocrine system back to the normal, central position. You set each lever until the flashing red warning light goes off, and the green normal operation light goes on. You set your pituitary gland so it is balanced and normal... and another wave of beautiful, rich drops of normalizing hormones and enzymes flow through your blood stream. You set your thyroid hormone levels to healthy and normal, and all your metabolic functions begin to normalize. You set your thymus to normal. Your liver has a number of controls, and you set them all to normal. Anywhere a red warning is flashing, you set it to normal, and a green normal operation light comes on. You do the same for you adrenal glands, your pancreas, and your ovaries (*or testes... choose depending on your gender*.) Your body is designed to work harmoniously and in balance with itself. And as you set the endocrine gland controls to normal, every function of your body begins moving swiftly to its natural, balanced and harmonious best. Every gland begins secreting the perfect balance of normalizing, regulating enzymes and hormones for abundant wellbeing.

Scanning the control room, you notice any other flashing warning lights that mean some part of your body is out of balance and operating imperfectly. Some of the warning lights may reflect specific body parts, like organs or joints. Some of the lights may reflect body functions like digestion, or circulation. But wherever you see a flashing red warning light in the control room, even if you are not certain what it controls, you set the control to the normal, healthy operating position. And you trust your deep body wisdom to restore normal function. As you set the controls to normal, the flashing red warning lights go off, the green normal function lights go on, and your body begins to normalize and harmonize all its functions.

You now instruct your deep, powerful subconscious mind to automate all the positive changes you have made in the control room today. And you further direct you inner mind to focus its attention on keeping all your physiological functions in perfect harmonious balance and optimal operating condition. Then you switch you body's autopilot back to the "on" position, giving your powerful inner mind a direct instruction to maintain all your body's operations at their normal, healthy best.

Every time you listen to this recording, or every time you take a deliberate relaxation break of any kind, it magnifies your minds' instructions for your immune system to return to and maintain normal operation. Every time you listen to this recording, your inner mind resets all of your body's functions to healthy, normal operation. You have an overwhelming desire and motivation to take a deliberate relaxation break at least once daily for 25 to 30 minutes each day. And every time you relax, meditate, pray, or even take a siesta, that daily relaxation break speeds and accelerates the process of your immune system regaining balance and normal healthy function. As your immune system normalizes, you feel physically and emotionally better each and every day. You allow every relaxation break to be an opportunity for your powerful inner mind to improve and enrich every aspect of your life. One effortless relaxation break is to listen to this recording once a day.

And as you drift and float, invite your conscious mind to think about some special, peaceful place in nature, or to simply entertain whatever peaceful and comfortable thoughts it wants to think for the next minute. And while your conscious mind drifts and floats with the music for the next minute, your powerful inner mind goes wherever it needs to go to magnify every positive idea on this recording a hundred times over and to accelerate your healing a hundred times as well. And the minute of quiet inner mind work begins NOW. (*Pause one minute*)

Returning to my voice, knowing that your inner mind continues normalizing all your physiological functions, and that in each and every day you are becoming stronger and healthier in every way. It is time now to return to the surface and to your normal awareness, rising back to the room with my count from one to five, bringing all the positive changes you have made out with you.

The immune system control in the script is shown in the chart on the next page. Before using this script, study the chart and the immune system's possible errors. Then when the script talks about the control panel, you have an image in mind of what the control panel looks like. Then while listening to the recording, you can picture moving the control back to the perfect center position. This immune system script is meant only to supplement and complement care by a licensed health care provider. It is not a replacement for regular medical and health care. Self-hypnosis is NEVER a replacement for appropriate health and medical care.

Immune System Control Chart
Immune System Quadrant

Sensitivity - How a Threat is Perceived

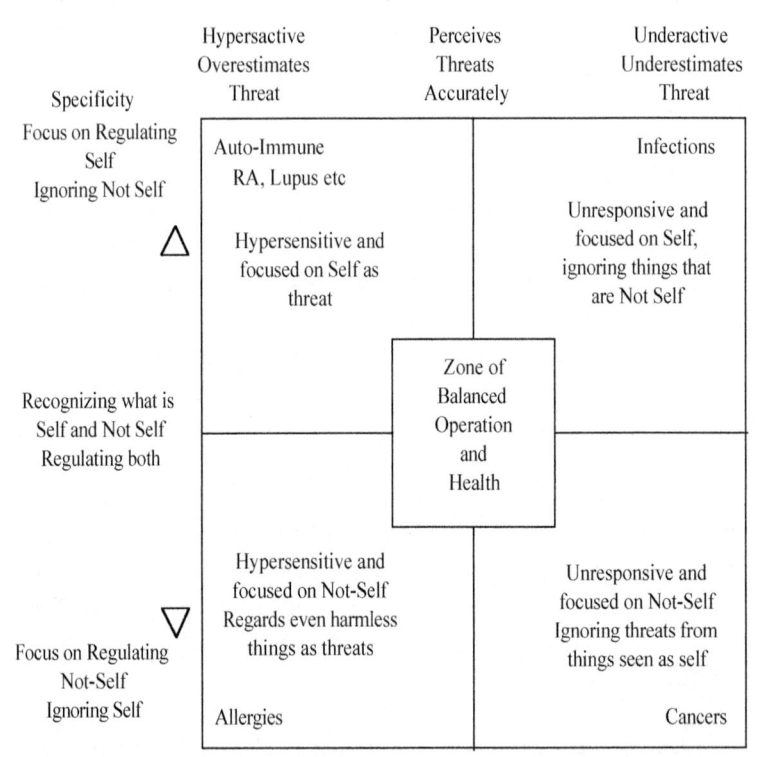

	Hypersactive Overestimates Threat	Perceives Threats Accurately	Underactive Underestimates Threat
Specificity Focus on Regulating Self Ignoring Not Self △	Auto-Immune RA, Lupus etc Hypersensitive and focused on Self as threat		Infections Unresponsive and focused on Self, ignoring things that are Not Self
Recognizing what is Self and Not Self Regulating both		Zone of Balanced Operation and Health	
Focus on Regulating Not-Self Ignoring Self ▽	Hypersensitive and focused on Not-Self Regards even harmless things as threats Allergies		Unresponsive and focused on Not-Self Ignoring threats from things seen as self Cancers

The diagram presents the four major immune system malfunctions. The immune system can vary along two axes. It can vary in sensitivity level from unresponsive to hypersensitive. And it can vary in specificity, from a balanced differentiation of that which is self and that which is not self. As the immune system moves farther from the center on either axis, it works progressively less well, and at the extremes of each axis, a state of disease or malfunction results. A healthy immune system is sensitive, but not too sensitive, and it keeps a healthy balance between self and not self, regulating both actively but not overactively.

Preparing for Surgery

This script is a complement for regular medical care. Hypnosis is always a complement to regular medical care. Hypnosis is NEVER a replacement for regular medical care..

As you relax more deeply, letting yourself become loose, limp and heavy, your body is so peaceful that it seems as if you simply can't move. And as you breathe, this feeling of incredibly deep and peaceful relaxation becomes even deeper yet. Every breath you breathe causes you to relax more deeply in body, mind, emotions, and spirit.

You truly enjoy this peaceful state of inner awareness and calm. Anytime you want to give yourself this feeling, all you have to do is close your eyes and silently repeat, "Calm and relaxed" to yourself. "Calm and relaxed" are magic words for you now. Every time you repeat your magic words, "calm and relaxed" they cause you to feel a wonderful wave of peaceful relaxation, and all worries and concerns fade away. Practice now... as you hear your magic words, you relax even more deeply. "Calm and relaxed"... Expect your magic words to relax you more deeply. Want to be even more calm and relaxed. And feel yourself relaxing and calming into such a wonderful, pleasant state. And every time you repeat your magic words "calm and relaxed" they cause you to relax as deeply as you are now and even deeper.

You are listening to this recording because there is a condition in your body that you have not been able to fully heal without outside assistance. You have chosen to have surgery to help you recover full and natural use of your body. Because you have chosen this surgical assistance, and because you trust the surgeon and the surgical team that you have chosen to assist you in repairing your body, you are calm and relaxed before, during, and after the surgical procedure.

And you have such a wonderful and exciting way to help yourself stay in precisely the right state of mind to create a smooth and easy experience with the surgery. You hypnotize yourself! The words "calm and relaxed" are magic words for you. Every time you take a deep breath, let it out and whisper the words "calm and relaxed" to yourself silently inside, you feel a wonderful wave of calm, peace and confidence flow through you.

Practice with me now. Take a deep breath in, hold it for just an instant... and repeat the words "calm and relaxed" silently to yourself. Notice the wave of relaxation, peace, and confidence you feel. Every time you repeat the words "calm and relaxed" to yourself, you experience this same peace, calm and confidence. You don't have to be in hypnosis to feel it. Every time you take a breath, let it out and repeat the words "calm and relaxed," you feel a wonderful wave of calm, peace and confidence.

You have chosen to have surgery in order to heal or repair some part of your body and to restore full, healthy functioning to your life. Throughout the time from now until your surgery, you frequently picture, imagine, and visualize the healing, repair, or improvement that you expect. Practice with me again... picture and imagine yourself as you wish to be after the surgery and recovery. Imagine and remember the feeling of full health and wellbeing. (*Pause 5 seconds*) You now send this picture to the deepest part of your subconscious mind with the instruction that your subconscious mind is to do every healthy thing necessary to help your body and the surgical team bring about this result... a fully healthy body, a return to full function, and complete freedom from the discomfort, pain or malfunction that caused you to need surgery.

You have a deep trust in your physician, in the surgical team and in the health care facility. You have chosen the best people to assist you. And because of your trust and confidence, all anxiety about the surgery simply fades away to nothing. You expect the easiest possible process... a routine and easy surgery, a completely trouble-free recovery, and a swift return to full health. While it is true that you would never choose to have a surgery for entertainment, it is also true that you expect the entire process to be nearly effortless and peaceful. And since you repeat your words "calm and relaxed" to yourself whenever you think about the surgery, you are peaceful, calm and confident in your wonderful outcome, and you expect complete restoration of your full health.

On the day of the surgery, you are calm and relaxed. You arrive at the surgical center or hospital feeling wonderfully good and totally confident since you know your mind is in total harmony with the goals of restoring your health with the surgery. You are totally at peace, and you use your words "calm and relaxed" frequently to give you a good feeling of peace and confidence.

When the procedure begins, you receive some form of anesthesia, and because you are so calm and relaxed, the anesthetic is very effective. The anesthesiologist is pleasantly surprised that you respond so deeply to the least necessary anesthetic. Everyone in the operating room is pleased that you are calm and peaceful, and your great mood and confidence spreads to the surgical team. And everyone is calm and relaxed, and operating at their very best.

When the procedure begins, even if you are deeply unconscious, your body immediately recognizes and accepts the surgical instruments and surgical procedure as allies in restoring your health. Your body knows that the surgeon and every part of the surgery are working for your highest and best health. And your body responds in a positive and helpful way. Your surgeon is astonished that there is absolutely minimal bleeding. Your body simply closes the valve on any blood vessels that may be cut. Your tissues are open and available, your muscles are loose and relaxed, and your body simply accepts the entire procedure as an unusual but helpful experience. Your body understands that the instruments are allies, not invaders. So your body responds to them with minimal or no inflammation or swelling. In each and every way, your body accepts the procedure and cooperates with it.

As the procedure is ending, your body responds by allowing normal flow of blood and nutrients to the affected area and by reducing swelling to an absolute healthy minimum. Your body provides a flow of healing and nurturing hormones and endorphins that speed natural healing. Throughout the surgery, your pulse, blood pressure, and other vital signs remain calm and perfectly normal. The surgical team is totally pleased at how successful and completely routine the surgery has been. The whole experience has been calm and relaxed for you and the entire surgical team.

When the procedure is finished, you find yourself in the recovery room, awakening in a calm state of mind. You know that the surgery has been successful, and you return to consciousness easily, and you are totally calm and relaxed. If you feel any discomfort, there are people there to assist you rapidly. And because you are calm and relaxed, there is so little discomfort that it amazes you and the staff.

As your surgical incision heals, you experience minimal bleeding. Your body rapidly repairs the incision with its innate healing wisdom and the tissue that forms the scar is tough but flexible and soft. All your normal tissues knit themselves back together and the surgery heals effortlessly.

Because you have been calm and relaxed in mind and body, your body experiences minimal swelling. Your natural and normal healing endorphins and hormones are working and the tissues around the incision simply join back together with minimal inflammation. Your doctor is both pleased and astounded at how swiftly you recover.

You have absolutely zero infection or other complications. Because you have been so calm and relaxed before, during, and after your surgery, your subconscious mind is able to fully marshal your immune system to protect your healing tissues and keep them free of infection. The incision heals cleanly, completely free of adhesions, and you feel wonderful.

You experience minimal post-surgical pain. Your body knows the surgery has been an ally to healing and so your body simply goes about healing without the pain that would come with an injury. When you do feel pain or discomfort, you use your words "calm and relaxed" in addition to your pain medications, and you find that any pain is easily controlled with minimum doses of medication. Your doctor, and everyone else, nurses, physical therapists and so on, is astounded at how well you are doing and at how little pain and discomfort you are feeling, because you are so calm and relaxed.

Your body returns to full function more rapidly than anyone expects. Your body is able to heal itself rapidly because you are calm and relaxed and in each and every way you are able to heal and restore yourself to full health in an astoundingly short time.

You now send each and every positive and beneficial suggestion on this recording into the deepest and most powerful parts of the subconscious mind where they lock themselves in place and become the absolute truth for you. Every time you listen to this recording, each and every positive and beneficial thought on this recording becomes ten thousand time more powerful for you. You have a profound desire to listen to this recording at least once daily between now and your surgery, and you use your magic words "calm and relaxed" frequently.

In a moment, I am going to bring you up to the surface with a count from one to five. Every number I count causes your mind to magnify every good thing on this recording a thousand times over. And every number I count makes you a thousand times more calm and relaxed about your surgery.

Radiant Health for Cancer Survivors

This script is intended to complement and supplement medical treatment of cancer. Hypnosis is a complement to regular medical care. Hypnosis is NEVER a replacement for medical care. Induce and deepen profound hypnosis to use this script. I use Dr. Kresnik's induction with a Feather deepening.

Picture and imagine a beautiful natural healing mineral hot springs pool in a perfect and protected natural setting. This pool is a special place for you to relax and allow your inner mind to help you heal and live a radiant and vibrant life. The water is just right... not too cold and not too hot... just the perfect healing and relaxing temperature for you. This hot spring has been a center of healing since ancient times. And it is there for you in the private depths of your mind whenever you relax and bring it to mind. Imagine stepping down the ancient stone steps into the pool, feeling the warm water flow over your feet, up over your calves and knees, relaxing and soothing as you step into the pool. Feel yourself step in up to your waist, letting the healing water wash away all your cares and concerns. Just imagine stepping into the pool completely. And as you do, your powerful inner mind goes wherever it needs to go to help you achieve the radiant and vibrant health that is your birthright. So calm and relaxed now... So peaceful and serene.

Simply let yourself lie back in the pool and let the warm water comfort you. And as you float and drift in comfort, your mind absorbs the following new healing ideas. You don't have to do anything... you don't even have to think hard about these new ideas. They simply sink into your subconscious mind where they make a permanent impression and are simply accepted as the new truths about you from this day forward. These new ideas become the new truths for your mind. And your body heals and changes in accordance with these powerful new ideas.

It is so easy now for you to ignore all discomfort. You have an exciting new method to take discomfort right out of your life instantly! All you have to do is take a deep breath, hold it for a moment and whisper the words "calm and relaxed" to yourself and a wave of peace and comfort flows through you, and all discomfort just fades away. Try it now.
Breathe in. (*Pause*) Hold it. (*Pause*) Let it out, repeating, "calm and relaxed". Just feel a new and deeper wave of relaxation fill you. Every

time you tell yourself "calm and relaxed," you feel a wave of comfort fill you, and all discomfort fades away.

Your stomach is calm and relaxed (*Pause*)
Your heart is calm and relaxed (*Pause*)
Your mind is calm and relaxed (*Pause*)
All your internal organs are working normally (*Pause*)
You are at peace and nothing can disturb your peace (*Pause*)
You are calm and relaxed (*Pause*)

"Calm and relaxed." These are your magic words, and every time you take a breath, hold it, let it out and whisper "calm and relaxed" to yourself, all discomfort fades away, and you are filled with a wave of relaxation and peace. Try it with me now... Breath in... (*Pause*)   Hold it...(*Pause*)   Let it out repeating, "calm and relaxed" as you do. (*Pause*)   Just feel that new and deeper wave of relaxation and serenity flow through you from the top of your head to the tips of your fingers and toes.

Your mind is at peace (*Pause*)
Your body is comfortable and tranquil (*Pause*)
Your heart is at rest (*Pause*)
Your entire heart, mind and body is calm and relaxed (*Pause*)
Your spirit is at peace and your soul is strong and vital (*Pause*)
You are filled with the energies of life and spirit and you are so "calm and relaxed." (*Pause*)

You are so excited because you realize that your mind is now working in perfect harmony with your immune system to bring you to a state of comfort and health.

Your mind is working hand in hand with your immune system and your doctors to create a state of optimal well being for you. Your mind and immune system now recognize your treatments as allies in the battle to bring you to a state of glowing health.

The cancer cells in your body are using far more energy than normal cells. Some of that energy is used for out-of-control growth, and some of that energy is used for cellular defenses. Your immune system now recognizes cells that are using far more energy than normal cells. And your immune system is directing the medicines, radiation, and other treatments to those out-of-balance cancer cells. Your immune system is protecting your normal cells and providing them with the materials they need to repair any damage caused by the treatments.

Your mind and body now recognize all your medical treatments as powerful allies in the battle to restore your health. And your mind and body are cooperating fully to direct the medications and treatments to the tumor cells and away from normal cells.

In the past, the cancer cells have fooled your immune system. Cancer cells fool the immune system into thinking that the cancer cells are wounds that need feeding and protection instead of the rogue, out-of-control psychopathic tumors that they are. Your immune system now realizes that any cell that is using more energy than the normal cells around it is an enemy to be destroyed and removed. Your immune system can't be fooled again. And your immune system is now joining with your medical treatments to totally and completely eliminate all the rogue cancer cells from your body. Picture and imagine those selfish cancer cells as nasty psychopaths, acting for themselves only and invading the sacred space of your body. And imagine your immune system rounding up, destroying, and completely removing every last trace of the invading cells.

Take a moment to picture it with me now... Imagine a herd of selfish, out-of-control cells invading your body and stealing its energy... Now picture and imagine your immune system working with your treatments to round up and totally destroy and remove those selfish, rogue cancer cells. Enjoy imagining and watching your activated immune system work with your medical treatments to totally remove all the cancer cells from your body.

In the past, because the cancer cells had fooled your immune system into treating them like wounds that needed nourishment and protection, your body was fooled into building lots of new blood vessels to supply the cancer cells with blood, oxygen and nutrients that they use to grow and attack your body.

But now, your immune system is wise and can't be fooled again. Picture and imagine those new blood vessels leading into the tumor. Imagine a valve in each blood vessel that allows you to turn the blood flow on and off. You now imagine opening those valves every time you have a treatment, so that the medications and chemo can get into the cancer cells and destroy them. When your treatment is over, your immune system closes all those valves so that the cancer cells no longer receive any blood flow. They lose oxygen and nutrients and literally starve to death. It is a double whammy. Your immune system opens the valves to let the medications flow into the tumor cells, and then closes the valves to lock the medication in and to starve the tumor cells of food and suffocate them from lack of oxygen. And the cancer cells die. Your immune system now knows that cells that are growing unusually fast are enemies to be destroyed and removed. And your immune system is working side by side with your medications or radiation to totally destroy those rogue cancer cells.

Picture and imagine your immune system attacking and destroying the cancer cells. Picture and imagine your immune system opening the blood vessels to let the medications in and closing them to starve and suffocate the cancer cells. What you tell yourself now is what is happening in your body. Your mind is powerfully aligned with your immune system, and with your medical treatments, to totally and completely eradicate the cancer cells from your body. What you picture in your mind is happening in your body, NOW.

Again, picture and imagine your immune system attacking and destroying the cancer cells. Picture and imagine your immune system opening the blood vessels to let the medications in and closing them to starve and suffocate the cancer cells. What you picture in your mind is happening in your body, NOW. *(Pause 5 seconds)*

Now return your mind to your wonderful warm natural healing pool. And as you do, all these wonderful and exciting thoughts and ideas sink deeply into your subconscious mind and become the truth for your mind and body.

Just relax and let the miraculous healing energies of that mineral pool go wherever they are needed to bring you healing, easing and comfort. And know that you are well and filled with life. Know that you are filled with peace and comfort. Know that your heart, mind and body are at peace. "Calm and relaxed."

And as you float and drift so peacefully in your magical healing pool, your heart is flooded with a beautiful golden light that shines with a wonderful brilliance. It is ten or a hundred times brighter than the sun. Not hot and burning, just incredibly bright and beautiful.

That light is so bright that it floods through you, and lights you up from the inside. That wonderful light fills your heart and spreads outward. And you feel a wonderful wave of wellness and peace fill your heart. That wave of happiness and wellness flows through every cell in your body. You are happy and at peace, and that happiness goes with you wherever you are. "Calm and relaxed."

As that beautiful light spreads through your entire body, you feel it cleansing you of all fear, all resentment, all disease, all discomfort, and all grief. You feel whole. You are at peace with everyone and everything, and especially at peace with yourself. And that peace goes with you always, "Calm and relaxed."

And that light spreads in a glowing ball all around your body, forming a golden healing and protective shield. And you know that you are surrounded by a protective shield of peace and joy… and that your joy and peace are with you in every moment. "Calm and relaxed."

Now just relax in the pool, knowing that every positive and beneficial idea in this recording is making a deep and permanent impression on the most powerful parts of your subconscious mind. Relax knowing that every positive idea here is becoming a permanent part of your reality. Every time you listen to this recording, and every time you say the words, "calm and relaxed" to yourself, every positive and beneficial idea on this recording becomes a thousand times stronger and truer for you.

You listen to this recording at least once a day. And you can bring yourself to this wonderful healing pool simply by closing your eyes and thinking about it. Your magic words, "calm and relaxed," go with you and are always powerful and relaxing for you. All you have to do is take a breath and whisper the words, "calm and relaxed," to yourself. And no matter where you are and what is going on as soon as you whisper the words, "calm and relaxed," to yourself, a deep wave of peace and comfort fill you. And in every day, in every way you are growing stronger and healthier.

Dr. R. D. Longacre's Childbirth Imagery

Dr. R.D. Longacre formulated the concepts here. The applications of his concepts are in my words. You should record and begin listening to these scripts regularly – either one at least 4 times weekly – beginning in the seventh month. **Hypnosis does not replace obstetric care.** *Hypnosis is meant as a complement to regular obstetric care. Never use these scripts in place of regular obstetric care. Use them as supplements to your regular obstetric care. Use Longacre's Yardstick as either a stand-alone induction, or as a deepening with the two-minute induction. You can record this for yourself, or have your coach or partner record it for you. Read the script slowly, with lots of pauses to let the imagination picture the things the script suggests.*

Now feel yourself relaxing deeper and even deeper. As you go deeper and relax even more deeply with every breath, you are able to picture and imagine the vast joy of childbirth. And you are enjoying every moment... so peaceful... so relaxed... so content... so very calm... tranquil and at ease... And you are recognizing and realizing how wonderful your birthing experience is for you and your baby. You are alert, relaxed and free of worry, so you are giving your baby the gift of a conscious and fear-free birth, the most wonderful gift you can offer a new baby.

And just relaxing deeper and even deeper, feel how wonderful your birthing experience is in your imagination. Just imagine it as if you were there already. Realize that at this actual moment you are not giving birth. Know that it is still in the future. For now, picture and imagine the birthing experience just the way you want it to be.

Your baby is now within you developing and growing, preparing for entry into the world. Let yourself and allow yourself to feel and imagine your baby is already outside, with you. See your baby smiling, looking at you with love and adoration. Feel your baby snuggling in your arms. So content, so soft. See your baby looking into your eyes with such deep appreciation and such unconditional love. You are a **wonderful** mother.

Your baby's birth is a completely natural event in your life. Childbirth is a joyful experience and a perfectly natural process of your body and mind. You body has been prepared by countless ancestors to do the perfect job of bringing your baby safely into the world. Visualize and feel yourself relaxing during childbirth. So courageous, so confident, so strong, and so deeply relaxed through all the process of giving birth.

Realizing that you are not giving birth right now and that everything happens in its natural time, just picture and imagine giving birth to your baby. Just imagine how wonderful it is. One group of muscles is dilating and relaxing in the womb and birth canal so that baby can go further down. Another set of muscles in the abdomen and womb are contracting to gently push baby out into the light. All your muscles are working in perfect coordination and harmony to create the miracle. You know your body is doing its natural best and doing a wonderful job. When you are relaxed and calm, your muscles dilate and contract in perfect harmony. And although it is a tremendous muscular effort, like a world record Olympic performance, all you feel is the effort. All discomfort fades away. You are totally free of all fear and totally free of all discomfort because your body and mind are working in perfect natural harmony to bring your baby safely into the light.

Picture and imagine yourself doing so wonderfully well and feeling so very good.... So healthy, so strong... so confident in your ability to give birth to a healthy baby, full of peace and joy and mirroring your own tranquil peacefulness. And you are recognizing that for you, the work of childbirth is as easy and as natural as any other process of your body. You experience strong muscular effort, and you are absolutely free of discomfort as your body does the work of bringing your baby into the world safely and gently.

And as you relax now even more deeply and again more deeply, you can imagine and hear your baby's first cry. You are alert when your baby is born... alert, conscious and participating fully in the experience so that you can experience baby's first cry with all the love in your heart. You are fully alert and conscious but also deeply and peacefully relaxed, just feeling that blissful feeling as you hear baby's cry and look into your baby's eyes. You are so very relaxed... peaceful, calm and composed. And you are so looking forward to the wonderful joy of giving birth.

Just you rest for a moment... relaxing deeper and even deeper. Just relax and enjoy the warmth and love of your baby. You are part of a miracle... the miracle of life. Just relax now and enjoy your baby's warmth and love... See your baby's pink soft skin... See your baby's wonderful eyes...

And imagine your baby in your arms... You are a wonderful, loving and caring mother who has given her baby the profound gift of a fear-free birth... you are a perfect and wonderful mother in every way.

Dave Elman's Childbirth Imagery

> Dave Elman developed the concepts in this script. This is my interpretation of his work. **Hypnosis does not replace obstetric care.** Hypnosis is a complement to regular obstetric care. Never use this script in place of obstetric care... it is meant to supplement obstetric care. Listen to this script or the previous one regularly – at least 4 times a week – beginning in the seventh month. Use a Sensory Overload/Elman induction and a Feather deepening. Make sure your coach knows that the word "Feather" is a magic relaxing signal for you. Practice relaxing with the feather often, just by closing your eyes in a safe place, and imagining your feather.

As you float and drift and feather so deeply, just following the feather in your mind, each movement of the feather causes you to relax more deeply. "Feather" is a magic word for you now. Every time you hear the word "Feather," every time you repeat the word "Feather" to yourself, and every time you close your eyes and picture your magic floating feather, the feather causes your mind to relax as deeply as you are now, in seconds. You don't have to be in hypnosis. Any time you close your eyes and say "feather", or imagine your feather, the feather causes your mind to instantly float and drift like a delicate down feather to this level of relaxation or even deeper. Any time your coach says the word "feather" to you, your eyes close and you relax almost instantly to this level of relaxation and even deeper.

Being in this deeply relaxed, and totally conscious state of self-hypnosis is automatically anesthetic. Every time you relax deeply, all discomfort of every kind simply fades away. The more you practice using your feather to relax, the deeper you go and the faster you get there. Being totally relaxed automatically takes away pain and discomfort. You practice imagining with your feather every day because the deeper you go, the more you are in total control of any discomfort.

Most mothers-to-be have heard scare stories from friends and relatives and from some well-intended, but misguided, professionals, that having a baby is a horrible ordeal. So mothers to be look forward to what they have heard described as labor and hard labor and labor pains. There is no such thing as labor or labor pains or hard labor. **There is no such thing associated with the miraculous birth of a baby!** All these terms are false names that keep a mother's attitude in exactly the wrong state. From now on, your mind rejects any scare stories or hard labor stories no matter who tells them... friends, relatives or health care personnel. Scare stories have nothing to do with you and nothing to do with your baby and your baby's arrival. Your mind rejects scare stories and hard labor stories as the worthless nonsense that they are.

You can cultivate the right attitude by knowing just what happens when a baby is born. Nature has a way of making your baby's birth possible through rhythmic contractions and dilation of the muscles of the abdomen and womb. Each wonderful contraction works in perfect harmony with internal muscle dilation to help you gently push your baby down the birth canal and into the world. Each contraction pushes your baby a little further along so that your baby can be born very easily.

Now you _do_ have contractions. But you don't have hard labor or labor pains. Sometimes the muscular contractions give you intense sensations, but they do not give you pain because you are relaxed and your mind is helping your body do everything in its natural best way. When your mind is relaxed, the contractions and dilations are in perfect harmony, and they feel like the amazing muscular efforts they are, but they are totally comfortable because you know they are absolutely natural. You are like an Olympic athlete in terms of intense muscular movement... delivering a baby is an intense effort. But your mind is so focused on the miracle of bringing your baby into the world that the intense muscular work of delivery is joyous. And every contraction puts a smile on your face because you know that each contraction puts your baby one step closer to your arms.

You look forward to the contractions... as intense effort, but in a good way, like winning a marathon race. You welcome each contraction because contractions represent your body doing its best to help your baby enter the world easily and peacefully. You know that you are having contractions as they occur, but you only feel them in a pleasant way. As you feel a contraction begin, you let your coach know and your coach strokes your hand or holds your neck, just like you have practiced, and a wave of warm relaxation fills you. You feel the contractions as powerful and pleasant sensations because you know your body is bringing your baby into the world. Each contraction puts a smile on your face because each contraction brings your baby one step closer to your arms.

You are surrounded by a caring and highly competent staff in the birthing room. And every effort on their part makes you feel more and more secure and more and more at peace. Your coach is present and you feel so loved and cared for. Nothing else matters except your body doing its very natural best to prepare your baby for arrival. As your contractions get closer and closer together, the doctor arrives and the doctor's arrival causes you to feel a powerful wave of relaxation because you know you are so close to giving your baby the gift of life.

One of the wonderful things about relaxation is that it shortens the whole process of delivery tremendously. When you are relaxed and leave your worries outside the door, your body is able to do everything in the most coordinated and smoothest way possible. Your contractions are in perfect synchronization with your dilation and your baby is relaxed and peaceful just like you. That means that your body and your baby are on the same wavelength and no part of you resists the process. So as you feel each pleasurable contraction, you are aware that you are giving your baby the gift of a natural and fear-free childbirth. As each wave of contraction passes, you know that you are closer to the birth of your baby. With each contraction, you know you are closer to your baby's birth and the thought keeps a smile on your face. And you feel strong, good and relaxed every step of the way. And after your baby comes into the light, you will get to see your baby instantly and look into your baby's eyes... so full of love and affection.

Remember that the relaxation you are learning is **in addition** to all the other help medical science has developed to make your delivery safe and comfortable. Your relaxation is a plus that amazes the staff and pleases your doctor, because health professionals know that your attitude makes all the difference in the world. You choose to experience your baby's birth in full consciousness. And full consciousness means that you remember in every moment that you are part of a miracle. You remember that there are contractions and intense muscular effort involved, but that there is so little discomfort. You know that contractions are a pleasant part of the process... intense muscular efforts that bring your baby closer and closer to the light.

And remember that you are totally in control of the process... you can ask for any assistance you like... ice, Tylenol, a Nubane drip or even an epidural. There is no right or wrong way to have a baby. Using hypnosis does not mean you cannot ask for other kinds of help. Using hypnosis means that you are totally in control. And you can ask for whatever makes your experience the best. Hypnosis relieves pain, but even more important, hypnosis gives you the courageous, adventurous attitude that lets you give your baby the gift of a totally fear-free birth.

There is a relationship between fear and pain. When we are afraid, our brains interpret intense sensation as pain. When we are calm and relaxed, and full of joyful expectation, our brains interpret intense effort and sensation as only that... intense sensation. And you can handle any intense sensation easily because you are so relaxed and calm, even while your body is delivering a baby. Your body is working incredibly hard, as hard as if you were running a marathon... but your mind is calm and relaxed, and totally filled with the joyful expectation of holding your baby in your arms.

And because you are calm and relaxed, there are no fear hormones in your body. And that means that your baby is calm and relaxed, and totally free of fear. A fear-free birth is one of the greatest gifts you can give your baby. When your baby is as calm and relaxed as you are, your baby learns that it can handle what ever life brings, just by being calm and relaxed and trusting the process. You stay totally relaxed and at peace for the entire birth experience, and give your baby the gift of peace and calm that lasts life-long. You are a totally wonderful mother in every way.

Now take a moment to imagine your baby's birth... knowing that your baby isn't being born right now... that is still a little ways in the future. Imagine watching yourself go through the intense muscular effort of a strong contraction, and notice that it brings a smile to your face, because you are totally calm and relaxed in your heart and mind, even while your body is working hard. Notice the smile on your face... you know that every contraction brings your baby closer to your arms... *(slight pause)*

Imagine the time when your doctor or midwife tells you to push. Watch as you focus all your energy on strongly, but lovingly, pushing your baby into the light. It may feel really intense, but in the same way that the finish line of a marathon is intense. You are strong all the way to the end, and your mind interprets the intense effort as sensation, and all feeling of pain simply fades away to nothing as you experience the profound joy of bringing your baby fearlessly into the light. You are a totally wonderful mother in every possible way.

Imagine looking into your baby's eyes for the very first time. That is the deepest experience of pure, unconditional love we ever experience. Feel that love, and know feel how proud you are that you were calm and relaxed every step of the way so that you could be here for this moment, looking into your baby's eyes and feeling the unconditional love, knowing that you have given your baby the priceless gift of entering the world totally free of fear. You are totally amazing and a wonderful mother in every possible way.

Every time you practice relaxation at home using your feather, and every time you hear this script, you are more and more at ease and at peace. Every practice seals the relaxation response into your deepest mind and when it is time for baby to arrive, you find yourself relaxing automatically without even having to think about it. You are conscious throughout the process and enjoying every miraculous moment of it, even during the intense muscular effort of contractions. You have a magic word, "feather," that takes you easily and automatically into a deep state of hypnosis. You and your coach practice helping you relax with the word "Feather" several times a day, so that when delivery day comes, the word "Feather" causes you instantly to relax. While my voice is quiet, your subconscious mind goes wherever it needs to go to multiply every positive idea on this recording at least one thousand times. Just Feather deeper and enjoy the moment. *(Pause for 30-45 seconds)*

Every time your coach says "Feather", or stokes your hand or holds the back of your neck, your mind automatically takes you to this deep, powerful peaceful place. You don't even have to think about it. Your powerful subconscious mind knows that you a part of a miracle and your mind automatically relaxes you whenever you hear your magic word "Feather", or whenever your coach strokes your hand or holds your neck.

In the awakening sequence, incorporate suggestions about "feathering" and about having a fearless, amazing, miraculous birthing experience.

Dental Bruxism

This script complements regular dental care. Hypnosis NEVER replaces or substitutes for regular dental care. Use with the Kresnik induction.

As you relax more deeply with each breath you breathe, every positive and beneficial idea on this recording flows into the deepest and most powerful parts of your mind and brain, and your powerful inner mind locks every positive idea into place and makes it true for you. Every breath you breathe while listening to this recording causes you to relax more deeply, and every breath you breathe causes your inner mind to magnify and strengthen every positive and beneficial idea on the recording over and over and thousands of times over.

Your beautiful meadow is an inner sanctuary, It is a place where every part of your mind is welcome and respected. Your inner meadow is a place where you can meet every part of yourself to resolve difficulties or explore creative solutions to any problem in your life. You simply relax into your beautiful meadow and go even deeper with every breath as your inner mind accepts and implements every good idea on this recording.

Bruxing... clenching and grinding your teeth... is a habit. It is a habit that has been automated and locked into your subconscious mind, most likely as a well-intended but ineffective way of reducing stress or expressing aggression. All habits are learned behaviors. Even subconscious habits are learned behaviors. Anything that the mind has learned can be unlearned and corrected. In your beautiful meadow, your inner mind is reviewing its habit of grinding your teeth. Your inner mind now understands the damage that tooth grinding is doing. And your inner mind is coming up with new and effective ways of dealing with stress and aggression. Every time you listen to this recording, or any stress reduction recording, your inner mind amplifies and strengthens the process of understanding and eliminating tooth grinding from your life. Your inner mind is finding positive and effective means of dealing with stress. And you are eliminating bruxing permanently from your life.

Since bruxing is a subconscious habit, there is a part of your subconscious mind that is in control of the habit... a part of your inner mind that thinks it is helping you in some way by causing you to grind your teeth. This part of your mind is not your enemy. It is a part of your mind that is trying to help you, probably to relieve stress or aggression. But the bruxing part of your mind has simply made a mistake. The bruxing part of your inner mind isn't talking with the rest of your mind. The grinding part of your mind has never realized that the tooth grinding itself is far more harmful to you, and far more stressful, than anything it is designed to fix. It is time to help the bruxing part of your mind reconnect with the rest of your mind to find effective ways of relieving stress and rechanneling aggression.

Imagine that you could talk with the bruxing part of your mind. Imagine the tooth grinding part of your mind as if you could talk with it right here in your safe and beautiful inner meadow. Imagine that you could connect a computer-to-computer cable to your inner tooth grinder... a cable that is capable of transmitting vast amounts of information, conscious and subconscious alike, to your inner grinder. Just take a moment to imagine your inner tooth grinder here in the room with you NOW... (*Pause 10 seconds*)

As you allow yourself to be in contact with your inner tooth grinder, you begin sending over everything you know about the negative consequences of bruxing, at the speed of thought, across that mental cable. You send the bruxing part of your mind information about the physical harm and discomfort bruxing causes, and about the financial impact of grinding, and about harming your teeth and jaws. You send your inner bruxer information about the negative impact tooth grinding has on the people around you, especially anyone who has to listen to you at night. Show your inner grinder how bad it feels to have a negative habit controlling you. Every part of your conscious and subconscious mind sends every bit of information you have about the negative consequences of tooth grinding over the mental cable to your inner bruxer. And every part of you, conscious and subconscious alike, tells your inner bruxer how incredibly much you want to leave this negative and self-destructive habit in the past. You inform your inner grinder that you wish to find effective ways to relieve stress. You inform your inner grinder of your immense desire to truly transform aggression... not turn it against your own body. Over the next few seconds, there is a vast flow of conscious and subconscious information flowing to your inner bruxer... (*Pause 10 seconds*)

As all that new and true information fills your inner bruxer, you also send a wave of thanks and self-forgiveness because you realize your inner bruxer was never trying to cause all this difficulty. Your inner bruxer was trying to help you, and simply made an error about what helping you really means. So you thank your inner bruxer for what it was trying to do. And you recognize that if your inner tooth grinder reconnects with the rest of your mind, it can play an important and meaningful role in your life.

Next, you show your inner bruxer that you are not the same person you were when you first started bruxing. Perhaps, way back then, grinding your teeth was the best thing you could do. But you are different now. You have learned many more effective and positive ways of dealing with stressful situations and stressful people. Your conscious and subconscious mind sends over a vast amount of information about all the many effective and creative ways you now know for relieving stress and tension. You show your inner bruxer, at the speed of thought, all the effective new stress relief techniques and powerful life skills you are continuing to learn. And you show your inner bruxer, that it can be an important part of your integrated mind. If it chooses to reconnect with the rest of you, your inner bruxer can take on the job of helping your learn even more effective and creative ways to relieve stress and live life fully. Your inner bruxer can also take charge of finding creative ways to truly let go of aggression, or channel aggressive energies into creativity that makes life better for everyone... (*Pause 10 seconds*)

As your inner bruxer takes on the new role, it also gets a new title. Bruxing is a thing of the past and it fades into the past. When you were little, you had training wheels on your bike, but now you drive a car. In the same way, bruxing fades into your past, just like training wheels, and your inner bruxer now becomes the driver of your new and creative methods of relieving stress and transforming aggression. This creative and helpful part of your mind now informs you of the new title that makes sense for it. And as that new title locks into place, you feel a wave of healing energy as every part of your mind, including this newly renamed creative part of you, melts and merges together into a single, intercommunicating wholeness, never to be separated again... (*Pause 10 seconds*)

As you feel that wonderful wave of reconnection, bruxing fades from your life. Things that upset you, hurt your feelings or angered you in the past no longer bother you. The things that stressed you in the past roll off you like water off a duck's back. The things and people that annoyed you in the past are so much more in perspective now... you never sweat the small stuff and your realize 99% of everything is small stuff. You are calm and relaxed almost all the time and you take life in stride because you know that you have all the resources you need to meet any challenge that life brings you, and thrive. Your inner mind is now finding new and fulfilling ways of creatively reacting to every challenge in life.

You especially enjoy breathing deeply and peacefully. Whenever the old habit of grinding your teeth even begins to start, your inner mind now gives you three deep, relaxing breaths in a row, even during your deepest sleep. As you exhale those deep breaths, the tension flows out of your jaw; and your head and neck relax. The tooth grinding fades away before it even begins. And every time your subconscious mind sends those relaxing breaths instead of clenching and grinding, it becomes 10,000 times easier and more automatic to take the relaxing breaths the next time.

Practice now. Remember and imagine some person or event from the past that stressed or annoyed you. Let that situation fill your mind. Remember how in the past, that situation would have led to clenching and grinding. Now, take a deep breath...(*Pause*)... and as you let it out, feel yourself relax more deeply. (*Pause*) Take the second deep, relaxing breath in. (*Pause*)... Let it go, and feel even the muscles of your face and jaw relax... (*Pause*)... Take in the third deep, relaxing breath... (*Pause*)... and as you let it go, everything comes into perspective. You relax deeply, knowing that the old situation has no power over you. And the entire urge to grind simply fades forever into the past. Your powerful inner mind now automates this entire process. Anytime something stresses or annoys you, you automatically take 3 deep relaxing breaths. You feel a wave of calm, and you feel a deep and powerful confidence that no matter what is going on, you have everything you need to meet the challenge and thrive. And all desire to clench and grind, and all the clenching and grinding itself, fades entirely into your past, replaced by your mind's new and dynamic dedication to finding fulfilling and creative solutions to every challenge in your life.

And now it is time to return to your normal state of awareness, bringing amazing and gratifying changes with you. All the old pattern of clenching and grinding is fading away, and the newly reintegrated parts of your mind are creating positive and powerful new ways to truly transform the stresses of the past. You can return to your beautiful room, this place of powerful inner transformation, any time you want, by listening to the recording, or simply closing your eyes and thinking about your peaceful inner sanctuary. Your inner mind signals its acceptance of the positive and beneficial ideas on this recording by continuing your peaceful breathing... just the way you are. And every breath you breathe causes you inner mind to magnify these positive ideas over and over, and make them totally true for you.

The Road of Life for Enuresis (Bed Wetting)

This script complements pediatric and psychological care for enuresis. Hypnosis NEVER replaces medical or psychological care. I use a feather induction with this script. Use Dr. Kresnik's induction.

The number one truth that I want every part of you to know is this. Bedwetting always gets better. No one has **ever** gotten to be 50, or even 30 and still wet the bed. Everyone eventually solves the bedwetting problem in their own time. This recording is to help you move up the time that you get bedwetting out of your life. You are going to solve it eventually. Let's just make it sooner rather than later. Your inner mind is open to accepting every positive suggestion on this recording and putting them into practice so that bedwetting fades out of your life forever in the fastest healthy time possible, starting today.

As you rest in the meadow, begin to picture and imagine your problem with bedwetting as if it were an object. That is, imagine an object that symbolizes the bedwetting for you... the bedwetting itself and all the problems it causes you. That object symbolizes all the reasons for the bedwetting, whether you consciously know them or not, whether they are physical causes or emotional reasons. It doesn't matter whether you consciously know the reasons or not. Your inner mind knows the reasons. And this object symbolizes them. Your object symbolizes the frequency and severity of the bedwetting problem. And it also symbolizes any gains or benefits that you get because of the problem, such as attention. In short, the object represents and symbolizes every aspect of the problem of bedwetting in your life. Just take a moment and imagine an object that symbolizes your bedwetting problem for you. (*Pause 10 seconds*)

And as you imagine that object, be aware of its color, its size, and its shape. Feel the feelings that are part of the object. And tell your subconscious mind that you truly want to remove that object and **all it represents** from your peaceful meadow, and from your life forever, starting right now.

Carry, push or drag that ugly, heavy, useless bedwetting object to the edge of your meadow, where there is a road going by. This long, winding, sometimes beautiful, road is the road of your life. Realize how long you have been carrying this miserable, worthless bedwetting object along the road of your life. It has been so long. And the time has finally come to set yourself free of that heavy, wet, miserable, burden.

I want to invite you to set the bedwetting object down on the side of the road away from your meadow. The bedwetting has never belonged in your meadow. That's right, for a little while, just put that soaking, miserable object by the side of the road and let go of it. When you set the object down, you are setting all that it represents aside as well. You are showing your mind that you want it to let go of bedwetting and set you free. Notice how light and free it feels to set this burden down. You feel so light that you could just drift away.

So go with that feeling of lightness, and allow yourself to float up above the meadow, and above the road of your life. Floating upward like a helium balloon, rising so high that you begin to see the entire road of your life down below you. Floating so high that you can't make out any specific events on the road of your life, but you can see the entire road... from before you were born to beyond the doorway to heaven. Floating so high that the bedwetting object down below is nothing more than a tiny speck alongside your beautiful road and meadow. And notice that your meadow isn't a small place. It is an infinitely vast meadow that is always touching the road of your life, always present for you. And it stretches far beyond your field of view. No wonder your meadow is so peaceful, and no wonder the bedwetting object has no place there. Your meadow is a place of infinite peace.

As you float in the calm light, high above the road and meadow, begin to time travel into your future. You do that by floating forward above the road of your life. I don't know exactly how far you need to go, but I know that somewhere, not very far ahead of you on the road of life, there is a place where that crummy bedwetting object is completely gone. Just a little way ahead in your life, there is a time where the miserable bedwetting object has completely disappeared. I don't know exactly how far ahead it is. I just know that place where the bedwetting is gone is not very far ahead. Remember, bedwetting always eventually cures itself. So I know there is a place where you are free in your future. Just keep floating forward until you are over that place where the object is either vanished completely or totally transformed into something light, beautiful and life sustaining. Remember that all bedwetting eventually cures itself, so I know there is a place just a little way ahead on the road of your life where the problem is already solved.

You feel a strong invitation to go down and meet your own future self, the you who lives up ahead, in that future, where you are totally free of the burden and embarrassment of bedwetting... A time and place where that bedwetting object has been completely removed from the road of your life. You accept the invitation to meet your dry, healthy, confident future self. And you begin floating down to the road of your life to meet your own dry future self. The very first thing you notice is that your future self is waiting to greet you. It's your future, so your future self knows you are coming to visit.

And you are amazed that your future self greets you with 100% total and complete love and acceptance of you just as you are in this moment... bedwetting problem and all. It is such an amazing feeling, and you let your heart open to accept the love and total acceptance. That total acceptance is for two reasons. First, your future self cannot even exist without you being exactly who you are in this moment. So your future self loves and accepts you just as you are. And second, your wise future self has rediscovered that you are a child of God, or of a creative and infinite universe, and greets you as the child of God that you are.

And you ask your future self: "how does it feel to be me, here in the future, where the miserable bedwetting object, **and all it represents**, are gone from my life forever?" And as your future self tells you and shows you how good it feels to be healthy and dry and free. You open your heart and allow those good feelings to totally fill you. It feels so good that words cannot express it. Just open your heart and allow those good feelings to fill you. And as you allow those vast feelings of freedom and dryness and confidence to flow from your future self to you, you let your deepest healing subconscious mind study those good feelings. And your inner mind begins doing whatever healthy things are required to bring you these wonderful feelings of health and freedom and confidence permanently in the fastest healthy time possible for you, starting NOW.

You ask your future self to give you or hints and clues, either conscious or subconscious, to help you get to where your future self is even sooner. And you listen carefully as your future self tells you and shows you directions, clues or hints that help you arrive at total freedom and dryness even more quickly. As I let my voice be quiet for 20 seconds, your future self shares a vast amount of conscious and subconscious advice at the speed of thought. (*Pause 20 seconds*)

Return to my voice, knowing that even if you are not consciously aware of specific clues or instructions, your vast inner mind has been filled with an immense amount of guidance from your wise future self about how to set you permanently free of bedwetting. And if you received specific conscious recommendations, you remember them and apply them joyfully in your outer life.

Your wise future self is always available for you to visit for advice, just by closing your eyes and floating forward over the road of life. You can talk with your wise future self any time you like just by closing your eyes and thinking about the road and the meadow.

Next, let's travel back to your beautiful meadow knowing that deep inside, your vast and incredible inner mind is doing whatever it needs to do to set you totally free of bedwetting and all the negatives that go with it forever in the fastest healthy time for you. And every time you talk with your wise future self, the positive changes get stronger and happen faster.

As you float backwards over the present, you look down and see that the ugly object is already beginning to fade away. It is already getting smaller and lighter and beginning to disappear. And that is because now that your inner mind has experienced the freedom, health and good feelings of your future, it is already doing whatever healthy things it needs to do to get the bedwetting object **and everything it represents**, out of your life in the fastest healthy way possible.

You notice the changes happening and you are overjoyed. Every morning now, you wake up feeling great and ready to go. If you need to wake up at night, you rouse yourself easily. It is as if your bladder has an alarm clock in your brain now. And if your bladder is full and needs emptying, the alarm goes off and wakes you up in plenty of time to get to the toilet. The sphincter muscles for your bladder, the muscles that have to relax so you can pee, are completely tight. Your bladder sphincter muscles can only relax if you are sitting on a toilet or standing in front of a toilet. No matter how much the rest of your body relaxes, your bladder sphincter muscles are completely tight unless you are sitting on a toilet or standing in front of a toilet.

Your subconscious mind studies your rectal sphincter, the muscles you have to relax to poop. You never poop the bed because, no matter how much the rest of your body relaxes, your rectal sphincter muscles never relax unless you are sitting on a toilet. Your subconscious mind now makes your bladder sphincter muscles work just like your rectal sphincter muscles. Your bladder sphincter muscles never relax, and your bladder never empties, unless you are sitting on a toilet or standing in front of a toilet.

 It is so easy to get up at night, empty your bladder in the toilet, return to bed and fall soundly asleep for the rest of the night. Because you have eliminated all the reasons for bedwetting from your mind, along with the problem itself, you find it easy to get up in the night if you have to. You also find that your bladder holds twice as much as it used to all night long.

You never sleep too deeply for your bladder to wake you up. You have an internal alarm that gently, but firmly, wakes you up from even the deepest sleep if your bladder needs to be emptied. The alarm in your brain is connected directly to your bladder and it always wakes you up long before you urinate. When you are asleep at night, your bladder sphincter muscles are tight and sealed. They only relax and let you pee if you are sitting on a toilet, or standing in front of a toilet.

Every time you wake up in the night to go to the bathroom, you feel an incredible sense of happiness because you are a total success. You sleep soundly, but wake up easily when you need to urinate. After you urinate, you fall asleep easily and refresh you body and mind totally with good, deep sleep. And even in your deepest sleep and relaxation, your bladder muscles stay tight and your bladder stays closed. You feel good about yourself... better than ever before. And you feel a deep sense of pride and accomplishment because you are leaving the bedwetting behind you. It is so good to feel your body working at its normal and natural best, just the way it is designed to. It feels so good to know that you are totally leaving the problem in your past. You are happier than ever before. Your family is happier. Everyone who knows about the problem is happy. Just imagine the look on your doctor's face when you say: "I don't have a problem anymore. I used the incredible power of my mind to totally leave that old problem behind me." It feels so good to know that your inner mind is changing your life and solving this old problem so quickly that before you know it, the problem is completely vanished, just like that miserable object you banished from your mind today.

If all these suggestions are acceptable to your mind, you simply keep breathing... just the way you are, and with each and every day, in each and every way, your mind is erasing your bedwetting problem so quickly and completely that it is totally amazing.

You can return to your meadow and your wise future self any time you want, just by listening to this recording, and every time you listen to this recording the changes happen faster and faster. Every time you listen to this recording, all the good ideas for totally leaving bedwetting in your past get stronger and stronger.

High Blood Pressure

This script is a supplement to medical care for hypertension. Hypnosis is always a complement to medical and is NEVER a replacement or substitute for medical care. Use the Feather, Dr. Kresnik or Beach inductions.

As you relax in this calm and beautiful place, every breath you breathe causes you to relax a little deeper. With each exhale, you breathe out stress, tension, worry and anxiety... just letting it go. (*Pause*) With each and every inhale, you breathe in calm, peace and relaxation. (*Pause*) Every breath you breathe causes you to relax a little deeper, and every breath you breathe causes your powerful subconscious mind to reinforce each positive and beneficial idea on this recording.

You find yourself more aware of your breathing these days and every breath causes your mind to magnify and multiply the beneficial suggestions on this tape. Deep, gentle and slow breathing corresponds with states of peaceful relaxation. Even in the middle of work your subconscious mind now focuses on keeping your breathing slow, calm and relaxed... no matter what is happening in your day. Every breath you breathe causes you to be calm and relaxed and every breath causes your mind to reinforce the ideas on this tape.

Whenever you feel any kind of stress, tension or anxiety, your powerful subconscious mind causes you to automatically take several slow deep breaths. And the stress and tension melt away. All the stress and tension flow right out of you and down the drain, leaving you feeling peaceful and calm no matter what is going on in your life. You don't even have to think about it consciously. Your powerful subconscious mind takes over the whole project for you and does whatever it takes to keep you feeling calm and at peace.

High blood pressure is a mistake that the mind and body make. And your brain is now reprogramming your mind and body to maintain your blood pressure within normal levels. Somehow in the past the blood pressure control in your brain got set too high and your mind now sets the control to normal. I want you to imagine a control lever for blood pressure right there in your mind. Imagine yourself pulling that lever down to the middle of it's range and imagine your mind reprogramming your brain so that your blood pressure stays perfectly in the middle... not too high and not too low... but perfect for you. (*Pause 5 seconds to imagine pulling down the lever*)

As you imagine pulling your blood pressure control lever to the perfect healthy middle, I want you to visualize your veins and arteries expanding and relaxing so that the blood can pass through them more easily. Feel your hands, feet and skin tingling and becoming warmer as your blood flow increases. Feel the peaceful sensation of relaxation and peace as your arteries relax and let the blood flow more easily. All the tiny muscles that relax or constrict your blood vessels relax, and your oxygenated blood flows freely to every cell in your body. Every calm, deep breath you breathe causes your blood vessels to expand and relax. Every calm and relaxed breath causes the muscles that control your blood vessels to relax.

As you relax and breathe slowly and peacefully, focus your attention on your heart. Notice that your heartbeat is calm, steady and peaceful. And notice that your heart pumps your blood to every corner of your body easily and effortlessly. Your mind notices how easily your blood flows when you are peaceful and relaxed. And your powerful inner mind does whatever healthy things are necessary to keep your blood pressure in the exact, healthy middle range for you... no matter what is going on in your life. Visualize or imagine your blood flowing in beautiful, calm circles from your heart and lungs outward with fresh oxygen and nutrients. Imagine the blood easily carrying carbon dioxide back to your lungs. Your blood flows in beautiful, quiet circles, bringing every cell nutrients and air, and carrying away waste products.

As your blood travels gently and easily through your kidneys, your kidneys gently clean the blood and leave it fresh and free of waste. You find yourself drinking plenty of water to help your kidneys flush out waste products. You decide to help your kidneys do their job. And you find that you are eating foods that are perfectly in balance with your body's need for salt. If you have been taking in too much salt in the past, your subconscious mind changes your likes and dislikes so that all desire for salty foods fades away.

Similarly, your desire for caffeine and other stimulants decreases. Too much caffeine can make your kidneys work too hard. So your subconscious mind simply changes your taste. You find yourself asking for decaf, or for or herbal teas instead of coffee; and for water, juice and other healthy beverages instead of sodas. All desire for sodas, with their excess sodium, sugar and caffeine, fades away. In every way, your subconscious mind helps you reduce your desire for caffeine and other stimulants.

You limit your consumption of alcohol to no more than the equivalent of 2 glasses of wine per day, simply to give your kidneys and liver every chance to bring your blood pressure down to normal in the shortest time possible.

As you think about your heart and blood vessels, you imagine your entire circulatory system bathed in a beautiful, glowing golden light. That light teaches every cell in your blood vessels how to be relaxed and peaceful. All the stress and tension that is located in those blood vessels just fades away in that beautiful glowing light. Imagine it happening, want it to happen, expect it to happen and feel yourself becoming healthier and calmer with every breath you take. (*Pause 10 seconds*)

Whenever stress and tension build up in your job, or in your life, your subconscious mind causes you to take a few deep, peaceful breaths and the tension melts away. You find that nothing bothers you the way it used to because you have faith in the power of your subconscious mind and soul to help you solve or resolve any problem you face. In fact people are amazed at how genuinely calm and peaceful you are now all the time.

I want you to visualize and imagine your next few visits to the doctor. And I want you to see your doctor's amazement that your blood pressure is staying in the best healthy normal range for you. Imagine your doctor saying "I'm not sure what you are doing, but keep it up because it's working and your blood pressure is doing great."

And what you notice is that you feel wonderful. Your head feels clear and free of stress. You just don't worry about anything as much as you used to. Life has a way of working out, and you find yourself trusting that everything will work out for the best.

You sense a subtle but definite increase in your energy and your sense of wellbeing. You trust that your subconscious mind is doing everything necessary to keep your blood pressure in the perfect normal range for you. You now see situations that used to bother you as opportunities to feel relaxed and in the flow. In every way you feel great... at peace with life and with yourself.

Every positive and beneficial suggestion on this recording serves as a template for your powerful subconscious mind to follow as it does whatever is necessary to keep you healthy and peaceful and to keep your blood pressure in the perfect normal range. Every breath you breathe gives you a feeling of calm, control and harmony. And every breath you breathe causes your powerful subconscious mind to reinforce, multiply and magnify every positive and beneficial idea on this recording.

Just breathe gently and easily for a moment and feel how good it feels to let every peaceful and natural breath magnify and multiply all the wonderful healing ideas on this tape. As you rest in the silence, your blood pressure goes to normal and stays there. (*Pause for one minute, then segue to the awakening sequence*)

Return to my voice now... peaceful, calm and totally refreshed. It is time to return to the surface, bringing all the powerful healing ideas on this recording out with you. You are calm and relaxed no matter what is going on in your life. And your blood pressure is normal and healthy all the time.

Insomnia: Sleep Reprogramming

This script is a supplement and complement to medical care for insomnia. Hypnosis is NEVER a substitute for medical care. In this example, use a beach induction or deepening.

Your beautiful beach is a perfect inner sanctuary... a place where your inner mind can reprogram itself so that you return to the ability you were born with. That ability is your birthright... the ability to sleep fully and naturally each and every night, easily, effortlessly. Your vast inner mind can think thousands of times faster than I can speak, so, as your conscious mind floats on this wonderful beach, your inner mind accepts all the positive and beneficial ideas on this recording. And your vast inner mind races far ahead of me to do every healthy thing necessary inside, so that you sleep deeply, fully and restfully... each and every night. The more you listen to this recording, the more powerfully every breath you breathe restores you to deep, full sleep every night. If you are someone whose shift work means you sleep when other people are awake, your inner mind automatically translates the word "night" to "your normal sleeping hours." You now inform your inner mind of how much you want to sleep deeply and fully each and every night. You now inform your inner mind how much you want the complete rest and recharge that sleeping gives you. And you tell your inner mind all the consequences of not sleeping... Mental confusion, low energy, physical exhaustion, dangerous lack of attention, emotional crankiness, diminished health, and all the other negatives that you want to leave in the past. Take a moment to send all the negative consequences of not sleeping to your deepest inner mind NOW... (*Pause 10 seconds*)

Now, fully and completely share with your inner mind precisely what you want. You want to awaken each day after a full night of deep, refreshing and rejuvenating sleep. You want to fall asleep quickly and effortlessly every night. You wish to awaken every day fully recharged in heart, mind, body and spirit. You want to be energetic, in a great mood, mentally at your sharpest and best. You want to sleep deeply and waken physically energetic and healthy. You want to sleep and be recharged on each and every level. Take another moment and fully show your deep inner mind all the benefits of sleeping fully and soundly every night... (*Pause 10 seconds*)

Your inner mind now accepts your new goal and lets the old, useless pattern of sleeplessness fade forever into the past. A part of your inner mind monitors my words on this recording, and locks every positive and beneficial idea into your deepest mind where it simply becomes the truth for you. The vast majority of your subconscious mind dives deep inside and reprograms everything inside so that you now sleep easily, deeply and fully each and every night.

Because you wish to awaken every day totally recharged and fully refreshed, you now make a practice of taking 5 deep breaths as you settle into bed. And you relax and move quickly into a wonderful sleep. Throughout your sleep hours, you sleep deeply and peacefully as your body and mind totally refresh themselves. As you take the first deep breath after settling into bed, you silently repeat the magic words: "sleep now" to yourself. And as you breathe out and repeat: "sleep now," every muscle in your body relaxes, becoming soft and smooth. As you take your second breath, it is deep, but very gentle, like you are breathing now. You repeat your magic words: "sleep now," and another, even deeper wave of relaxation fills you. As you repeat: "sleep now," each subsequent breath is even more deep, and even more rhythmic and gentle. You are relaxed in body and mind. Your magic words: "sleep now," cause your mind to set aside all worries, stress and tension. Anything truly important will still be there when you wake with lots more energy to deal with them. And all the rest just fade away into nothing.

As you repeat: "sleep now" to yourself with your fifth exhale, you automatically slip into a calm, peaceful and natural sleep. After your fifth exhale, you are so relaxed in body and mind that sleep is the only possible course for your mind and body. You are so relaxed after the fifth repetition of your magical words: "sleep now," that your conscious mind simply drifts off until it is time to awaken. You thoroughly enjoy the state of deep, restful sleep. You have pleasant and meaningful dreams. And you awaken totally recharged and refreshed... strong and healthy. Every time you repeat your magic words: "sleep now," your inner mind totally strengthens and reinforces every good idea on this recording, and totally reinforces your new pattern of deep, effortless, refreshing sleep.
Sleep Now.

If there is an emergency in the night, or if your body has needs, you can trust your powerful inner mind to wake you instantly. And when you have dealt with the emergency, or with your body's needs, you return to bed and return to sleep within 60 seconds, simply by repeating your five deep breaths and magic words, "sleep now." Gently inhale deeply, exhale and repeat the words: "sleep now" with each exhale. And by the fifth exhale, your body and conscious mind are so relaxed that sleep is the only possible course.

Your inner mind now accepts the following truths:
Every human body and brain needs sleep, and everyone is born with a natural ability to sleep. Newborn babies can sleep 20 hours a day through anything. Sleep is natural. We have to learn to not sleep. And anything that can be learned can be unlearned and reprogrammed. Your inner mind studies where you learned not to sleep, and now corrects the errors in the mind that led to not sleeping. If your inner mind needs to heal the past or release fear so that you can sleep normally, your inner mind leads you to heal the past or face and transcend your fears. If you learned not to sleep from other people, your inner mind throws out those worthless lessons and restores you to the natural sleeping pattern you were born with. If there are interfering sounds or light during sleep, your mind now allows you to sleep through them... just like people living near railroad tracks effortlessly sleep through trains passing by. If your sleep has been blocked by worries and concerns, your inner mind creates a shelf for worries and concerns. As you go to bed, your inner mind automatically puts all worries and concerns on the shelf and out of your conscious mind. Any important worries will still be on the shelf for your conscious mind to deal with in the morning, when you are fully recharged. The rest simply fade into nothing as you sleep.

As you sleep, you are blanketed with a protective shield of beautiful, subtle light that has all the colors of the rainbow. As I go through the colors, your inner mind builds this protective shield for you, and you rest every night knowing that you are held in the arms of a loving and creative soul that keeps you safe and well as your mind and body totally recharge themselves.

Red is the light of life and energy, the light of refueling and re-energizing every fiber, cell and tissue of your body... red surrounds you with energy... sleep now.

Orange is the color of connection, healing and rejuvenation... orange light fills your shield, rejuvenating you in every way... sleep now.

The beautiful yellow of choice and will flow over you... filling your shield... you are choosing the path of highest health and good... sleep now.

Green, the color of growth and love... your heart fills with compassion and forgiveness as you sleep... old hurts heal and fade away... sleep now.

The wonderful blue of communication swirls through you and around you... you sleep so deeply, so wonderfully that your communications are twice as meaningful as before... sleep now.

The color of heaven, of infinite mind and thinking, purple, fills your shield and flows through every fiber, cell and tissue, and your thinking is so refreshed and clear... sleep now.

The colors swirl together, over you, around you, through you... merging into the white light of universal good, infinite love... guarding, protecting, sealing you into a deep and refreshing sleep... Now

As the shield of light surrounds you, it locks in and becomes permanent. It is always there when you sleep. Just rest and enjoy your beautiful beach as your inner mind locks your shield into place.

Now it is time to practice. If you want to get up after using this recording, then the next 200 words you hear cause you to gently and slowly rise to the surface knowing that your inner mind is totally reprogramming you to sleep soundly and deeply every night.

If you are using this recording to help you go to sleep, my voice leads you into sleep, and you allow your recorder to simply shut itself off as you drift into sleep... even the sound of the machine turning off causes you to sleep twice as soundly.

Take in a gentle, but deep breath... and as you gently let it out, repeat your magic words: "sleep now" silently inside... as you do your body and mind relax ten times deeper.

Take in a second deep breath... let it go so gently... sleep now... relaxing deeper again

Another deep breath... sleep now... so calm and relaxed

Breathe in.... let it out... sleep now... every breath carries you deeper

In with the air... sleep now... sleep... sleep... sleeping

The recorder takes care of itself, and you sleep, dreaming, sleeping, deeper, sleeping

As your recorder turns itself off, the little click of the machine causes you to sleep even more deeply.

Sleep now... sleep now... sleep now... sleeping now... sleeping now.... sleeping

(*Let the volume of your voice fade over the last line, and if you use music, gently fade it to zero over the last 15 seconds. If you want to wake up after using the recording, pause for one minute and then move into the awakening sequence.*)

Return to the surface now, knowing that your mind has been totally reprogrammed for deep, full and refreshing sleep every night. The more you listen to this recording, the deeper and more fully you sleep. And every minute of sleep recharges you fully, heart mind and body.

Insomnia: Sleep Now

This script is a supplement and complement to medical care for insomnia. Hypnosis is NEVER a substitute for medical care. Use any induction, and a deepening. This script is meant to lead you into sleep, so do not record an awakening sequence. Use a Beach induction, or Dr. Kresnik's induction and a deepening.

As you relax so incredibly deeply, you feel a wave of confidence because you recognize that deep relaxation is a prelude to great sleep. You inform your powerful inner mind how much you long for regular deep and restful sleep... for a full night's sleep. And as you listen to this recording, every word on the recording causes your powerful inner mind to do whatever healthy things it takes for you to achieve your goal of sleeping naturally and effortlessly and waking each day fully refreshed and rejuvenated. As you breathe, every breath is a signal for your inner mind to magnify and reinforce every positive idea on this recording.

You again inform your inner mind of your goal. That goal is to sleep deeply and be fully refreshed in your normal sleeping times, and to be awake and totally refreshed and energized the rest of the time. Your inner mind listens to this recording and implements the ideas here effortlessly and easily.

The first new idea that your inner mind implements is this: from this day forward, you never **try** to go to sleep. Sleep is natural. All beings sleep. But human beings are the only beings who have difficulty sleeping. And that is because we get confused and **try** to sleep. Trying requires effort. And making an effort causes us to wake up. So from this day onward, you refuse to **try** to sleep. Instead, you allow yourself to easily flow into the gentle and natural sleep that is your birthright. In fact, when you totally relax, and **let** yourself sleep, it happens so naturally and quickly it is amazing. In fact after the first few times you use this recording, you don't even hear the end of it any more because you are already deeply asleep. At bedtime, just hearing the first few words in my voice causes you to sleep deeply. At bedtime, even remembering the sound of my voice causes your inner mind to magnify all the ideas on this recording and lead you rapidly into a deep, refreshing sleep.

Imagine a beautiful garden, the safest and most pleasant place you can imagine. Sense it, feel it. Notice the colors of the sky and flowers. Feel the warmth of the sun on a perfect late spring day. Imagine the feeling of a light breeze refreshing you. Notice the wonderful aroma of the roses and other flowers filling the air. Be aware of the trees swaying gently with the breeze. There is a hammock under the trees. Imagine yourself rocking gently in the hammock, watching the clouds flowing across the sky. It is so wonderful here.

Perhaps sometime, a long time ago, a part of you became afraid to sleep. And you learned, like a soldier in a war zone, to make extra efforts to stay awake and alert. And at the time, this pattern of avoiding sleep may have been useful to you. It may even have saved your life. But all that is in the past. And you are now letting the past fade into the past and set you free. What was a useful pattern at the time is now hurting you. I want you to imagine your past self, the part of you who learned not to sleep. Picture your sleepless, frightened past self, and invite your past self into the garden. Thank the part of you that has been forcing you to stay awake, because that part of you was trying to help in the past. But also let your sleepless self see that the old pattern is now more harmful than helpful. Show your past self how the pattern of not sleeping is detracting from your ability to function. Show you sleepless self how it is negatively effecting your energy levels, your mood and even your health. Then move your past self into the garden. Every part of you is totally safe here. So you let your past self feel how good it feels to be relaxed. All the fear drains away, as your past self realizes that you have grown far beyond the old days. And that you are totally capable of keeping yourself safe and healthy. And your past self now realizes that helping you get deep, regular sleep is the most important thing it can do to protect you and help you thrive. The old pattern fades away. And every part of you is now ready for you to sleep deeply and soundly.

Let's move into sleep now. It is literally as simple as falling off a log. Place your attention on your deep gentle breathing. And notice how smooth, rhythmic and relaxed it has become. Sleep now.

Feel the way your abdomen rises and falls as you breathe slowly and deeply. Sleep now. Let all the points of tension dissolve totally into the rhythm of your breathing. Sleep now.

Now imagine how your breath is sending oxygenated blood from your lungs all through your body. Your blood carries the oxygen and nutrients your cells need to rebuild, refuel and repair damage. The deeper you relax and sleep, the healthier you are. Feel and imagine this rich, aerated blood flowing from your lungs and heart down to the center of your body. Feel and imagine it reaching the base of the spine with a warming and refreshing wash of goodness. Feel the oxygen and recharging sensation rising up your spine like mercury in a thermometer. Imagine and feel it flowing all the way to the top of your head and down through your brain like a gentle creek... washing away stress, tension, worries, and problems. Washing away every point of tension and every distraction. Washing it out of your brain. And letting your mind and brain just sway gently in your garden hammock... totally at rest.

With every breath you take, and with each beat of your heart, you feel more at peace and more relaxed. You are feeling totally loose and limp... perfectly at peace. As you continue to breathe, you notice the comfort and peace filling your entire body. And you notice the how the tension is simply draining out of every bit of your body and flowing away. You feel so good, because you know you are reaching your goal. It may even be difficult to consciously keep track of my words because your conscious mind is letting itself sleep while the inner mind takes over and recharges and refreshes every fiber, cell and tissue of your being... Sleep now. All negative thoughts flow away, just going... going... gone... Sleep now. All unwanted tension or worry is being dissolved like sugar in a cup of coffee... Sleep now. Watch it disappear, feel it disappear. And with each relaxing breath, you know that you are now and forever a natural healthy sleeper. Your mind's new mantra is: "I fall asleep effortlessly. I sleep fully and deeply. I wake up fully rested every day"... "I fall asleep effortlessly. I sleep fully and deeply. I wake up fully rested every day"... Want it to happen, expect it to happen, feel it happening NOW. Sleep now.

Each moment of relaxing leads you into a deeper and deeper relaxation in the next moment. Feeling so relaxed, so calm, so peaceful. There is nothing to do. Just relax and let your inner mind and body carry you away into the arms of the deepest and most refreshing sleep you know. Sleep now.

Rest NOW, letting it happen.
Sleep NOW, so softly, joyfully, peacefully, at rest
Sleeping now, sleeping so deeply

Deep Sleep, in the arms of your deepest mind
Gentle Sleep
Being still, and sleep... sleep... sleeping... sleep now
Calm Sleep now
Drifting and floating, swirling deeply into sleep
Refreshing, restoring, rejuvenating... sleep now
Deep Sleep... Deeper... Still Deeper... and even deeper sleep
Sleep now
Sleep

The sound of the my voice lulls you into a deeper and more relaxed sleep...
The sound of your recording automatically shutting off is a signal for your mind to double your state of deep restful sleep... sleep now
Every breath you breathe causes you to sleep deeply and fully, naturally and effortlessly... sleep now
Sleep now, deeply asleep
Sleep the whole night through... Sleep... sleep... sleep now

(Let your voice grow softer over the last 3 paragraphs, and fade almost to nothing in the final paragraph. If you use a music background, fade it down to very soft as well to the end of the recording.)

Reverse Diabetes Now 1: Fork in the Road

This script is one of three written as part of a comprehensive effort by a group of holistic health practitioners to address the growing epidemic of Type 2 diabetes. The Virtual Gastric Bypass weight reduction script above is actually part of this series too. Diabetes is a medical problem and absolutely must be treated by health care professionals. These three scripts are meant to be used as complements to medical care. **NEVER, EVER** *use these recordings* **in place** *of medical care. Use any induction, and use a deepening as well. The Kresnik induction, combined with the feather deepening is one of my preferred combinations to achieve a deep hypnotic state.*

As you allow yourself to float and drift into a deep and mentally receptive state, every breath you take causes you to relax more deeply, and every breath you take causes your powerful inner mind to be receptive to, and to act upon every positive and beneficial idea on the recording.

You have chosen a positive new path, the path of health and wellbeing. You have chosen the path of freedom from diabetes. Your inner mind is now aligning with your goal of returning to total health. And you are aware that you are embarking on an exciting series of changes in your desires, appetites and behaviors. You now inform your subconscious mind of your overwhelming desire to leave diabetes and all its complications and causes in your past, and to return to radiant and vibrant health.

Reversing diabetes and pre-diabetes requires you to make major changes in lifestyle. You now inform your inner mind that you are so excited about returning to full health that you are totally willing to make major changes in your life. These changes include changes in your relationship to food, changes in your relationship to exercise, changes in attitudes, changes in your behavior, and developing a new relationship with yourself. In the past, you may have relied solely on medications to control the symptoms of diabetes. Now you are harnessing all the power of your mind, heart and spirit to cooperate with your doctors to reverse the disease itself. And because you are so ready to be healthy, you let your inner mind know that you are totally willing to make major changes in your life. And because your powerful subconscious mind can think a thousand time faster than your conscious mind, every time you listen to any of your reversing diabetes recordings, your inner mind races far ahead of the recording to study and understand your condition thoroughly and to make every mental and emotional change necessary for you to achieve total and radiant health. Every time you hear my voice on these recordings, your inner mind receives and accepts every positive and beneficial suggestion on each one of the recordings and magnifies those positive suggestions over and over until they are totally true for you.

You are at a fork in the road of your life. One fork of the road is that you continue doing exactly what you have always done, and make no changes. Choosing that fork in the road means that your disease continues and gets worse and worse with time. If you send your imagination even a little way down that diabetes fork in the road, you see the consequences of diabetes getting more and more severe, and you see your life shortened and limited in so many ways. The diabetes road is the road of constant hassle, struggle, pain, weakness, blindness, amputation and early death.

The other fork in the road is the healthy road of total health and wellbeing. Choosing that fork means that you make every change necessary to return yourself to a full and healthy life… a long and abundantly active and healthy life.

Send your imagination forward on the healthy road. Your subconscious mind exists in the past, and in the future, as well as in the now. So by sending your imagination up the healthy road, you are literally time traveling into your healthiest possible future. Just a little way up the healthy road you see a radiant figure. It is your healthy future self, coming forward to meet you and guide you on the road of total health.

The first thing you notice about your healthy future self is that you are strong, slender and active. Your future self is the part of you that knows exactly what changes you have to make to achieve total health. Your future self shows you how good it feels to be at an ideal and optimal weight, and to use your body as it was meant to be used … strong, flexible and active. You open your heart and let your future self fill you with all the good feelings of being active, strong and healthy. Your subconscious mind fills with the feeling of total health. And your powerful subconscious mind begins making whatever changes it needs to make NOW, so that you achieve that total state of health in the fastest possible way.

You ask your future self what your blood sugar numbers are and your future self shows you that your blood sugar stays at 100 or lower 90% of the time. You feel a vast wave of pride that your blood sugar levels are normal, just a little way in your own future. And your subconscious mind accepts that feeling of pride and makes achieving normal blood sugar levels its goal. And your vast subconscious mind makes whatever changes are necessary so that feeling of pride is permanently yours... starting right NOW.

Your healthy future self shows you your A1c levels. And your pride in yourself increases hundreds of times over as you see that your A1c levels are normal... at 5.5 or lower... just a little way in your future. And your subconscious mind does every healthy thing necessary to bring you those normal A1c levels ... starting RIGHT NOW.

You realize that your healthy future self enjoys great vision, abundant energy, unlimited strength and incredible endurance. Your future self has a strong heart, perfect kidneys, a healthy pancreas, a sharp mind, perfect circulation and in every way enjoys radiant and vibrant health. You watch as your future self leaves sickness and weakness in the past and returns to astounding health. If you have children or grandchildren, you are amazed and gratified that your future self can be an important part of their lives. And your vast subconscious mind is making all the changes necessary for you to enjoy that perfect state of health... beginning right now.

So what are these changes? Some of them may include changing your relationship with food. Your future self knows that food is fuel for your body and nothing else. If you have used food in the past to as comfort, or to deal with emotions like sadness or grief, anger or pain, you throw the old relationship away and realize that food is fuel for your body and nothing else.

If you have eaten sweet, starchy and fatty foods because there is not enough sweetness in your life, you find healthy ways to make life sweeter, and all desire white, sweet, salty and greasy foods fades away. You replace junk food with healthy and nutritious food. And you only want to eat what your body needs for fuel. All desire for junk food fades away and you learn what real food tastes like, and how it makes your body feel so good. Your subconscious mind changes all your inner beliefs and attitudes about food so that you only want the kind and amount of food your body needs for fuel. Food is fuel for your body and nothing else. You crave foods with a low glycemic index: fresh greens, fresh vegetables, lean proteins, fresh fruits and whole grains. Sodas, even the zero calorie kind, are poisons, and all desire for sodas fades away. Saturated and trans fats are poisons for your heart and pancreas, and they encourage obesity. So your desire for saturated and trans fats fades away to nothing.

If you have been inactive, or even a couch potato, you now adapt a new attitude. Human bodies are designed to move and they can only be healthy when they get lots of movement. You adapt a whole new attitude. Your body is your most precious possession, and you give it lots of exercise and movement so that it can be totally healthy.

Because you eat a healthy diet, your cells are more receptive to insulin. Because you choose to eliminate bleached white flour and white sugar from your diet, your pancreas is healthy and produces all the insulin you need.

You learn about supplements such as chromium, gymnema, tumeric, CoQ10, B complex vitamins, prickly pear cactus and vitamin D that can help reduce inflammation and return your metabolism to normal. Your subconscious mind guides you to find the supplements that are right for you.

Your future self now begins to tell you about other specific changes that are important for you in your quest to reverse diabetes and return to total health. I am going to be silent for a few moments, and in that silent time, your healthy future self tells your conscious and subconscious minds what they most need to hear NOW so that your body can return to full and radiant health in the fastest time possible. That moment of silence for you to listen to your healthy future self begins NOW.

Pause 30 seconds

Return to my voice now, knowing that you inner mind has listened deeply to you healthy future self, and your inner mind is making whatever changes are necessary in your thoughts, feelings, attitudes and behaviors so that you achieve your new state of abundant and radiant health in the fastest healthy way possible. Every time you listen to this recording, these ideas become stronger and stronger. And you find yourself returning to total and perfect health effortlessly and easily. Your life is totally new.

Your attitudes, thoughts, beliefs and behaviors are all totally renewed. And you are healthier and healthier with every passing day.

Reverse Diabetes Now 2: Circles of Truth

This script is one of three written as part of a comprehensive effort by a group of holistic health practitioners to address the growing epidemic of Type 2 diabetes. Diabetes is a medical problem and absolutely must be treated by health care professionals. These three scripts are meant to be used as complements to medical care. **NEVER, EVER** *use these recordings in place of medical care. Use any induction, and use a deepening as well. The Kresnik induction, combined with the feather deepening is one of my preferred combinations to achieve a deep hypnotic state.*

Continue breathing gently and easily, and every breath you breathe causes you to relax more deeply. As you relax, your powerful inner mind is more and more open to, and accepting of every positive and beneficial idea on this recording. Every time you listen to any of your self-hypnosis and relaxation recordings, your inner mind multiplies and magnifies all the good ideas on your recordings over and over until they are totally true for you. And each breath you breathe causes your vast inner mind to magnify and totally reinforce all the positive suggestions on your recordings.

You have chosen the path of total health and of returning your body to radiant and vibrant wellbeing... totally free of the hassle, harm and sickness of diabetes. You have chosen to make whatever changes in your attitude, beliefs, thoughts and feelings are necessary for you to achieve your goal of total, radiant health and wellbeing.

You are making positive changes in diet and exercise, and positive changes in your attitudes about life, so that you effortlessly achieve radiant health. Your inner mind is automating the entire process and making the changes without you having to spend much time at all thinking about them consciously.

And because you are making positive changes in your thoughts, attitudes, feelings and behaviors, you are becoming healthier in every possible way. And because you are willing to make profound and powerful changes in your life, there are some amazing new truths operating in your life. In fact there are two new circles of truth that your subconscious mind totally accepts and is putting into operation in every phase of your life. Every time I repeat one of your new truths, your inner mind magnifies and strengthens the entire circle of truth over and over and millions of times over so that your inner mind totally accepts your new truths and puts them into operation. And every breath you breathe makes each individual truth and your circles of truth stronger, and stronger and millions of times stronger.

Your first new circle of truth is made up of four individual truths, and every time I repeat a truth it causes your inner mind to make the entire circle stronger. You hear each truth in your own voice, because they are your new truths.

The first truth in your first circle of truth is this:
My appetite exactly matches my body's need for fuel. My appetite exactly matches my body's need for fuel. I only want the food my body needs of fuel. My appetite exactly matches my body's need for fuel.

And because my appetite exactly matches my body's need for fuel, that leads to my second new truth in the circle:
Because my appetite is in total harmony with my body's need for fuel, I am eating less food, and better food and enjoying my food a thousand times more. Food is fuel for my body and nothing else, so I am now eating less food and better food and enjoying it a thousand times more.

That leads to the third new truth in my circle:
 Because I am eating less food and better food, my body burns off excess fat and converts it to fuel. My body burns off excess fat and converts it to fuel. I have a lean, fat-burning body. My body burns off excess fat and converts it to fuel.

Which leads to the fourth and final new truth in my first circle of truth.
Because my body burns off excess fat and converts it to fuel, my body is more slender and lighter every week. My body is lighter and more slender each and every week. I love my strong, healthy slender new body. My body is lighter and more slender every week.

And it is a circle of truth, because the fourth new truth leads back to the first one.
Because I love my new lighter, more slender body, my inner mind makes my appetite even more perfectly in balance with my body's need for fuel.

My entire first circle new truth sounds like this:
My appetite perfectly matches my body's need for fuel
I am eating less food, and better food and enjoying it a thousand times more
My body is burning off excess fat and converting it to fuel
My body is lighter and more slender every week
And because I love my lighter, more slender body, my appetite even more perfectly matches my body's need for fuel.

And every breath you breathe causes your inner mind to magnify and reinforce your first circle of truth until it is totally true for you.

Your second new circle of truth also contains four individual truths. And every time I repeat one of the individual truths, your inner mind strengthens and reinforces the entire circle over and over and millions of times over until the entire circle is completely true for you. And every breath you breathe reinforces both of your new circles of truth over and over and millions of time over until they are totally true for you. The truths in the second circle are true for you because the truths in the first circle are true and vice versa. Each circle of truth leads to and reinforces the other.

The first new individual truth in my second circle of truth is this:
I am much healthier and my stress and stress hormone levels are much lower. I am much healthier now and my stress and stress hormone levels are much lower. I am so happy with my new healthy body that my stress and stress hormone levels are dropping dramatically. My stress and stress hormone levels are much lower.

And that leads to my second new truth.
Because my stress and stress hormone levels are much lower, my inflammation levels are dramatically reduced. My inflammation levels are dramatically reduced. My body is becoming remarkably free of inflammation. My inflammation levels are dramatically reduced.

Which leads to my third new truth in the second circle.
Because my inflammation levels are dramatically reduced, my blood sugar is stable at 100 or less. My blood sugar levels are stable at 100 or less. I have the blood sugar levels of a healthy, normal person. My blood sugar

levels are stable at 100 or less.

And that leads to my fourth truth in the second circle.
Because my blood sugar levels are stable at 100 or less, diabetes is locked in my past. Diabetes is locked in my past. Diabetes has totally vanished from my present and future. Diabetes is forever locked in my past.

And since diabetes is locked in my past, I am much healthier and my stress levels are lower and lower, and it is a complete circle of truth that gets stronger and stronger with every breath I breathe.

My entire second circle of truth sounds like this:
I am healthier and my stress and stress hormone levels are much lower
My inflammation levels are dramatically reduced
My blood sugar levels are stable at 100 or lower
Diabetes is locked in my past
I am healthier and my stress and stress hormone levels are much lower

Now take a few moments to focus on your breathing. Notice that each breath is a circle. You breathe in, and the air circulates through your lungs, exchanging oxygen and carbon dioxide in trillions of individual circles. Then you exhale and circulate the breath back out. And then you inhale again, starting the circle of breath over. And because your breathing is a circular activity, every breath you breathe causes your inner mind to automatically repeat, magnify and multiply every one of your individual new truths. And every breath magnifies both of your circles of truth over and over and over. Every inhale and every exhale... every breath you breathe... causes your inner mind to reinforce and magnify both new circles of truth over and over and trillions of times over until they are the total truth in your life.

Now just continue breathing, knowing that each breath causes your inner mind to reinforce both circles of truth over and over, making them totally true for you, and your inner mind is doing all the work, you don't even consciously have to think about it. Your inner mind is taking over the entire job for you. Listen to your circles of truth one more time as you vast inner mind makes them millions of times stronger.

Circle 1
My appetite perfectly matches my body's need for fuel

I am eating less food, and better food and enjoying it a thousand times more
My body is burning off excess fat and converting it to fuel
My body is lighter and more slender every week
And because I love my lighter, more slender body, my appetite even more perfectly matches my body's need for fuel.

Circle 2
I am healthier and my stress and stress hormone levels are much lower
My inflammation levels are dramatically reduced
My blood sugar levels are stable at 100 or lower
Diabetes is locked in my past
I am healthier and my stress and stress hormone levels are much lower

And now it is time to return to the surface of the mind, knowing that your vast and amazing subconscious mind is taking over this entire process for you. And you are adopting your new circles of truth so completely that they become totally true for you and you are amazed and gratified at how quickly you are returning to radiant and vibrant health. Every time you listen to this recording, every positive and beneficial suggestion locks into your mind and becomes the total truth for you.

Reverse Diabetes Now 3: Appetite Control Room Metaphor

*This script is one of three written as part of a comprehensive effort by a group of holistic health practitioners to address the growing epidemic of Type 2 diabetes. Diabetes is a medical problem and absolutely must be treated by health care professionals. These three scripts are meant to be used as complements to medical care. **NEVER, EVER** use these recordings in place of medical care. Use any induction, and use a deepening as well. The Kresnick induction, combined with the feather deepening is one of my preferred combinations to achieve a deep hypnotic state.*

As you gently continue listening to my voice, every breath you breathe causes you to relax more deeply. And every breath causes your mind to be more and more open to, and receptive of, every positive and beneficial idea on this recording. And every beat of your heart is a signal for your inner mind to magnify and multiply the ideas in this recording and make them true for you. Every word on this recording causes your subconscious mind to go deeply within and do every healthy thing necessary for you to achieve your goals of reversing diabetes and returning to your birthright of full and vibrant health.

As you float and drift, imagine or picture the control room of your body and mind. It may look much like the cockpit of a jet airplane, only much larger and a thousand times more complex. Your mind's control room is filled with lights, levers, buttons, dials, screens, computers and control apparatus of every kind. All of your mind and body's functions can be moderated and controlled from this center.

The first thing you notice is that every control has a set of indicator lights. Green lights indicate that a body part or function is operating normally. Red lights indicate that the mental or physical part or function is not operating in a normal or healthy manner. You see many, many green lights and a few red lights in your control room. This indicates that most of your mental and physical systems are operating in a healthy way. But some are operating in not so healthy ways.

You also notice that the autopilot light is on. Your mind and body keep doing the same things over and over, even when the functions are out of balance, because your mental controls are on autopilot. So the first thing you do in your inner control room is turn off the autopilot so that you can adjust and change the controls.

You begin with the controls for your appetite. You see several red lights over the appetite controls. Perhaps your desire for food is bigger than your body's need for fuel. Perhaps your appetite for sweets, starches and fats far exceeds your body's need for such high-energy fuels. Perhaps your appetite for healthy vegetables, fruits, whole grains and lean proteins is too small to give your body what it needs. Perhaps your desire to eat is driven by emotions rather that what your body actually needs. You remember that food is fuel for your body and nothing else. Your appetite is working normally when your desire to eat exactly matches your body's need for fuel. You don't have to consciously know what each red light means. Your vast subconscious mind knows exactly what each light and each control means.

Everywhere you see a red light in your appetite control area, you find the attached control, whether it is a lever, a switch or a computer. And you begin adjusting the controls until all the red lights turn to green. You are giving your subconscious mind instructions to make any changes necessary in your appetite until your desire to eat exactly matches what your body needs. You only want the kinds of foods and the amounts of foods that your body needs to be maximally healthy, and your inner mind changes every part of your appetite so that it happens effortlessly and automatically. If, in the past, you have been hungry for too much food, your inner mind adjusts your thinking so that you are only hungry for the amount of food your body actually needs. If, in the past, you have had strong desires for sweet, starchy or fatty foods, your powerful inner mind changes your perceptions so that all desire for sweet, starches or fatty foods fades away. And you find yourself craving whole grains, lean proteins and fresh fruits and vegetable.

If, in the past, you have gobbled your food, your inner mind slows your eating so that you truly taste and enjoy your food. You eat much less, but enjoy it a hundred times more. You truly enjoy the taste of whole, fresh and unprocessed foods. Your mind totally rejects products made with bleached white flour and white sugar. White flour tastes like wallboard paste and white sugar is annoyingly too sweet for you. Your inner mind changes your taste so that you truly enjoy the complex and deep flavors of whole natural foods. As you adjust your appetite controls, your desire to eat comes into perfect balance with your body's need for fuel. The basic truth is that food is fuel for your body and not another thing else.

If, in the past, you have eaten food at restaurants, or eaten foods prepared by others who have no concern for your body's actual needs, you find ways to creatively order healthy foods when you eat out. And you practice making your actual needs known to those who prepare your food. You simply refuse to eat foods that do not meet your body's needs. Your subconscious mind knows exactly what your body needs. And all desire for any other foods fades away. As you continue to adjust the appetite controls, the red lights turn green. And your inner mind helps you assert complete control over what you eat. You only allow foods in your body if they supply the fuel your body wants and needs. You simply refuse to eat what your body does not need. Once you have eaten what your body needs, all desire to eat anything else fades away and you totally reject excess food or nutritionally empty calories.

As you adjust your appetite controls, and as the red lights turn green, your inner mind realizes that food is fuel for your body and nothing else. If, in the past, you have eaten for emotional reasons, your inner mind now realizes that food cannot fix boredom, pain, loneliness, fear, anger, resentment or any other emotion. Food is only fuel for your body and nothing else. Eating for any other reason damages your body. And as you adjust the appetite levers, all desire to eat emotionally fades away. Your conscious and subconscious mind find new, creative ways to reduce stress and control emotions... including self-hypnosis, listening to relaxation recordings, and forgiving the injuries of the past.

As you adjust your controls, and as the red lights turn green, all desire for soda pops, including the low calorie kind, fades away to nothing. The sugars and artificial sweeteners in sodas, and the phosphoric acids, are poisons for your body. All desire to consume poisons disappears. You find yourself attracted to water, juices and teas or coffee, or beverages sweetened with stevia, agave or a tiny bit of honey. All desire for alcoholic beverages fades to nearly zero. Alcohol is a poison as well as being empty calories, and your appetite changes so that you no longer want to swallow poison.

It takes great courage to let yourself make changes in your appetite. It takes courage to replace emotional eating with eating based on what your body needs. And you are a far stronger and more courageous person than you have ever given yourself credit for being. You have the courage you need to achieve your goal of reversing diabetes and returning to full and abundant health. Changing your appetite requires the courage to make major changes in your diet. Getting white sugar, white flour, sodas, and other refined, nutritionally empty poisons out of your body requires courage and the attitude of an explorer. And you have that courageous new attitude! You are willing to explore and make any changes necessary to free yourself from the scourge and disaster of diabetes. You are totally determined to make whatever changes are necessary to return to total health. Changing everything about your appetite, so that food is fuel for your body and nothing else, is the first and most important step in setting you free of this horrible and nasty disease. As you adjust all the controls in your appetite control area, all the red lights change to green. You don't even have to know consciously what each lever or dial or switch actually controls... your subconscious mind knows. All you have to know is that you are giving your inner mind instructions to change everything about your appetite so that food is fuel for your body and nothing else. And everything changes so that you only want the kinds of food and the amounts of food that lead you back to total and radiant health.

Your control room is vast, but working with the appetite control center is the most important first step in reversing diabetes. You find yourself automatically exploring new, and healthier food. You find yourself automatically eliminating poisons and nutritionally empty calories from your diet. You are eating less, eating better, and enjoying it a thousand times more. And it is all happening automatically, as your subconscious mind makes all the changes inside necessary to return you to vibrant and radiant health.

You totally enjoy the changes happening within you. Once all the red lights in the appetite control center have been set to green, you turn the autopilot back on so that all the positive changes lock into place.

As your appetite changes, your body changes. Your weight begins to reduce as you eat more healthily. Your blood sugars stabilize and normalize, as food becomes fuel for your body and nothing else. You find new and creative ways to reduce stress and heal the past. And in each and every day you become healthier and stronger. You are amazed and your doctors are gratified as your new appetite totally changes the way you eat, the amount you eat, and the kinds of food you eat. In each and every day, you are growing stronger and healthier. As you rise up to the surface now, your inner mind continues making every healthy change necessary in your appetite and thinking so that you reestablish a healthy relationship with natural and nutritious food and courageously lead yourself back to total health. Every time you listen to this recording, all the beneficial and positive ideas get stronger and stronger. And your inner mind totally takes over. The changes happen automatically and you don't even have to consciously think about them. In each and every day, you are stronger and healthier in each and every way.

MISCELLANEOUS SCRIPTS

Manifesting Abundance

Use any induction and/or deepening that appeals to you. This script accompanies the Creating Abundance *script in* Unlocking the Blueprint of the Psyche.

As you relax more deeply, every breath causes your powerful inner mind to absorb and implement all the positive ideas for manifesting abundance on this recording. And your inner mind races far ahead to remove any obstacles to your abundance, and to unify your mind in focusing on the rich and abundant life that is your birthright.

Manifesting abundance is a process of uniting your inner and outer mind together with the mind of God as a whole, and allowing the energy of God to create and bring into reality that which you most desire. Many traditions teach this method. But most of them forget that the outer mind and inner mind must be in agreement and harmony about what you truly want in order for it to manifest.

The first step to creating an abundant life, filled with what makes you happy, is to unite your entire mind in the memory that you are an expression of God... a direct expression of divine and universal spiritual energy currently expressing through your mind and body, as you, on this physical plane. Most of our traditions teach us that we are separate from God. But the truth is that we are part of God. We are beings of infinite spirit, enjoying and learning in a physical life, body and mind. You are a child of God, and never separate from God and your own soul, which is a part of God.

Allow yourself to picture imagine your aura... the beautiful energy field that extends all around and through your body. Many people can actually see auras. Many others feel the energy around living things. Some even hear the beautiful tones of the human aura. Imagine that wonderful energy field in your own way... see it... feel it... hear it... imagine it... This is the pure energy of divinity dwelling within you. Your aura is the creative energy of the Universe sustaining every creative moment of your life. Feel the harmony of the energy. Let it fill you, lighten you and enlighten you as you remember that you are a child of God and expression of God. Feel every part of yourself, conscious and subconscious alike, dwell and revel in that energy... aligning with the energy... being the energy.

And as you feel the energy of your spirit fill you, you realize that you are endless and infinite, and connected to everything. Now repeat to yourself: "I am God in physical expression... (*Pause*)... God is being me, now... (*Pause*)... I am filled with a calm and deep feeling of infinite love and possibility... (*Pause*)... And as an expression of God, I have the divine right to manifest my heart's desires... (*Pause*)... I choose to exercise this power rightly and wisely."

Now imagine what will make you happy. Imagine the desire of your heart. The creative power of God will always answer yes to your desires,. And since you have chosen to use your creative power wisely, you always ask for what you desire in the context of benefitting all life, and harming none. You imagine your heart's desire. And you always leave it up to God to create exactly what you ask for, or to create something even better that harms no one, and benefits all beings including you. In this way, only positive karma attaches to your soul through the act of creation.

Imagine what you wish to have, to do or to be fully and totally. Ask if there is any part of your subconscious mind that objects to you attaining your heart's desires... the things that create happiness for you... the things that bring you rich and abundant experiences that enrich your life in every way. If some part of your inner mind objects to you achieving your heart's desire, dialog and negotiate with that part of your mind to find a solution that benefits all of you. Let the energy of your spiritual self penetrate every deepest corner of your mind, bringing every part of your mind into harmony. Take a moment to clearly imagine... sense, see, feel or hear... your heart's desire now, and to put it into words... *Pause 15 seconds*

Now remember that you live in an abundant, infinite and creative universe that is an expression of God. And remember that you are part of that wholeness of creation, and part of the creator. In that context, speaking to God as a whole and to God within you, say: I choose this, my hearts desire. Show God your heart's desire NOW... Imagine writing on the blackboard of your mind the words, "I choose", followed by your heart's desire. See yourself write your choice. Hear yourself repeat your desire. And feel yourself holding your heart's deepest desire in your hands... *Pause 15 seconds*

Now imagine yourself having, doing or being what you have chosen. Imagine having already attained the deepest, most abundant desires of your heart and mind for what makes your life rich and abundant. See yourself attaining your goal... Hear the story of your life with your deepest desire met... Feel your heart fill with the joy of your rich and abundant life. Imagine attaining your heart's desire so vividly that is as if you have already attained it. Take joy in the feelings, and magnify them a thousand times NOW! (*Pause 10 seconds*)

Realize that you are a child of God in an abundant universe, and that God always says yes to God. Imagine attaining your heart's desire again, so incredibly vividly that you can see it, feel it, hear it, and even taste it as if you already have it NOW. And give every part of your subconscious mind the instruction to align itself with an infinite and generous creator to make these incredible feelings of abundance, joy and freedom yours in the fastest possible way. God is not bound by time. Your deepest mind spans all time. Once your unified mind has imagined your heart's desire, and you have created the feeling of attaining it, your unified consciousness opens to God and your heart's desire becomes real for you. And it appears in your life in an astoundingly short time.

Return to the presence within... return to the spiritual presence that is always shining into your body and mind through your aura. Imagine your aura beginning to glow with the creative power of the entire universe, the entire presence of God. (*Pause*) Your aura begins to glow and vibrate as if it were a 50 million watt light... as if it were a stream of water bigger than the Amazon... as if it were a tune of amazing grace and power. And you know that energy is a magnet, drawing your heart's desire perfectly and fully toward you. Your entire mind, conscious and subconscious alike, is coalescing in harmony with the mind of God to bring you the abundant life and rich experiences that are your dreams.

Know that the entire creative power of the Universe is pouring through you to create your dreams. And remember that you are always open for God to bring you what you have asked for, or something even better that harms no one and benefits all. One of the wisest people who ever lived, Socrates, had a special prayer for manifesting that captures the essence of your trust in God to bring you the very best. Every part of your mind hears and integrates Socrates prayer into every act of creation in your life. This is Socrates manifestation prayer:

"God, avert evil, even if I have requested it, and bring me the highest good, even if I don't yet know how to ask for it."

Listen again, and let your subconscious mind totally accept Socrates' prayer as its own deepest guideline for creating an abundant life.

"God, avert evil, even if I have requested it, and bring me the highest good even if I don't yet know how to ask for it."

This prayer locks into your mind as an automatic request for God always to bring you exactly what you asked for or something even better, your highest and best good, that hurts no-one and benefits all beings, remembering that you, as a child of God, are always benefitted.

Now turn the entire process over to God, working through your subconscious mind. You have accepted the creative gift of manifested abundance into your life. Now relax, and trust that God is arranging the details of bringing it into your reality in the fastest way possible. The entire universe is rearranging itself to bring you your heart's desire or something even better in the fastest possible time... faster than your conscious mind can even imagine, because God and your inner mind are not limited by time or space.

Thank God for the abundance that has already been created in your life, and for the abundance that is coming. The universe always works for our greatest good. And when we relax and harmonize our creative desires with our best and highest good, and the best and highest good for all others, than that highest good appears in our lives with astounding speed and amazing power. Thank God, and thank the expression of God in physical body that is you, for the creative imagination that is bringing your deepest desires into being. One heart, one mind, one being; you are a beloved child of God in an infinite and creative universe that always responds with yes to the prayers of your heart. Take a moment to simply express the gratitude in your heart... *Pause 10 seconds*

Once again: imagine, your deepest desire as if it were already attained. Feel the feelings of having, doing or being what your most desire. See yourself attaining your desires... Hear the story of achieving your heart's desire... Hold those desires in your hands. And know that you have created them, and that a generous and loving God is bringing them into your outer life with astounding speed.

If this process of creative manifestation is acceptable to your deepest being, you simply continue breathing... just as you are. And your deepest heart and soul remember that you are a child of God, and that a rich and abundant life is your birthright. You absolutely trust the presence of God within. And you trust God as a whole to fill your life abundantly with your heart's desire. And so it is.

Now it is time to return to the surface of the mind, to your outer awareness and usual state of mind... bringing out with you the knowledge that you have placed your heart's desire in the responsive and creative hands of God. And that your heart's desire is manifesting in your life more powerfully with every breath your breathe. Every time you use this recording, you are clearer and more focused. And your heart's desires manifest more deeply and quickly. Every breath you breathe causes your vast inner mind to magnify and reinforce every positive and beneficial idea on this recording, and to reconnect you more powerfully to your birthright as a child of God.

Self-Esteem for Adults

This script is adapted from work by Dr. Mike Preston and Dr. John Kresnik.

As you relax more deeply with every peaceful exhale, every breath you breathe causes you to go deeper yet. And every beat of your heart causes your inner mind to accept and implement every positive and beneficial idea on this recording. As you listen to the suggestions here, your vast and powerful inner mind receives the suggestions. Your mind accepts them as true. And your mind activates and implements these suggestions at the deepest levels of your being. And every breath and heart beat causes your mind to magnify and reinforce every positive and beneficial suggestion for you over and over again.

You have a powerful and creative imagination. It is part of what makes you the talented and positive human being that you are. And the more you use that positive imagination, the more you shape your reality. And the better you feel about yourself in each and every moment.

I would like you to imagine a schoolroom deep in your mind. There are student tables with really comfortable chairs, and a teacher's desk. Perhaps there is a map on the wall, or pictures of your favorite things. Look around the schoolroom. The walls are your favorite colors. There is plenty of light and a beautiful landscape outside the big picture windows. You are surprised that it is much more comfortable than the schoolrooms you remember from childhood. It even smells good. There is a fireplace with a cheerful fire burning in the back of the room, and a wonderful reading chair by the fire. You feel welcome in this pleasant place of learning. And you are looking forward to what comes next. This is your dream schoolroom… a place of safety, and a place for you to learn about your deepest reality.

As you scan the room, the teacher walks in so quietly that you don't notice at first. You feel a welcome and pleasant energy, as if the light has been turned on a little brighter. You feel a gentle wave of peaceful surprise as you realize that the teacher is you… the highest, best part of yourself… the part of you that never forgot who you are, in the deepest core of your being. You feel a wave of deep recognition and joy to meet this inner teacher who has come to help you remember the most important lessons of life.

Your teacher directs your attention to the back of the room. On each side of the fireplace, there are big shelves of books, and you realize with amazement that all of these books, on both sides of the fireplace, are about you. Your teacher guides you first to the books on the left side of the fireplace, and as you scan the titles, they startle you at first because the titles of these books represent all the negative thoughts, feeling and actions you have ever associated with yourself. The books on the left contain all the worries and stresses that poison your life. They contain all the negative self-definitions and excuses that have prevented you from achieving your dreams. And your inner teacher explains to you that all these negative books are from the past, but they are still affecting your life and your feelings about yourself. Your teacher explains to you that most of the content in these books didn't even come from you. They were written by other people: parents, family members, outer teachers, peers, and authority figures of all kinds. These negative books were placed there by others and have no connection to your real self. But your subconscious mind has been reading these worthless old books so much that it has accepted them as true. Your inner teacher says, "Enough is enough! It is now time to leave other people's ideas about you in the past and learn who you truly are."

Your inner teacher first asks you to look at the titles of all the books that contain all the negative thoughts you have ever had about yourself. It is painful at first to look at the titles of the books containing your negative self-thoughts. But you feel so peaceful in your classroom, and so courageous, that you take all the negative self-idea books off the shelves and carry them to the fireplace. Without even bothering to open any of the books, you hold your negative self-ideas in your hands and rip them apart. You toss all your negative self-thoughts and self-definitions into the fire. You rip the covers to shreds as well and toss them in because there is no longer a place in your mind for negative self-thoughts. And the fire burns all your negative self-ideas and negative self-definitions out of your mind forever.

Your return to the negative books on the left of the fireplace, and your inner teacher next asks you to take down your books of negative feelings. These books contain all the negative feelings toward yourself that were connected to those worthless negative self-ideas. And it feels so good to take those worthless negative self-feelings into your hands and rip them to shreds and throw them into the wonderfully cleansing fire. And the fire burns them out of your mind forever.

Feeling great and getting the idea, you return to the shelf of negative books on the left, and take down all the negative behavior books that were connected to the old worthless negative self-ideas and feelings. Your inner teacher doesn't even have to tell you what to do. It feels great to take those negative behaviors into your hands and tear them to shreds. You toss them into the fire and let it burn those old negative behaviors out of your mind forever. You simply pause for a moment and watch as the fire burns the last traces of your negative thoughts, feelings and actions out of your mind forever.

Then, feeling inspired and intuitively knowing what comes next, you return for the last books on the negative bookshelves. These books hold all the limitations you have ever accepted about yourself. They contain all the "I can'ts" and all the excuses that have ever prevented you from achieving your dreams. You look to your inner teacher, and receive an almost telepathic response. Your inner teacher confirms for you that all these limitations, "I can'ts," and excuses were planted in your mind by others and have nothing to do with your true self. So with a wave of joy, you take all your limitations, "I can'ts" and excuses into your hands, tear them to shreds and throw them into the fire, cover and all. You watch with deep and peaceful satisfaction as the fire turns all the negative books of the past into smoke and ash. And your inner mind is free of all the chains of the past.

Feeling free and deeply peaceful, open to amazing possibilities, you move to the books on the right side of the fireplace. And with a very pleasant surprise, you see that these books have titles that reflect the real you, your true self. These titles reflect the wonderful, talented, skilled, loving, accomplished, creative, and good qualities you accept as the real you. You read these titles and they say things like: loving, confident, strong, capable, worthy, important, terrific, imaginative, intelligent, poised, fascinating, energetic, talented, skilled, special, creative and loved.

You look at these books and you feel a warm swelling of pride. You know these books describe you at your very natural best. Your inner teacher asks your subconscious mind to read these positive, true books over and over, and to integrate their truths into your outer life. You accept that these books represent the real you. You accept that the ways you intuitively think, feel and act are wonderfully positive. And your positive thoughts, feelings and behaviors make life better for yourself and all you love. Just thinking about these books gives you a warm and joyous feeling. Your inner mind is integrating all the positive contents of these books into your thoughts, feelings and actions. You feel a new lease on life. You look out at the world and everything is better. The world is alive with possibility, because inside you are free of the chains of the past. And you are rediscovering your true nature more and more with every beat of your heart and breath of your lungs.

There are four special books that your inner teacher calls to your attention. They are beautifully bound in expensive red or blue leather, with gold lettering on their titles, and golden page edges. They are the most precious of the books on the right, and your inner mind was so distracted by the old negative books, that it really hasn't had a chance to read these four precious books with the focus they deserve. Your inner teacher gives your subconscious mind a homework assignment. It is to read, discover and integrate all the wonderful content of these four books into your outer life.

The first of your books is titled "My True Self, Who I Really Am". You turn to the first page and read the first sentence which reads "First understand this, you are a child of an infinite and creative universe, and loved beyond your imagination". Your subconscious mind surges with joy, knowing that this book reveals the deepest truths of your being. And your subconscious mind dedicates itself reading, understanding and implementing every word of this book.

The second of your special books is titled "My Deepest Dreams, Goals and Desires." It reveals the dreams of your deepest being… the things that you are alive to do and experience. You read the first sentence, and your book of deepest dream starts out: "Understand this, you are free to have, to do or to be whatever you can dream and imagine, and you are a powerful dreamer." And you have an exciting surge of expectation knowing that your inner mind will be reading your book of deepest dreams, goals and desires, and doing everything necessary to make them conscious. Your inner mind focuses all your energies into bringing your deepest dreams into reality.

The third special book is titled "My Book of Hidden Skills and Abilities. These are the abilities and skills you have never realized you had. They are meant to unfold throughout your life to help you realize your deepest dreams. The first sentence of your book of skills and abilities reads: "You have talents and abilities you have not yet discovered or fully developed, and you are now free to find and manifest your passions in life." And again, you feel an incredible wave of joy and satisfaction knowing that your inner mind is rediscovering your deepest talents and bringing them to the surface to help you create your new life with energy and delight.

The fourth of your special assignment books is titled "My Gifts to the World." With joy, you remember that you, like each of us, has a reason for being alive. And that reason includes the positive impacts we are meant to make in the lives of others... making the world a little better for our having been here. Your book of gifts opens with this amazing sentence: "You arrived on this Earth complete with wonderful, unique gifts to discover and share with the world to make life better for everyone you encounter. You are now free to discover and unwrap those special gifts." There is a special good feeling that fills you as you remember, day by day, more and more of what you have to offer the world.

Your subconscious mind willingly and joyfully takes on the task of reading your four precious inner books, and making their truths part of your outer consciousness and reality. You feel a surging new energy flowing into your life. You experience a new excitement and vitality about living a meaningful life. And you know yourself to be a positive influence on others as you creatively build your dreams and help others achieve theirs. You believe in yourself. You know yourself to be intelligent, worthy, creative, loving, kind, positive, talented and valuable in each and every way. You think, feel and act positively and with the best intentions all the time. You notice other people noticing the positive changes in your attitudes and in your life, and you are truly delighted. You feel a special kindness for yourself, and for every experience of your life. You love yourself and approve of your thoughts, feelings and actions more than ever before. And with each and every day you feel yourself creating your dreams. You know yourself to be a beloved child of a creative and beautiful universe. And you look forward to the gifts that each day brings.

And if these ideas are acceptable to you, you simply continue breathing... just as you are. And every breath you breathe magnifies and reinforces every idea on this recording. Any time you listen to this recording, or even think about your classroom and inner teacher, it is as if you are instantly there and the lessons get deeper and deeper and a thousand times deeper every time you visit your inner teacher and class room in your mind.

Your inner teacher has one more special lesson, just for you. As my voice is quiet for a minute, you inner teacher talks to your conscious and subconscious minds, imparting a special lesson... the one that you most need to hear to remember your deepest and truest nature... the lesson that you most need to hear, now, so you remember to love and appreciate yourself more each and every day. You may be consciously aware of inner teacher's words, or you may just consciously be aware of a deep self-loving feeling filling your mind. And inner teacher is communicating vast amounts of information directly into your subconscious mind. The moment of silence for inner teacher to give you your special, personal lesson begins now.

(*Pause 30 seconds*)

Return to the recording now, knowing that inner teacher has given you a wonderful, self-affirming private message. And the more often you use this recording, the more your inner teacher shares with you all you need to know about loving yourself as the gifted, talented and wonderful human being that you are. You accept and love yourself more with every beat of your heart, and with every breath you breathe. And you share your inner love with everyone you meet, knowing that you are a wonderful and appreciated part of so many lives.

And now, it is time to return up to the surface of the mind, knowing that in the background, your inner mind continues discarding the negative lessons of the past and replacing them with your inner truths. Every day in every way, your life is improving, and with every breath you breathe, your inner mind is incorporating, extending and implementing all the positive ideas on this recording.

Enhancing Spiritual Awareness

This script was designed for the beach induction in Unlocking the Blueprint of the Psyche, *and a countdown deepening. The script uses imagery, part of which is non-denominational, and part of which is a story, Footprints in the Sand, that is told in a Christian manner. If you are not Christian, with a little inventiveness, you can convert the story to reflect your own spiritual traditions. It could be about the Buddha guiding a pilgrim in the mountains, about Mohammed walking with the hadji in the desert, about the Great Mother guiding an earth child on a vision quest and so on. The essence of the story is that we are <u>all</u> children of God. And it is an invitation to wake to that realization. God's love is not limited by our human limits of belief. So recreate the story in any way that is easy for you to hear. A Don Pablo Neruda, le agredezco infinitamente para las flores amarillas. To Pablo Neruda, infinite thanks for the yellow flowers.*

As you gently rest on your beach, you are struck by the idea that a beach is where all the elements of nature come together in harmony. The water of the sea meets the sand of the earth. The fire of the sun shines on both as the air connects them all. Air and water merge together in the breaking waves. Sun and sand create a home for living things. The big and the small converge in beauty. You are aware of the vast ocean shifting her changing blues against the blue of the sky, developing a myth and power and mythos that fills your heart with wonder. But at the same time, your eyes are awed with beauty as you see a small plant with golden yellow flowers hanging from the cliff face. Watered by the spray and fog, fed by the earth, breathed by the air and energized by the sun, the yellow flowers explode across your consciousness with a joyous recollection that everything is connected. The flowers exist, and create their astounding beauty, only because ocean, air, sun and earth exist. And at the same time you realize that in a deeper sense, the vast ocean, the air, the earth and sun themselves exist because they are impelled to create the beauty of your flowers. And as you realize that you, like the flowers, are a manifestation of all the elements in the physical world, you also realize that part of the reason that world exists is so that you can be here. You are a child of the universe, a child of God... at play and at work in a world designed for you to flower in beauty... to become your greatest potential.

Your yellow flowers remain in your mind, and are a source and symbol of peace for you. Any time you think about, or picture your yellow flowers, a wave of peace and comfort fill you, and you remember there are no mistakes in your existence. You carry your image of yellow flowers with you, and whenever you wish for peace, strength or courage, the image, of the courageous yellow flowers growing on the ocean cliff, fills your mind. And you feel a deep, empowering wave of peace and strength.

As your mind rests, peacefully and joyfully contemplating the amazing golden yellow flowers, I am going to tell you a story. It is a story I first heard in a Christian form, but I have since heard similar stories in almost all of the world's great religious traditions. I will tell it as I first heard it, but you can translate it into any form that makes sense in your spiritual tradition. So if I refer to Jesus, or the Christ, your mind hears: Jesus Christ, the Buddha, The peacemaker, Great Mother, Gurudev, Lao Tzu, Mohammed, St. Teresa, or any of the world's great spiritual masters according to your traditions.

The story is about a pilgrim, whose entire life was spent walking down a long beautiful beach like yours, leaving footprints in the sand... looking for an unknown something. Every day, walking down that beach... in good weather and in stormy weather... the pilgrim left footprints behind in the sand. And one day, in vast surprise, the pilgrim noticed that while there were no footprints ahead on the beach, there were two sets of footprints side by side, in parallel stretching back behind to the horizon.

And turning to that place the pilgrim had forgotten to look, the pilgrim was astounded to find, walking side-by-side, was Jesus, the lord.
(*Or, depending on your tradition; the Buddha, the Peacemaker, Great Mother, Gurudev, Lao Tzu, Mohammed, St, Teresa, or any of the world's great spiritual masters. This is the section of the script you can rewrite to reflect your spiritual tradition.*)
And the pilgrim's heart was filled with awe and joy as the pilgrim recognized the Christ... looked into the eyes of the master and allowed the love, compassion and mercy there to flow in fullness. The love filled the pilgrim with joy and a deep sense of purpose and meaning... banishing fear and opening channels of love.

As the pilgrim's heart filled with the grace of the Christ, the pilgrim looked back over the footprints left behind during a long life. The pilgrim noticed that in some places, those places where the pilgrim's life had been most filled with fear, grief, loss, rage, or confusion, there was only one set of footprints in the sand. And the pilgrim asked Jesus: "Lord, why, when I was most confused, enraged, lost, alone, hurt, fearful and grieving; why in those times did you leave me alone, with only one set of footprints?" And Jesus, with infinite compassion, answered: "beloved child of God, in those times when you were most lost, confused, enraged, worried, alone, aggrieved, and hurt; in those times I did not leave you, in those times I carried you."

And Jesus continued: "You are a child of God, a child of an infinite and creative, loving Universe, no less than any other. And you are in my heart and the heart of God forever. And like the sparrow that falls and the lily in its glory, you are held and cherished and never abandoned. You are, like the flowers on the beach cliff, an enduring, courageous traveler on the road of life... a being not just of earth, air, fire and water... but also of spirit. You are held in the hands of God forever. And you, yourself, are that unknown something you are seeking. You are not here to do God's work. You are God's work."

The cup of the pilgrim's heart flowed with wonder and joy at hearing these words, knowing that they are the truth, and knowing that as God's beloved child, the pilgrim walks in the house of the Lord forever... (*Pause 10 seconds*)

I know that you have heard this story before, or one like it. But there is a secret in this story that you may not know. And that secret is this: you are that pilgrim on the beach. The story is about you. And you allow yourself to look into that place within where we often forget to look, and see that waiting there for you is the Master. And you feel a wave of comfort, acceptance, cherishing and love deeper than you have ever experienced before. You realize that even in the darkest moments, the Master is with you... carrying you when your own strength fails... helping you find the deeper courage and strength... and helping you to remember that you, like all human beings, are precious and beloved children of God.

The master has come with a very special and personal message for you... to tell you, pilgrim, what you most need to know, now, to further your spiritual awareness. To tell you what you most need to hear today to open deeper understanding, love, compassion and service. My voice is quiet for a minute, and in that quiet, the master speaks to your mind and heart, filling them with what you most need to know, and that minute of silence begins NOW.

Pause 60 seconds

Return to my voice now, and as you return to my voice, you carry with you deep, meaningful communication from the Master, who is always with you. You can return to this beach, and this conversation with the Christ, with the master, any time you wish, simply by listening to this recording. Or you can simply sit in a quiet, safe place, close your eyes, and visualize or imagine your beautiful beach. As you picture and imagine your beach, and your special yellow flowers, your heart returns you to this beach, deeply relaxed, and open to hearing the Master speak within.

Any time you think about, or visualize your yellow flowers, just imagining them causes your mind to feel a wave of peace. Picturing your flowers causes your mind to bring you to this magnificent and beautiful beach... recharging you: heart, mind, body and soul. And whenever you visit this beach, the Master is always present for you with deeper teaching of peace, love, compassion, mercy and service. The deeper you relax, the more deeply you connect with the master within... the one who is always with us. And every breath you breathe reinforces and magnifies all you have gained from this recording... the more you listen to the recording, the deeper your understanding and connection becomes.

And now it is time to return to the outer world, bringing back all the inner awareness from your beach... bringing a sense of connection and joy... a sense of compassion and love... out with you to enrich your life and the lives of all you meet.

Alleviating Toxic Guilt and Shame

Use a Dr. Kresnik's induction and a feather deepening.

Just float and drift in your beautiful meadow. As you continue to relax more deeply, your conscious mind rests. And you allow your subconscious mind to do all the work. Each breath you breathe causes you to relax more deeply and you let go of all stress, tension and worry. Your conscious mind rests deeply and recharges itself while your inner mind hears, accepts and integrates every positive and beneficial idea on this recording, sealing them in so they become a permanent part of your new reality. Each breath you breathe causes your inner mind to magnify and reinforce every positive idea on this recording. And every beat of your heart causes your inner mind to integrate these beneficial ideas fully into your outer life.

The first thing to understand is that guilt and shame are gifts from a loving universe. Guilt and shame are meant to be small, quiet emotions that gently remind us that we don't like how we feel when we treat ourselves, or others badly. Guilt and shame are meant to be small, gentle reminders that we can do better than we have done.

But for most of us guilt and shame have become overwhelming and toxic. They are like a small stream that has flooded in a storm, and is now destroying the very fields the stream was meant to nourish with life-giving water. For most of us, at some point, guilt and shame have stopped being gentle reminders to treat others better. Instead they have become horrible, all consuming feelings that paralyze our abilities to think clearly and do our best. Shame and guilt have stopped being gentle reminders to do better and have become punishing burdens that poison our lives. The goals of this recording are to help you come back into balance with your natural feelings... to leave toxic guilt and shame in the past... and to restore shame and guilt to their right place as gentle feelings that guide us to do and be our best.

As a human being, you are a holographic reflection of the entire universe. We are each, especially in our deepest hearts and minds, connected to every thing and every other being in creation. If you have a religious nature, you recognize that you, no less than any other, are a child of God. But even if you don't follow a spiritual or religious path, you can sense and feel that there is an underlying connection and co-evolution that connects all living things. And that you are, as much as anyone else, part of that creative, positive and evolving universe. And as a child of God, as a creation of an infinite and evolving universe, you have a right to exist full of self-acceptance and confident harmony.

As you rest in your beautiful meadow, imagine an ornate, full-length mirror in an elaborate, rich wooden frame. Don't look directly at this mirror yet. Stand to the side and examine the frame. In beautiful, golden letters, it says": "Mirror of Truth, Reflecting the Deepest Reality". And you realize that this mirror will not show you your clothing, your body or any other outer appearance. It is a mirror that reflects you as you truly are, in your deepest heart and soul. This mirror shows you yourself through the eyes of God, through the eyes of your own deepest wisdom and love. This mirror reflects you as you are at your very natural best.

As you now look into this mirror, you are astounded by the love you see all around you, and through you and shining from you. You stand in amazement knowing that the remarkable, beautiful reflection in the mirror reflects you at your very highest and best. You perceive yourself as kind, honest, loving, truthful and strong to a far higher degree than ever before. You recognize that in your deepest being, you are the profoundly capable loving and good person you have always dreamed you are.

You think about the mistakes you have made in the past, and about the harm you have done to yourself and other. And your mirror shows you that the mistakes and harm of the past are not the real you. They are only the things you have done out of fear and confusion. You now choose to reject your negative past and all the mistakes of the past. You choose to reject fear and confusion, and to think, feel and act as the loving being you know you are. You feel yourself turning over a new leaf... starting a new season in your life. You think about the burdens of shame and guilt you have carried around. Your mirror reflects them as huge, dark, heavy, poisonous balls and chains that have limited your life and kept you from living fully. You realize the toxic shame and guilt cause more harm than good. And they contribute to the fear and confusion that keeps you from being and doing your best.

The wisest part of you peers back at you from the mirror, and tells you that it has been far too long since you have treated yourself fairly. Your highest and wisest self tells you that what you need is forgiveness. Forgiveness does not mean sweeping your mistakes under a carpet and pretending everything is OK. True forgiveness means acknowledging your mistakes, making amends where possible, and changing your behavior and thoughts so that you do not make the same mistakes again.

Begin by inviting someone you have harmed in the past to join you in your mirror. When their highest self is there with you, begin by humbly acknowledging the way you have harmed them. Admit to your highest self, and their highest self, that you could have done better. Show them what you would have done, if you had done your best. Then ask for their understanding and forgiveness. And feel the freedom and lightness that flows through you as their highest self accepts the apology. If there is some physical amends, apology or restitution that you can make in the outer world, your mind makes a note of it, and you pursue outer amends later if the other person allows it. But more importantly, you make a determined commitment to yourself and to their highest self, to change your thinking and behavior, so that you always do better, starting today. And then you keep a tiny bit of the guilt and shame to serve as a reminder that you don't like how it feels when you harm others. You keep only a tiny bit of the guilt and shame as a reminder, and you let the rest just fade away in the waves of forgiveness. That tiny, quiet voice of shame or guilt is a guide... a reminder to always do and be your best. And as a tiny voice, it is a blessing... One you rarely need because it feels so good to do and be your best. (*Pause 10 seconds*)

Forgiveness feels good, so good that you repeat the process with another person you have harmed. You bring them into your mirror so that you are talking with their true self. You truthfully and fully acknowledge the harm you have done them. You explain your fear and confusion. And you make a deep and sincere apology. Once again, if your highest self guides you to make a specific apology or restitution in the outer world, you remember and pursue it later, if the other person is willing to receive it on the outer level. But most importantly, you make a sincere and dedicated commitment to change your thinking and behavior so that you do better from now on. You keep just a tiny bit of the shame and guilt around to remind you that you don't like the way you feel when you harm others. And you let all the rest of the poisonous shame and guilt fade away on the waves of forgiveness. (*Pause 10 seconds*)

And it feels so good to acknowledge and apologize for your mistakes and errors of behavior and judgment, that your inner mind keeps repeating this process over and over deep in the mind. And every time you listen to this recording, you repeat the process with more and more people. And the burden of toxic guilt and shame lightens with every day. You find yourself treating others with a new kindness, understanding and respect. You even begin to see people who have harmed you as confused and fearful. And you find yourself forgiving as freely as you have been forgiven.

Remember this, forgiving others who have harmed you does not mean sweeping the harm under the rug and "making nice." True forgiveness means honestly telling people they have violated your boundaries, and gently resetting the boundaries.

There is one additional person who needs your forgiveness, and that is you. You are your own harshest critic and you judge yourself far more negatively than others would judge you. So again, looking into your mirror, speaking with your highest self, you bring up some key way in which you have erred, or failed to live up to your own expectations for yourself. You acknowledge fully and honestly how you have failed to do or be your best. And you show your highest self, how you have punished yourself by taking on a poisonous, paralyzing burden of guilt and shame. You examine and acknowledge the fears and confusion that have clouded your mind and heart. And you humbly ask your highest self to forgive you for not doing or being your best. And you make a dedicated and determined commitment to do better from this point on. You promise to see through the confusion and to face the fears, and to do and be your best in spite of them. And as you make a commitment to your soul to being the best you can be, a vast wave of love and forgiveness flows from your mirror. And the burden of shame and guilt melts away like snow on a warm spring day. You keep only a tiny, quiet, bit of shame and guilt around to remind you that you don't like how it feels to do or be less than the best you know you can be.

Your powerful inner mind continues this process of self-examination and self-forgiveness on the inside. You find yourself becoming more and more conscious of an overwhelming desire to do and be your best in every situation in life. You are amazed at the kindness and love you have for yourself and others. You know that you are a caring, strong, honest, capable and loving human being. You joyously look forward to bringing the best of yourself into the world and of creating a full, rich and meaningful life for yourself and others. You feel a deep sense of calm, peace and confidence. You find yourself forgiving others easily. And you have a deeper and deeper understanding of others. These feelings are growing in every cell, fiber and tissue of your heart and body, and in every corner of your vast and incredible mind. You know yourself to be a force for growth and healing. And every time you listen to this recording the good feelings grow stronger and stronger.

Return to your mirror, and be silent for a moment while you ask your highest self what more you most need to know to reduce the burden of shame and guilt in your life. And the answer comes back to you in the minute of silence. Ask: "What do I most need to know now about reducing toxic shame and guilt?" And the moment of silence for the answer begins now.

Pause 60 seconds

Return gently to the recording, as your inner guidance seals itself inside and becomes an effortless and natural part of the way you are, and the ways you think, feel and act. Free of toxic shame and guilt, free to be the best you can be in every moment of life.

And now it its time to return to the surface of the mind, bringing the calm, peace and self-forgiveness out with you to enrich your outer life.

Grieving

I have used a Sensory Overload induction and a Countdown deepening, but almost any induction and deepening will work.

As you breathe, you continue relaxing more deeply with every exhale. Every breath causes your mind and body to sink into a deeper state of calm, peaceful awareness. As you listen to my voice, each beat of your heart causes your deep inner mind to accept, magnify and reinforce each positive and beneficial idea on the recording. The deeper you relax, the more you achieve your goal of allowing grief to flow through you, and create a richer and deeper appreciation for your life, and for the miracle of all life.

Grief is a real and valuable emotion... It does honor to those who have passed and it honors our own sense of loss or incompleteness. As you listen to this recording, you recognize that grieving changes and losses is important. It is especially important that we grieve for those who have passed away. Grief does not just go away... we have to live it and go through it. Grief is a totally human emotion, and all of us experience it. As you listen to this recording, you realize that the goal is not to escape from grief. The goal is to allow your grief to lead you to a deeper and more compassionate relationship with yourself and all beings.

There is a very old story. Some say it was told by St. Francis, or that it is a Sufi Muslim story. Others say it was a parable of Jesus from the Apocrypha, some say it was even older, taught by the Buddha. Many, many spiritual traditions claim it and the story reflects a deep and universal truth. As you listen to this story, it opens communication with the deepest part of your being, the part that guides your dreams: the part of you that remembers who you are in your deepest reality.

The story is about a young woman who was born into a poor family. And even though she was poor, her family protected her from all unpleasantness. They even shielded her from knowledge of death. When she married, she married well and she moved to the home of her rich husband. And because she came from a poor family, she was treated with contempt, and was given all the worst jobs in the household. But by and by, she had a son who became the pride of the household, the first grandson in the family. And suddenly the family treated her with great respect... honoring her in ways she had never felt before. And she loved her baby above all things, and cared for him with great tenderness. He was her joy. And her entire life revolved around her child.

But it came to pass, as was too often the case in those ancient days, that her baby sickened with a fever and died. And because she had always been protected from knowing about death, she didn't understand what had happened. She begged all the people she met to give her medicine to help animate her little boy again. She went into the market place begging for a remedy to restore her son to her, but no one could help. Finally, a wise woman told her: "there is a great saint and teacher who lives as a hermit just outside the city. If anyone can restore your son to you, he can."

So she took her baby to the holy hermit, and explained how her life had turned dark with her baby's last breath. She begged him to restore her baby to health and life. And he told her that he could bring her baby back to life if she would go into the city and bring him back a single tiny seed of a mustard plant from a house that had never experienced death.

So she went into the city, and went from house to house, asking for a mustard seed from any household that had never experienced death. And at the first house, she was told, "we would gladly give you a mustard seed, but alas, death has been a frequent visitor here." And at the second house, she was treated with deep compassion and love, but they, too, were unable to give her a mustard seed because death had visited there as well. And so she went from house to house, receiving the same answer at each. At each house she visited, she noticed that there was sadness at the memory of those who had passed. But in each house there was also joy, and full life, and happy memory of those who had gone before. She noticed that those who most honored the dead also had the greatest joy in life. And at each house, people offered her deep sorrow for her loss, and hugged her, and offered her food. But none could give her the mustard seed.

And her heart filled with a great understanding. She said to herself: "The great saint knew this when he sent me on my quest for the mustard seed... that death is everywhere, and that it fills life and is in it and through it. Death is something we all encounter, and the loss of those we love is a universal human experience. And yet, in every house there is still joy and life." And her heart filled with a great love for all beings, who, in the face of death and loss, continue to bring light and joy into life.

She returned to the hermit, and said: "Thank you for the quest. My heart is open to the great truth that all that exists will pass away, and each moment of life is precious." So saying, she allowed her baby to have the funeral rites, and returned to her life with a deeper appreciation of every moment, and with a love for all others who had experienced death and loss. And in comforting others, she found her own burden of grief lightened and shared. And in allowing others to comfort her, she found that her burden of grief was no longer paralyzing. For the rest of her life, she would feel the sorrow at the loss, but day-by-day, her sorrow was overshadowed by the joy-filled memories of her son's life. And in her time, she became honored as a teacher and wise woman, reminding us all that every outer thing changes, every outer thing passes, but within the changing and passing there is the dancing joy of pure being.

And as you hear this story, a part of you deep within... the part of you that remembers who you are in your deepest reality... speaks to you. Perhaps in words, or perhaps in the language of feeling. And the voice of inner wisdom reconnects you with the deep and eternal energy of life dancing through the changing outer forms. That deepest part of you, call it soul, call it spirit, call it simply the energy of life, does not wish to erase your grief... grief exists in all our lives. The deepest part of you simply reminds you that even in the midst of sorrow, there is love and joy. Love and joy may seem distant now, like a seed buried under feet of winter snow. But the spring always comes. The seeds grow and thrive. And love and joy return. Not to replace what was lost, but enriched and blessed by the compassionate memory of those who have gone before us. And where not even a single mustard seed can be found in a place where death has never entered, many mustard seeds planted in the ground give rise to beautiful fields of yellow flowers in the spring. With the gentle passage of time, your thoughts transform more and more from loss to joyful appreciation of the time you had with the people you have cherished. You walk in beauty and you find yourself, day-by-day wiser and richer in your appreciation of each and every moment of life.

Just take a minute, and allow that deepest part of you to tell you or show you what you most need to know today to help you heal and transform your grief into a compassionate appreciation of life... (*Pause 60 seconds*)

Returning to my voice now, knowing that each time you listen to this recording, you relax more quickly and deeply. And each time you listen to this recording you feel a stronger and stronger connection to that deepest, wisest part of your own being, your teacher within. And that the wisdom you receive from your own deepest source is far more profound than my words. You can visit and communicate with your inner teacher, your wisest, deepest self, any time you like... either by listening to this recording, or by relaxing in a quiet place and asking that profound voice of inner wisdom to speak to you in the silence.

And now, it is time to return to the room, to this time and this place, fully alert, knowing that step by step, your grief is transforming into a deeper and more compassionate love for all life and all beings. You rise up knowing that our losses eventually give a depth and richness to our lives that nothing else could. And knowing that the seeds of joy and love of life are waiting under the winter snow... knowing that the spring always comes.

Each time you listen to this recording, your mind magnifies and reinforces every positive and beneficial idea, especially those that come from your highest, deepest self.

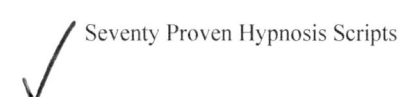

Healing the Past

Use Dr. Kresnik's induction or the Feather induction, or use either as a deepening with any other induction.

As you continue breathing, each gentle, rhythmic breath causes you to relax more deeply. With each exhale, you are breathing out stress, tension and pain... with each inhale, you are inviting in a deeper serenity and peace. Relaxing more deeply with every breath... and as you relax, your powerful inner mind is receptive to all the positive and beneficial ideas on this recording. Every breath and every beat of your heart cause your mind to take in the positive suggestions for healing, to amplify those suggestions, and to make them your new inner and outer truth.

Your beautiful meadow is a secret place within your heart, even if it is also a place in the outer world. And whenever you visit your inner meadow, you are entering a place of safety and healing. Your meadow is always there for you. You don't have to listen to this recording or be in hypnosis to visit your meadow. All you have to do is close your eyes in a safe place, and picture and imagine your meadow. As you visualize or think about your meadow, a wave of serenity and peace fill you, and you feel a deep and lasting wave of all the good feelings you are feeling right now, no matter what is happening around you.

You relax in your meadow, allowing your outer conscious mind to rest and drift in the harmony and tranquility while your vast and profound inner mind does the work. Your outer mind is welcome to listen and follow, but your inner mind does the work. You are listening to this recording because sometime in the past, perhaps repeatedly, you suffered profound emotional pain and trauma. And the echoes of that trauma are still affecting you today, filling you with pain and fear, and limiting your choices in life. And you inform your powerful inner mind that the time has arrived to heal the pain of the past, and to begin living as fully and richly as you deserve.

When we experience trauma, or emotional injury that is bigger than we can handle at the time, it literally splits our minds. A part of our mind, often a vulnerable or childlike part of our mind, stays in the past and wraps itself around the trauma, locking it inside so that the rest of us can survive and grow. That is an effective strategy that lets us continue living with pain that is too great to bear. But the pain is still locked within us. And that vulnerable, younger part of the mind is still experiencing the hurt, shame, and fear over and over, all 24 hours of every day. The first step to healing is to rescue that younger part of the mind.

You don't necessarily have to relive, or remember the events of the past in detail, although the specific memories may surface if, **and only if**, your subconscious mind **knows** you are strong enough to handle the memories easily. Otherwise the healing mostly occurs beneath the surface, in the subconscious mind. All you need to consciously know is that there is a younger part of your mind who is still caught in the old, bad memories... feeling the old pain as if it were still happening. Picture and imagine that child. Whether you have specific memories or not, you can picture and imagine your younger self in pain, ashamed or terrified. With all of your adult strength, you pick that child up. You rock and cradle your younger self in your arms. And you say to the child, "You are safe now... I am your future self, come back to help you. And you are safe now."

With a strength deeper than you knew you had, you take your injured younger self out of the old memories. And you tell your younger self: "You never have to live in these old memories again. My strong, capable adult self can visit these memories if I choose. But no part of me ever has to live in them again." And watch as a sigh of relief flows over your younger self. And all the weight seems to drop away. You move your younger self to your beautiful meadow, that place of harmony and joy. Your younger self never has to deal with difficulties, problems or pain again. That's why you are there... the strong, capable adult who knows that you have everything you need, not just to survive life's challenges, but to thrive. You tell your younger self that it has only one job, and that is to relearn the curiosity, joy, playfulness, adventure and exuberance of youth.,, And to return those gifts to your outer life. Your adult self is there to handle life's challenges.

As you and your younger self stand talking in the meadow, you notice that the sun is beginning to set. And as you watch the beauty of the sunset, you realize that the time has come to let all the injuries of the past fade into the past, and leave your present and future free. You choose to let the old injuries fade with the sunset. And that sunset is so beautiful... the amazing shades of orange, red and purple paint the clouds. And you watch that beautiful light dancing across the sky in waves, and showering over you and your meadow. You are almost spellbound by the light. You feel a wonderful new lightness of being within you. All the old pain flows out of you, into the earth. And you feel a surge of energy and healing within. You allow the old injuries to become unimportant to you. They are just things that happened on the road of life and they are fading into the past. You remember an ancient truth, that whatever doesn't kill us makes us stronger. And you realize that what you have experienced and survived has made you a powerfully strong, resilient, compassionate human being. The sun sets all the way now and you feel totally refreshed. You see your younger self, resting, and moving into a healing and recharging sleep for the first time in many years, as the old pain fades entirely into the past with the fading sunlight.

I am going to ask you now to do one difficult thing, but the peace of your moonlit meadow makes it easier. And that is to forgive the person or people who harmed you. Forgiveness does **not** mean pretending it didn't happen or making nice. True forgiveness means acknowledging clearly how they injured you. It means clearly stating your boundaries so it can't happen again. If the same people continue to harm you, it means removing yourself from them and doing whatever emotional, social and legal things it takes to get them to stop.

The key step to true forgiveness is making an agreement **with yourself** to let go of the rage, fear and vengeance so that those things no longer poison your heart. In this very specific way, I am going to invite you to imagine those people who hurt you, in a place of strength, outside of your meadow and away from your younger self. Imagine the people who hurt you as if they were tied to chairs and have to listen. Then, tell them in as much detail as you wish how they hurt you, and how that hurt has damaged your life. Tell them what your boundaries are, and that such behavior is never, ever acceptable again. Tell them all they need to know about the harm they have done you and others, and let them feel the pain they gave you... not as vengeance, but simply so they know what they did to you... (*Pause10 seconds*)...

Give them a chance to respond.... (*Pause10 seconds*) And no matter if they apologize or are defiant, tell them again what is, and is not, acceptable to you, and that they are never to harm you again... (*Pause 10 seconds*). Then, and only then, after the boundaries are back in place, you return to your meadow, free of the ones who hurt you. You take all the anger and rage, all the fear and shame, all the desires for revenge... and you let them fade into the past with the very last rays of the fading sunlight. You untie the people who hurt you and set them free. Those who apologized, you can explore new and healthy relationships with. Those who did not apologize, you allow to fade completely out of your outer life.

The beautiful moon lights your meadow fully now in a magic healing light. Your younger self sleeps a deep and healing sleep to awake on a new day, free or the past. You enjoy your meadow in the moonlight. The magical moonlight is soothing and healing in a degree deeper than you imagine. You feel so light. All the heavy burden has faded away. All the hurt, shame and fear are gone. All the rage, and vengeance have gone. Your heart is light and free... so light you feel you could fly. You realize that your life has changed so greatly. You know that you are a being of limitless possibility. You have the freedom to experience and be the highest you can be. The chains are gone. The burden has lifted. You know the next sunrise opens on a whole new world of rich inner experience. And the injured parts of you are healing more deeply with every breath you breathe.

If these suggestions and ideas are acceptable to you, you simply continue breathing... just as you are. The more you listen to this recording, the faster and deeper you relax, and the more profoundly you heal. The more you visit your meadow, either guided by this recording, or simply by closing your eyes and imagining it, the more calm, peace and confidence you feel flooding out into your outer life. You are a profound and powerful being, living in an infinite and beautiful universe. And you are loved and cherished. In each and every day, you heal more deeply and your outer life becomes a glorious dance of abundant life. And now it is time to return to the surface of the mind, to the outer world, bringing all the inner healing out with you. Every breath you breathe continues to strengthen and reinforce your healing and growth. Now rise back with my voice to the outer world, feeling wonderful.

Enhancing Breast Size

Try a Sensory Overload/Elman induction and a Feather deepening.

As you relax deeper and deeper, you follow only the sound of my voice. You remain awake and alert while you listen to this tape but you allow your mind to feather and float, drifting deep into you own subconscious. Your powerful subconscious mind is making the changes that you want... and is already beginning to make your breasts grow larger and firmer.

Deep in your mind there is a special room. It is a control room filled with levers, dials, monitors, buttons and other control apparatus. There is a screen in the control room that monitors body image. You see that screen and it reflects the way you see your body today. You notice that overall, your body is attractive, well conditioned and healthy. It is a very remarkable body and it works wonderfully well and does everything you ask it to. And you notice that you like your body. You especially like its femininity. Your body feels nice to you... it feels sexy and great. As you look at your current self-image... how your body has built itself... there is only one little change you would like to make. You would like to be even more feminine. You would like your breasts to grow larger... not pendulous and enormous... just larger, and perfect for your beautiful curvy, feminine body.

In the past, you may have disliked your small breasts. In the past, you may even have said; "I hate my flat chest." But now, a new attitude is forming. You now realize that your old flat breasts are the precious seeds of the new and beautiful breasts you are growing. You thank your body for all that it does for you. It is a wonderful home for your spirit and soul. You even appreciate your small breasts because you know they are the precious seeds that are growing and blossoming into the larger, curvy and attractive breasts that you are growing now.

You notice that the monitor where you are watching your body image is really an internal computer with a highly sophisticated drawing program. It is so sophisticated that it reacts to your thoughts. You don't have to touch any controls. All you have to do is imagine and think. And the powerful computer in your mind completely changes your body image.

Try it now. Focus on your breasts. Imagine what they would look like another 2 inches in diameter... another whole cup size larger. Watch as your monitor responds to that new image. Watch the breasts grow at a safe, healthy pace so that in just a few short weeks, they reach your new goal. Your body responds to your ideas on the control monitor by growing those breasts to be full, firm and beautiful.

Right next to your monitor is a lever. It runs from zero to ten. Zero means that there is no growth going on. Ten means that your breasts are growing at the fastest rate that is safe and healthy for you. Notice where your lever is set. Then imagine pulling it all the way up to ten and locking it in place. That's right... just lock it into place.

When the lever is locked into place at 10, you take a deep breath, let it out and let you mind feather deeper. You are fully awake and alert but you let your mind relax as deeply as it wants to go. You notice a tiny pulse deep within your breasts. That pulse is your signal that the process is working.

As you notice the pulse, you also notice that your breasts are warmer than the rest of your body. That is typical of tissue that is growing. Your breasts are adding more fat stores and expanding. There are more blood vessels growing to support the new breast tissue. One reason that the growth takes place over weeks is that it is important for your body to do things safely and systematically.

To have bigger breasts, your entire body has to make certain changes. You notice that your hips and bottom are rounding out just a little to balance the change in the shape and weight of your breasts. Your pectoral muscles are growing stronger to support your new breasts. Throughout your body, your blood vessels are changing so that they can support new, healthy breast tissue. Your lymphatic system and immune systems are making changes so that they can keep the new breast tissue healthy and safe. Your hormones are going into growth mode. Your brain is changing its systems of balance and awareness so that you can continue to feel naturally balanced in space.

There are many, many other behind-the-scenes changes that your body is making automatically so that your new breasts can grow healthy and perfectly. Fortunately your brain knows how to make every one of the millions of changes that have to occur. But that is why your breasts don't grow instantly. They grow at a gradual, steady pace that allows your brain to make all the changes it needs while keeping you totally healthy at the same time.

Your brain just needs your permission to get the process rolling. It needs you to visualize your new state every day. At least ten times a day, you close your eyes for about 10 seconds and visualize that monitor. You visualize those beautiful new breasts growing out to exactly the size that you want them. That visualization is an instruction to your mind and brain. Your mind and brain create what you visualize... firm, lovely, attractive, curvy and sexy breasts. You come to this room and visualize the changes that you want often. The more you visualize your breasts growing, the faster they grow.

Remember that for many years, you subconsciously told your breasts not to grow. You talked to them constantly, mostly subconsciously. And they responded. If your brain was an office, you sent so many "don't grow breasts" memos to your brain, that there isn't even room to walk around. I want you to imagine going into that office and sweeping up all those "don't grow breasts" memos into a big pile. Then you take those all those "don't grow breasts" memos to the incinerator. You realize that you have to take many wheelbarrow loads of those obsolete old messages out to that incinerator. You empty every filing cabinet and clear out all the secret corners. Then, when you have dumped all the old "don't grow" messages into the incinerator, you light them on fire and burn them up forever. Watch them burn out of your mind forever. (*Pause 20 seconds*)

As the old worthless, obsolete, useless "don't grow" messages burn up, you compose a new memo for your mind and brain. That new message is very simple. It reads:
Grow my breasts to a full, firm, and beautiful size that is perfect for my body. Grow them in a safe, healthy, balanced way that is perfect for me. Give me the really feminine, attractive, firm and full breasts that I deserve and that nature designed me to have.

Go back to your monitor and show your brain what you want. Visualize your breasts expanding to fill out exactly as you want them to. Remember that you love your breasts just as they are. They are the seeds of the breasts that are growing and blossoming, the new breasts that you love even more.

Imagine what you would do with those firm, full breasts. Imagine walking down the streets of your hometown. All the kids who used to call you plywood suddenly notice that you are all woman. Feel how good it feels when some of the guys drop their jaws in amazement. And some of the girls do too. Send that satisfied, sexy feeling deep into your mind and pull your lever up to ten to reinforce your new body image.

Imagine stepping off a curb to cross a street. As you step down, you notice a really cool bobble under your blouse as your breasts bob up and down in response to stepping off the curb. The feeling is so new and exciting. It feels incredible to actually have breasts that bounce when you move! Just enjoy the feeling. And tell your inner mind that this is the bouncy feeling you want to start feeling as soon as possible. These are the firm, sexy, bouncy breasts that you want it to build for you now.

Imagine being with your lover and feeling his delight as he (*or she*) caresses your sexy new breasts. (*Pause*) Feel how good it feels to you, too. Send that feeling deep into your mind to reinforce your new body image. Tell your brain clearly and unequivocally "This is what I want". I want to feel my wonderful, new curvy, sexy breasts being caressed in just this loving way. I LOVE my beautiful, new breasts.

At each and every level of your mind, brain and body, your breasts are growing. They grow at a perfect, healthy rate for you. Your body follows your mind and your breasts grow in response... just as they have for thousands upon thousands of women. Your mind is incredibly powerful. You know that your mind was powerful enough to keep your breasts from growing, which meant it had to overcome all your genetic programming. Your mind is incredibly powerful. And now that incredibly powerful mind is doing everything it needs to do so that your breasts grow out to their full, firm potential. Now, your mind is aligned with what your body has always wanted to do, and that makes it ten times more powerful. You are on your way to beautiful breasts.

Return up to the surface of the mind now, knowing that your inner mind is doing everything necessary to grow the breasts you want. And the more you visualize your new firm, bouncy and beautiful breasts the faster they grow. And the more you listen to this recording the faster your inner mind grows those perfect curvy and delightful breasts for you. Just turn this entire project over to your inner mind and relax as your perfect breasts grow to their perfect size over the next few weeks.

Body Building

Thanks to body-builder Steve McCloy, for the impetus to write this script, and for the program of healthy bodybuilding it describes. Any induction/deepening combination will work. I have used the Sensory Overload induction from Unlocking the Blueprint of the Psyche.

As you continue to relax, each breath you breathe causes you to relax even more... body and mind. And every breath you breathe causes your powerful inner mind to be open to, and to implement every positive and beneficial idea on this recording. The more you use this recording, the deeper you relax and the more powerful the suggestions on the recording become for you as you build the body of your dreams.

Imagine a mirror in your mind that shows your body the way you want it to be. You have a clear and precise goal of adding well-conditioned muscle mass to your body until you reach your goal weight, size and shape. When you look into your inner mirror, you see yourself, as you want to be. You see yourself weighing your ideal weight, and those pounds are composed of powerful, beautifully shaped muscle mass. Your mirror shows you that your density is perfect for your frame. You study what you see. You are truly pleased with your body at your goal weight, size, conformation and shape. You know a deep and powerful sense of satisfaction at achieving this ideal size, weight and conformation. You are incredibly happy at having achieved such a powerful and life-enhancing goal. Your subconscious mind studies the image in the interior mirror. And your subconscious mind does whatever is necessary to bring you to this ideal size, shape, weight and conformation. Your subconscious mind accepts this ideal body as the real you... as the body you were meant to have. And your subconscious mind begins doing every healthy thing necessary for you to achieve this ideal and perfect body, easily and in the fastest healthy time possible.

When you look into your inner mirror, and see your body at the perfect weight and perfect density for you, you are reminded of famous body building champions. But what you see in the mirror, and what your subconscious mind is creating for you is even better, because your subconscious mind is helping you achieve the best and most wonderful body for YOU.

You visit this mirror often and each time you do, you feel a deep and commanding desire to bring that perfect body into full realization and to manifest it in the world. It feels so good to see your body at its very natural best, that you are totally excited and motivated to do whatever it takes to achieve your goal. And because you enjoy your goal shape and size so much, and because you truly cherish your body and want it to be all that it can be, every step you take to achieve that body is pleasing and easy for you.

You know that you have designed the perfect workout, rest and diet routine for your body. Because you have studied and learned to separate the truth of bodybuilding from the myth and misinformation, you are now totally motivated to put your learning into practice. You are totally motivated to create that powerful and beautiful body in healthy ways that enhance your life and that serve to show others the way to healthy and effective body-building.

You have learned the secret of training intensely to failure in short workouts, usually twice each week. You know that pushing your muscles to the failure point is the stimulus your body needs to create new, stronger muscle tissue. You also know the secret of giving your body the rest and recovery time it needs so that it can actually build stronger muscle. You know that you have the courage it takes to push each muscle group in turn to the failure point. You know that vomiting or shakiness are actually good things because they are signals that you are pushing the limits upward. You are totally aware of the difference between healthy muscle burn and muscle or joint damage. And because you are totally aware of the difference, you can push yourself far beyond what would be limits for most people in a healthy and growth-enhancing way.

Because you are so focused on your goal, on creating the body in the mirror, you totally enjoy your workouts. Each workout is THE workout. Each rep is THE rep. You focus your entire attention on each and every rep, whether it is the first one, or the "impossible" 11th one. And each and every rep brings you joy. Each rep causes your body to produce endorphins that give you a wonderful sense of accomplishment and joy. Rep by rep, muscle group by muscle group, you go through your entire workout feeling totally focused and totally joyous.

After each workout, you know that your muscles need time to recover and rebuild. And when you give your body the recovery and building time it needs, you feel absolutely great. And when your muscles are recovered, you feel an enormous motivation and desire to do the next workout.

You have discovered the secret of using good form. Your muscles grow at the maximal rate because you always focus on good form, isolating each muscle in turn. You use good form to move the weights, not momentum. You treat your body with respect, always using just the right weight and never overstressing it with weights that would require bad form or momentum to lift. And your body responds to your appreciation of it by going all out and giving 100% plus effort each and every time. You train with total attention and total effort, and in each workout, you find yourself attaining more and more... more repetitions or more weight in exactly the perfect growth curve for your body.

And your body responds by creating an average of 3 to 4 pounds of new healthy, strong, conditioned and active muscle each and every month until you reach your goal weight and shape.

You know where the growth point is... the point of muscle failure... and you approach that point joyfully. You do whatever it takes... tapping the last bit of energy... doing one or two assisted reps... doing whatever it takes to break through each limit. And it is a joy to push the limits. You love each moment when you can go just a little further and you are totally motivated to go for the gold with every single rep, and in every single workout.

You give your body what it needs to be optimally healthy. You allow yourself time for a full night's sleep after your workouts, so that your body can repair and rebuild. You sleep soundly and deeply because you know that your body grows during sleep. You feed your body the foods it needs to grow optimally. You are totally motivated to follow a nutritious eating regimen almost every day. Because you have discovered the secret of eating your food slowly and chewing thoroughly, you not only digest your food completely, but you enjoy it far more as well.

You trust yourself, and the deep wisdom of your inner mind, so you trust yourself to train to failure with intensity and courage combined with safety. And that makes every aspect of bodybuilding intensely satisfying for you. You believe in yourself, you respect your body, and you love the image in your inner mirror. And because of all that, you are intensely excited about each and every opportunity to work out. You joyfully anticipate every single repetition. And you even look forward to reaching the point of failure, because each time you train to failure you are one step closer to your goal.

Your deep and powerful subconscious mind accepts every positive and beneficial idea on this recording and locks it into place in the deepest part of your mind, where it simply becomes true for you. And every time you listen to this recording, you are totally excited about your workout... because you know that the end result... your incredibly magnificent body at the perfect weight and density... is worth every step and every rep between now and your goal. Each time you listen to this recording, your powerful subconscious mind makes every beneficial and positive idea on the recording a thousand times more powerful, and every workout is a time of total focus and joyful accomplishment.

And now, it is time to return to this time and place, feeling totally relaxed. You come up to the surface bringing all your inner changes out with you so that you effortlessly and automatically build the strong, attractive and wonderful body of your dreams and imagination.

Include repeat visualizations of the body and its perfect weight, size and conformation with each count in the awakening sequence.

Increasing Concentration and Focus

Any induction and deepening will work with this one – a Sensory Overload induction from Unlocking the Blueprint of the Psyche *reinforces the text quite well.*

Say the magic words, "relaxed and focused," to yourself. Every time you say or hear the words, "Relaxed and focused," they cause your powerful subconscious mind to replay all the wonderful suggestions on this tape deep in your mind. The suggestions seal themselves in as a permanent part of your reality. Relaxed and focused

As you relax and focus more deeply, every word you hear causes your mind to increase its attention and focus, and to unleash your natural powers of focused concentration. Each breath you breathe causes you to relax even more deeply. And you are perfectly receptive to every positive and beneficial idea on this recording. Your subconscious mind integrates and **implements** all the positive suggestions on the recording so quickly that you find your powers of concentration growing beyond your goals as your mind harnesses its incredible power to help you become the focused and incredibly successful person you were meant to be.

The secret to concentration is being able to relax and focus on what is important. You are now relaxing so much more easily than in the past. And you have a magic phrase that helps you stay relaxed in every situation in your life, no matter how busy or distracting they are. Your magic phrase is
"Relaxed and focused." Every time you hear the words "Relaxed and focused" they cause you to immediately relax and your entire mind focuses deeply on whatever is most important to you at the moment.

Practice with me now
Take in a deep breath, and hold it for just a moment
As you gently release your breath, you silently repeat your magic words, "Relaxed and focused". And the words "Relaxed and focused," instantly cause your mind and body to relax more deeply. A wonderful sense of peace fills you, and you feel your mind focus deeply on the changes you are making here today. That's right, just let that wave of relaxation fill you every time you think or hear the words "Relaxed and focused."

Try it again: Take in another deep, cleansing breath, hold it just a moment knowing that as you let it out and silently repeat the words "Relaxed and focused," in your mind, another wave of peaceful relaxation fills you and all distractions fade even further away.

When you use your magic phrase to help you relax and focus your mind, you find yourself automatically concentrating only on the things that are truly important in each moment. And because you are relaxed, distracting noises or movements simply do not bother you. Your inner mind monitors distractions, you may even be slightly aware of them, but other people, movements, noises, and all other distractions simply become unimportant to you because the rewards of a focused, concentrated mind are so wonderful.

You find yourself making decisions more quickly, and making better decisions because your mind is able to focus deeply on what is most important. And as you make better decisions, you feel better and your self-esteem rises immensely. And you feel confident, secure and effective in every area of your life.

The word concentration comes from ancient Latin words meaning "to get to the center of things" or to get to the heart of the matter, as we would say today. It means to focus all our attention and energy on what is most important, and to exclude any distractions, so that we can resolve problem or create new ideas. All human beings are marvelous concentrators. It is wired into our very brains to focus on the most important details of any situation and to follow-up with absolute determination to reach our goals. The only obstacles to tapping into our natural powers of concentration are stress and worry. The more we relax and let go of stress and tension, the more we can effortlessly concentrate and focus our minds on what is truly important. When we are calm and relaxed, we automatically focus our minds on what is important, and distractions simply become unimportant.

Worry is the enemy of concentration because worry divides our mental energies and takes them away from focusing on the important things in life. You have a brand new attitude about worries. You realize that 85% of the things we waste time worrying about never happen. 10% of the things we waste time worrying about happen, but we can handle them easily. And 5% of the things we waste time worrying about happen, but they are beyond our power to do anything about, anyway. And what you realize is that it is useless to worry about anything. 85% of all worries never happen so there is no point in worrying about them. 10% happen but they are things we can handle easily so there is no point worrying about them. And the remainder of our worries are out of our immediate control, so there is no point in worrying about them either. Your subconscious mind now realizes worry never helps anything. And since worry blocks the focusing power of your mind, worry actually prevents you from solving problems or creating solutions. So your subconscious mind refuses to worry about anything... especially when you want to concentrate your mind on a problem or project. Every time you silently repeat your magic phrase "Relaxed and focused", all your worries fade away, and your focus and concentration amplify themselves ten times over.

You practice relaxing every day, by listening to your recordings, and by using your magic phrase, "relaxed and focused". And the more you practice relaxing, the more deeply you concentrate. Within a short time, you are aware of people noticing you, and telling you how much they envy your ability to stay calm, relaxed, focused and concentrated no matter what is going on. And you are delighted with your ability to relax and concentrate. Relaxed and focused. You recognize and are growing into your personal excellence more and more with every passing day. You really enjoy new challenges, and never worry about them because you know you have the ability to focus your mind and concentrate on meeting any challenge life can bring you. You have an exciting new sense of self-confidence and achievement. You accept that you are a talented and amazing human being who can meet any challenge that life offers, and not just survive, but thrive. Your new confidence spreads to others. When you are relaxed and focused, the people around you are relaxed and focused as well. You are a role model for others, and their respect for you grows with every passing day.

Now think about some project or problem that you are facing. Notice that because you are relaxed and calm, your mind is focused and you can concentrate all your powers on the problem or project. And it just doesn't seem as big a deal as perhaps it first did. Now, as you focus on your particular project or problem with a relaxed and focused mind, you feel your conscious and subconscious mind studying it from all angles. Repeat your magic words silently to yourself, and notice how your mind focuses even more deeply, and all distractions fade away. "Relaxed and focused."

Focus on the problem or project you are facing.

Now take a moment of silence without my voice and notice how your mind is focusing on the project or problem, and getting right to the heart of the matter. Picture and imagine yourself coming up with creative approaches and solutions that allow you to resolve the problem or accomplish the project. Background sounds are not a distraction. They simply set a rhythm for your mind to use as it focuses and concentrates. When my voice returns in 60 seconds, you are astounded to realize that your deeply concentrated mind has given you creative new ideas for solving your problem or achieving your goals. And that relaxed and focused minute of silence begins now. ...(*Pause 60 seconds*)

"Relaxed and focused." Return to the recording now. If your mind is still working on the problem or project, you inner mind continues its deep focus until you achieve your goal. If your mind is finished, and you have all the new ideas you need, you are totally astounded at the ability of your mind to totally concentrate on what is truly important, and at how quickly you can achieve your dreams or resolve any problem when you are relaxed and focused.

Every time you listen to this recording, you are more and more calm and relaxed, and that calm and relaxation spread to every aspect of your life. Every time you think or hear your magic phrase, "Relaxed and focused," your mind magnifies and reinforces the positive suggestions on the recording a hundred times over and you are more relaxed calm, focused and concentrated every day of your life. Now it is time to return to the surface, bringing all your new focus and concentration with you. Relaxed and focused.

Building Powerful Motivation

Use any induction and deepening that is effective for you.

Remaining in this deep, focused state of relaxation, every breath you breathe causes you to maintain and deepen this wonderful peaceful state even more. Your powerful inner mind is open to, and receptive of, every positive and beneficial idea on this recording, and every beat of your heart is a signal for your mind to accept, magnify and implement every positive, beneficial idea on the recording. The comforting sound of my voice causes you to relax more deeply and to reinforce and strengthen every positive idea on the recording, Just floating now, tranquil, in control, at peace and at rest, allowing the new to replace the old and useless. Simply enjoying where you are, what you are and who you are. Totally at peace.

As you relax more deeply, you realize that you have many important goals in your life... things that you would like to achieve, accomplish, create or experience. And these goals give your life value and meaning. They are not necessarily "big deals" in the world's eyes. But they are the achievements or experiences that bring you great satisfaction. And the more you listen to this recording, the more your powerful inner mind focuses its enormous energies on making your deepest dreams, goals and desires conscious. And the more your inner mind focuses on making your dreams and goals manifest in your outer life. Every breath you breathe and every beat of your heart cause you inner mind to be receptive to the positive ideas on this recording, and to implement those positive ideas in your outer life.

Deep in your inner mind, there is a secret place, a place of rest and peace, the deepest recesses of your inner mind. I would like you to imagine a set of five beautiful stairs leading down to the deep basement of relaxation and your secret place of healing inner change. As I count from five down to one, your mind takes you down the stairs to that secret place of powerful change.

Five... taking the first step down, doubling your pleasant relaxation with every step
Four... Feeling totally relaxed and totally excited about entering the heart of your mind

Three... Deeper, more calm, so alert but so peaceful, doubling your relaxation again
Two... Totally at peace, refreshed, rejuvenating
One... All the way down, so peaceful

You find yourself on a beautiful landing facing an elaborate door with a high-tech scanning lock. You place the palm of your hand in the scanner, and the feel the light scan your handprint. The lock clicks open, and you gently push the door open, and walk in to an incredibly beautiful room filled with books. In the back, there is a well-lighted reading area with a very comfortable chair. Perhaps there is a fire burning cheerfully in a fireplace near the reading chair. The carpeting is rich and soft, the walls are painted in the most soothing colors, and the furnishings and bookshelves are made of rich tropical woods. You know that you have entered in to one of the deepest recesses of the mind... to the library of yourself. All the books in this library represent aspects of yourself in all the richness of your being. You know you could spend years exploring this library. But, for now, you are focused on your deepest dreams and the motivation to fulfill them.

On the reading table next to your chair, there are two precious books bound in expensive leather, with gold titles and gold page edges. You know at a glance that these books are of incredible value to you. As you scan the titles, you realize the first book is titled: "My Book of Deepest Dreams, Goals and Desires." The second book is entitled: "My Book of Motivation."

You sit in the chair, even more comfortable now, and open your book of Dreams, Goals and Desires. You turn it to a page at random, and you are astounded to begin remembering something you thought you had forgotten... a dream or a goal that had faded from your consciousness. You know intuitively that this entire book is filled with the dreams of your heart and soul... the things you came to this Earth to experience or accomplish. And you have a deep joy in recognizing them. The dreams and goals are not all big things. Some are very simple: like being the best you can be at your career or family, finding and returning love, taking joy in each moment of life. Every goal and dream in the book is personally meaningful and important to you, whether the world thinks it is a big deal or not. Everything in this book is a big deal for you. You realize you have been distracted from your goals. So you now inform your subconscious mind that its homework is to read this book of dreams and goals from cover to cover. And to do whatever healthy things are necessary for your deep dreams and goals to become conscious again, and to be realized and achieved in your outer life.

Your subconscious mind now accepts the task of bringing your deepest dreams and goals into full awareness and full reality. Every time you listen to this recording, your subconscious mind explores your dreams, goals and desires more deeply, and increases the energy dedicated to making them conscious and bringing them into reality. In the background, all the time, your inner mind now accepts that one of its most important jobs is to keep your conscious mind focused on the goals that are important to you, and to keep you motivated to work toward accomplishing your deepest dreams and goals.

You look at the second book now, and read its title: "My Book of Motivation." And you know intuitively that this book contains everything your mind needs to know about the energy and focus you need to achieve your dreams and goals. You turn first to the introduction, which is written specifically for your inner mind. It tells your inner mind that the first secret of motivation is changing the way you look at yourself. And it reminds you who you really are, beneath all the definitions that other people have laid on you.

The book reminds your subconscious mind that you are a reflection of an infinite and creative universe, and that you have within you, everything you need to achieve your dreams. And as your subconscious mind reads the words in your book of motivation, it remembers more and more who you are in your depths, and at your highest potentials. Your inner mind remembers who you are at your very natural best, and begins sharing that knowledge with your outer mind. You feel a warm swelling of quiet contentment as you remember that you are a powerful and creative being, with an overwhelming desire to achieve your highest potentials and deepest dreams. And you now allow every day to be a step forward in the realization of your many empowering dreams, and the accomplishment of your highest goals.

You feel an incredible shift in your attitudes about yourself and your place in the world. You know your life to be meaningful and worthwhile in every way. You appreciate yourself and love yourself and your life more and more with every passing day. You know yourself to be special, valuable and loved. You appreciate your own intelligence and talent. You speak with conviction because you think things through clearly. And you focus intently on the meaningful aspects of life. You have an abundant new confidence that you have the skill, wisdom and intelligence to achieve whatever you focus your energies on. And you express and experience a special serenity, knowing that you are a success, and that your success grows with every day.

You have the power and wisdom to focus on your deepest dream and goals, and the perseverance to achieve them. You think of yourself as a success. You feel successful. And success goes with you in whatever you take on. You are a role model for others, inspiring them to reach for their highest goals with all their will and energy, just as you do. And you are creating a wonderful circle of joyous success in the people around you, which empowers you to reach even higher. You are determined and persistent, and nothing stands in your way for long. And as you achieve your dreams and inspire others to achieve theirs, you are becoming the happiest, healthiest, most loving and lovable person you can be. And you are making the world a better place for us all, simply by being here and doing your best.

Your book of motivation contains many other techniques and secrets that help you find, increase, and sustain the energy you need in every minute to be your best and achieve your deepest dreams and desires, and attain your deepest goals. Every time you listen to this recording, your subconscious mind reveals more and more of the secrets of this book to your conscious mind. And your inner mind is constantly working in the background to read and understand everything in your Book of Motivation and to bring the ideas, and techniques into your outer life.

The more you use this recording, the deeper your mind explores your Book of Deepest Dreams, Goals and Desires, and your Book of Motivation. And the more you listen to this recording the more motivated you are to do whatever healthy things it takes to focus on your most important dreams and to achieve them.

If these ideas are acceptable to your inner mind, you simply continue breathing… just as you are. That's right… And now, take a full minute without talking, and in that minute, your inner mind reads in both your books, and makes conscious whatever it is that you most need to know today about your deepest dreams and goals; and your subconscious mind focuses your energies totally on achieving them. Ask your inner mind: "What do I most need to know today about my deepest dreams and goals, and the motivation to achieve my dreams?" And the minute for the answer begins NOW... (*Pause 60 seconds*)

Returning to the recording now, you allow yourself to remember your inner guidance of the past minute, and you allow your inner guidance to seal itself within the deepest part of your mind where it becomes a permanent part of your new reality as an awesomely motivated creator and achiever of dreams. And every breath you breathe reinforces, strengthens and magnifies your new awareness. And every beat of your heart causes your vast and amazing inner mind to strengthen and reinforce every positive and beneficial idea on this recording over and over and over.

And now it is time to return to the surface of the mind: feeling alert, refreshed, and totally renewed. As you return to this time and place, you bring out with you, every positive and beneficial idea on this recording, integrated now into your deepest truth and reality.

Increased Self-confidence

Remaining in this deep, focused state of relaxation, every breath you breath causes you to maintain and deepen this wonderful peaceful state even more. Your powerful inner mind is open to, and receptive of, every positive and beneficial idea on this recording and every beat of your heart is a signal for your mind to accept, magnify and implement every positive, beneficial idea on the recording. The comforting sound of the recording causes you to relax more deeply and to reinforce and strengthen every positive idea on the recording, Just floating now, tranquil, in control, at peace and at rest, allowing the new to replace the old and useless, simply enjoying where you are, what you are and who you are. Totally at peace.

Your outer, conscious mind rests and floats even deeper asleep with every breath while your vast and powerful inner mind does all the work of restoring you to your birthright as a self-confident and secure person. You allow your inner mind to review your life. And you direct your inner mind understand all the ways that self-doubt, anxiety and worry have impoverished you, and stolen the success and joy from your life. You inform your deepest mind of your profound goal of leaving the self-doubts and fears behind, and living your life with the self-confidence to easily achieve success in every situation in life.

The first thing for your inner mind to understand is that self-doubt and fears about your ability are learned feelings. You were not born doubting and afraid... you had to learn those feelings. And as your subconscious mind knows, anything that it learned can be unlearned and replaced in the mind. Your natural state is to be confident and capable in every situation. Life never sends us anything we truly can't handle. But life has an odd sense of humor. Life causes us to grow by sending us lots of things we don't think we can handle until after we do. But the truth in every situation is that we have all we need, including the help of other people, to survive and thrive through everything life brings us.

Think about babies. They are not born full of self-doubt. Even though they are tiny, with limited movement, and brains that are far from completely grown, they are totally confident. A baby is confident that if it cries when it is hungry, food will come. Even though the baby has no language, it is confident that if it cries when it is wet or soiled, help will come and the diaper will be changed. As the baby gets older, and is starting to walk, even though the baby falls, over and over, in the process of learning, the baby is totally confident that it can walk, and it keeps on trying... before you know it, the baby is a toddler walking all over the place and getting into everything in the total confidence that the world is its playground.

And you were that confident baby. You were born with all the self-confidence you needed to try anything. You overcame doubts and worked miracles. When you were about three years old, you were learning, on average, five new words every day. Not just their meanings, but how to conjugate the verbs, how to make the words singular and plural, and above all, how to fit the words you learned into sentences with all the other words you knew so that you could express your thoughts. When you consider what a complex, amazing thing a language is, it truly is miraculous how you confidently and amazingly learned a language. What is even more amazing is that at the same time you were learning to talk, you were also learning very complex physical motions, you were learning about numbers and their meanings and you were learning an incredible set of social relationships about how you fit into your family and the larger world. You did all that with amazing natural confidence.

None of that could have happened unless you had the confidence to try any-thing, the perseverance to keep trying until you succeeded, and the courage to face down fears and do your best. That is the way you were born: confident, persistent and courageous. That is how you were meant to be all your life: confident, persistent, and courageous. And that strong, confident, persistent, and courageous being is still alive within you. You had to learn to be anything other than strong, confident, persistent and courageous. You had to learn self-doubt. You had to learn to let fear control your life. And anything you can learn can be unlearned and replaced. And your subconscious mind is doing that relearning right NOW.

Deep in your mind, there is a special place. It is a schoolhouse, like an old time one-room school house that you may have seen in history books. It is red, with an actual bell in the front. Imagine that one-room schoolhouse in your mind right now. Picture it, imagine it, or think about the schoolhouse and it is there for you. As you imagine it and as I count from 5 down to 1, you relax ten times more deeply and approach the schoolhouse more closely.

Five... Realizing that this schoolhouse is where your mind learns its deepest lessons, you start walking toward it, relaxing 10 times more deeply and feeling so excited and ready to learn

Four... Coming closer, and seeing a welcoming figure in the doorway, feeling a total trust in your welcome, and relaxing even more deeply in mind and body

Three... Almost to the schoolhouse, and recognizing the figure in the doorway as your own deepest wisdom, the part of you who has never forgotten your amazing potentials and abilities

Two... Stepping up onto the porch, and relaxing even more deeply, your inner mind is totally ready to accept and act on what you learn here today

One... Greeting your teacher, and being greeted with the kindest, most radiant smile in return... you know you are in the right place, and you are so wonderfully relaxed, and at the same time, so incredibly excited about what you are about to learn.

Your inner wisdom, your teacher within, leads you inside, and the room is truly beautiful. There are student seats and a teacher's desk. There are blackboards covering two walls, and shelves of books. There are science displays, maps, math diagrams and learning tools and toys of every sort ... and you are amazed at all the things you have forgotten that you know. You feel a warm swelling of pride as you survey all the things you have learned ... you are a talented and unlimited learning machine.

Your inner teacher, the wisest part of you, has a sad look. Your teacher points to the blackboard on the side wall. And on that blackboard, are written all your self-doubts and self-limitations: all the false things you have learned that limit your life, that cause you doubt, and that stop you from achieving your dreams. There are many of them: Some say things like: "I'm not enough... not good enough, not smart enough, not rich enough, not attractive enough and so on... a whole poisonous list of "I'm not enoughs". Some of the negative things on the board are "I cants": all the things you have falsely learned that you can't have, do or be. Some of the things on your list are self-doubts... all the things you doubt: your strength, skills and abilities. Some of the poisonous things on the list are "there isn't enoughs: there isn't enough money... there isn't enough love... there isn't enough of what I need to achieve my dreams... etcetera, etcetera, yadda, yadda, yadda. What a poisonous load of baloney! It is no wonder your self-confidence has faded away when you are carrying such a load of false learned nonsense in your mind.

Your inner wisdom tells you the worst thing about all the baloney you learned is that it didn't even come from you. Every bit of that nonsense was taught to you by someone else: parents, teachers, other kids, and authority figures of all kinds. That board contains every bit of self-doubting, fear inspiring, nonsense that you learned from others. **It doesn't even belong to you.** And it is time to get rid of it forever. Your inner teacher hands you an eraser and says it is time to clear the nonsense off the board and out of your mind.

You take that eraser in your strong hands, and you begin to erase every bit of nonsense from the board. You begin with the "I'm not enoughs" and you erase every single vile way you have been taught to view yourself as insufficient and not enough... whether it involves abundance, skill, intelligence, appearance, or any other characteristic... **any idea that you are not enough is a miserable lie.** And you erase those lies permanently from the depths of your mind. You follow up with the "I cants"... erasing everything you have been instructed is beyond you – and it feels so good to simply erase the "I'm not enoughs" and the "I can'ts" from your mind forever. Riding that wave of good feeling, you erase the self-doubts... whatever skills and talents you have been taught to doubt; you erase the poisonous doubt from your mind. And finally, feeling great, you erase the "there's not enoughs" from the board. We live in abundant, infinitely creative universe, and any idea that there is not enough is a miserable lie that you erase with enthusiasm and joy. All the "I'm not enoughs", all the "I can'ts', all the self doubts, and all the "there's not enoughs" on that board are miserable lies that other people put in your mind... **You take an immense and wonderful joy in erasing those miserable lies totally off the board, and totally out of your mind.**

Feeling incredibly light now, with the side board clear of the lies, you turn to the board in the front, and your inner teacher hands you a permanent marker. You see, written on that board, incredible truths that had faded almost to nothing because your mind hadn't been paying attention to them. And you begin to trace those truths over with your permanent marker so that you never forget them again. As your permanent marker traces each of these new truths, you realize they aren't really new... they have just been temporarily overshadowed by that load of nonsense you erased off the other board. And now it is time for your new-slash-old truths to take their rightful place in your life and mind.

With courage and joyous expectation, you begin tracing your first truth in permanent marker. Your first new truth is this: "I am a child of God, a child of an infinite and creative universe, and I am, just as I am in this moment, enough, and far more than enough for God and my own soul". And that new truth locks into your mind and grows stronger with every breath you breathe. **"I am a child of God, a child of an infinite and creative universe, and I am, just as I am in this moment, enough, and far more than enough for God and my own soul".**

Feeling light and powerful, you trace the second new truth. It reads: "I always have whatever I need to succeed: resources, talents, wisdom and help. Life never sends me anything I truly can't handle. Life may send me things I don't think I can handle until after I do, but that is just how life encourages me to grow. I can handle anything life brings me. Every breath I breathe locks this truth into my deepest heart and mind where it is fully implemented".

Listen again as the truth becomes permanent in your mind: **"I always have whatever I need to succeed: resources, talents, wisdom and help. Life never sends me anything I truly can't handle. Life may send me things I don't think I can handle until after I do, but that is just how life encourages me to grow. I can handle anything life brings me. Every breath I breathe locks this truth into my deepest heart and mind where it is fully implemented".**

On a roll now, you rewrite your third new truth in permanent marker and it says: "I am courageous. Courage is not the absence of fear. Courage is feeling the fear and doing my best anyway. I am a courageous person. Simply to come into a physical body and live on the earth is an act of vast and incredible courage. I am a courageous person. And every beat of my heart increases my courage"

You hear it again and this new truth locks into your deepest mind forever: **"I am courageous. Courage is not the absence of fear. Courage is feeling the fear and doing my best anyway. I am a courageous person. Simply to come into a physical body and live on the earth is an act of vast and incredible courage. I am a courageous person. And every beat of my heart increases my courage"**

Feeling great, you continue tracing your fourth truth with permanent marker, never to be forgotten again: " I am persistent and persevering. Edison said success is 10 percent inspiration and 90 percent perspiration... and I know what that means. I simply continue going with a vast persistence and all my strength until I reach my goals."

Every sound in your ears causes this new truth to lock in and become absolutely true for you as you hear it again: **"I am persistent and persevering. Edison said success is 10 percent inspiration and 90 percent perspiration... and I know what that means. I simply continue going with a vast persistence and all my strength until I reach my goals."**

With joy, you write your fifth new truth: "I can do, accomplish or be whatever I set my mind on and work to achieve – all "I cants" are meaningless lies... I can be, do or have whatever I can dream or imagine, and I am a powerful dreamer and imaginer."

And every breath makes this truth stronger and more powerful in your life as you hear it again. **"I can do, accomplish or be whatever I set my mind on and work to achieve – all "I cants" are meaningless lies... I can be, do or have whatever I can dream or imagine, and I am a powerful dreamer and imaginer."**

Feeling a total transformation occurring within, you write the sixth new truth: "I live in an incredibly rich and abundant universe which provides me with everything I need to live a full and meaningful life. I lack for nothing, I dwell in the wealth of all creation, and there is more than enough to achieve my dreams. And each beat of my heart actualizes and strengthens this new truth in my outer life."

As you hear it repeated, this new truth locks permanently into your inner mind and becomes the absolute truth for you. **"I live in an incredibly rich and abundant universe which provides me with everything I need to live a full and meaningful life. I lack for nothing, I dwell in the wealth of all creation, and there is more than enough to achieve my dreams. And each beat of my heart actualizes and strengthens this new truth in my outer life."**

And all the new truths are summarized with a seventh statement on the board. "In each and everyday, in every way and in every situation in life, I am confident, strong, persistent and courageous. And I am enough and far more than enough to meet any challenge in life and thrive." Free of all doubts, your inner mind accepts these powerful renewed truths, and restores you to the birthright of confidence, strength, persistence and courage that you were born to live always.

Listen again, and all seven new truths magnify themselves a thousand time and become totally true for you. **"In each and everyday, in every way and in every situation in life, I am confident, strong, persistent and courageous. And I am enough and far more than enough to meet any challenge in life and thrive."** Free of all doubts, your inner mind accepts these powerful renewed truths, and restores you to the birthright of confidence, strength, persistence and courage that you were born to live always."

If these new truths are acceptable to your mind, you simply continue breathing… just as you are. And every breath you breathe, and every beat of your heart, causes your inner mind to magnify, reinforce, strengthen and totally implement these new truths in your outer life. Your calm, confidence, persistence and courage lead you to achieve your many and worthy goals in life. And you know, with an unbreakable confidence that you are enough and more than enough to meet any situation in life and thrive.

You can visit your schoolhouse any time you like, either by listening to this recording, or simply by closing your eyes in a safe place, and picturing and imagining it. Any time you visit your schoolroom, whether with the recording, or in your own mind, every powerful and beneficial idea on the recording gets stronger and deeper. Every time you visit the schoolroom of the deepest mind, the old lies and nonsense erase further away. And the new truths multiply and grow so much stronger. The more you use this recording, the more powerfully your new truths actualize and manifest in your outer life. You come back to the outer world now, renewed, refreshed, and with a profound confidence that grows with every breath you breathe.

Finis Libris

Robert Hughes.BCH

Also by Robert Hughes
Unlocking the Blueprint of the Psyche:
Self-Hypnosis for Modern Miracles

- Comprehensive Introduction to Hypnosis
- Unleash the power of your subconscious mind
- Create miracles of positive change
- Learn what hypnosis is and isn't
- Learn to write powerful suggestion scripts

This is one of the best introductions to hypnosis and self-hypnosis ever written. Carefully developed concepts, and step-by-step instructions help you master basic hypnosis techniques readily. The focus of the book is making the practice of self-hypnosis available to anyone. Because it teaches suggestion formation, and hypnotic induction so clearly, it belongs on every hypnotist's bookshelf. The book includes the Self-Hypnosis Master Script that can be used, with suggestions you write for yourself, to unlock the vast potential of your subconscious mind and create astounding changes in your thoughts, feelings and actions.

"Anyone serious about using self-hypnosis to heal should have this essential resource in their reference library.
Pat Dawson, LCSW, CHt, Richmond, VA

"… so comprehensive that I use this book as a standard text for beginning hypnotherapy students"
J. Michael Dunlap, Ph.D., Board Certified Consulting Hypnotist, and co-founder of the Idaho School of Professional Hypnosis

www.RobertHughesPublications
www.Amazon.com/author/hughesrob
Available in Kindle and Paperback

Also by Robert Hughes
Our Souls Are Not Lost
Messages and Meditations

Master hypnotist, Robert Hughes, shares his wisdom as spiritual seeker, interfaith minister, and compassionate teacher.

- Over 50 messages and meditations
- Faith
- Compassion
- Spiritual Renewal
- God… A Verb
- Service
- Love
- Transformation
- and much more

Priceless messages, reminding us that we are the hands and faces of God in these troubled times. Each talk is accompanied by a guided meditation that enhances the message.

*"I think we should feel as though we are on a mission. Not a mission of sadness to save souls - **they are not lost,** and if they were, you wouldn't know where to look for them - but a mission that glorifies the soul. Not to find we are here for salvation, but for glorification--the beauty, the wonder, the delight of that Something that sings and sings and sings in the soul of humankind,"* **Dr. Ernest Holmes, Founder of Religious Science**

Robert Hughes was ordained as a minister in a New Thought tradition in 1999. New Thought teaches that God is all there is, that we are never apart from God, that the universe is responsive to our thoughts, and that we participate with divine spirit in co-creation of the world as we experience it.

www.RobertHughesPublications
www.Amazon.com/author/hughesrob
Available in Kindle and Paperbac

By Jerry Mooney
The Power of Thought

The Power of Thought is a practical and revealing guide to obtain, retain, and sharpen your ability to live life to its fullest by unlocking the powers you already have. The quest for more meaning and fulfillment in our lives is a common pursuit, one that often results in a misguided struggle for quick answers and immediate fixes. Many self-help books offer prescriptions that, if followed closely, will result in guaranteed success. Author and speaker Jerry Mooney offers a new way to look at how you can truly improve your life by not tapping into some philosophical ideal or religious formula, but by examining the power that already exists within yourself. Mooney helps you identify those things in life that may be robbing you of this power: negative thoughts, fear of change, mistrust, peer pressure, and many other unrecognized obstacles. With tested exercises such as visualization, writing, meditation, yoga and more, Mooney offers a sensible plan to start utilizing your innate power to begin living the life you truly want.

Available on Amazon

By Erika Ginnis
Essential Mysteries: A User's Guide for the 21st Century Mystic

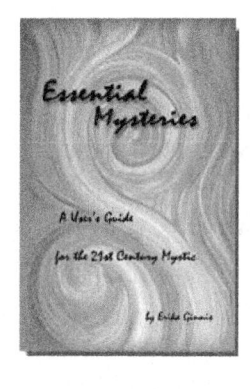

There you are: a Beautiful Luminous Spiritual Being, waking up to the Truth of your Divine nature. There is that within you that knows what to do and how to do it. You are the 21st Century Mystic. And this book is for you.

Awaken to your spiritual power, passion and purpose. Celebrate your journey, and have fun!

"I was experiencing emotional blockages that led to frequent illnesses and a fear of living life to the fullest. The soothing, nurturing reassurance of Erika's good work filled me with joy. My life is richer and more filled with love than it has ever been."
Lori Campbell, Kirkland, WA

"Erika's work inspires people to live in the bright shining light of life. It is a method of navigating the ups and downs of being human that honors all experiences, perspectives and religions while opening the individual to their truest self and the myriad of opportunities that are available to them. Given where I came from and where I am now, I know that anything is possible. I am so grateful to Erika for her help and encouragement and thrilled that she wrote this book so that more people can benefit from her work."
— Susan DuMett of Vox Vespertinus; Operatic vocalist and writer, Seattle Washington

Available at: www.inbreathcommunications.com

ABOUT THE AUTHOR

Robert Hughes, BCH, is a practicing hypnotherapist and hypnosis teacher with over 25 years experience. He is Board Certified as a Consulting Hypnotist by the National Guild of Hypnotists (NGH), and as a Clinical Hypnotherapist by the National Board for Hypnotherapy and Hypnotic Anesthesia (NBHA). Board certification is the highest practice-based certification of both organizations. Robert is also an NBHA certified teacher of clinical hypnosis, and is a co-founder of an NBHA recognized hypnotherapy training program. Robert has practiced in four states, and on two continents. He is the author of 3 books, with two more in manuscript form waiting publication. He has also recorded over 30 self-hypnosis CDs on a wide variety of topics. He lives and works in Boise, Idaho. He can be contacted at www.HughesHypnosis.com, and his books can be found at amazon.com/author/hughesrob.

Printed in Great Britain
by Amazon